The Churches and Inter-Community Relationships

by

Duncan Morrow, Derek Birrell, John Greer and Terry O'Keeffe

Centre for the Study of Conflict

University of Ulster

The Churches and Inter-Community Relationships

by

Duncan Morrow, Derek Birrell
John Greer and Terry O'Keeffe

Centre for the Study of Conflict
University of Ulster at Coleraine

ISBN 1 85923 085 7

Acknowledgements

This is a new printing of this report, first published by the Centre for the Study of Conflict in 1991. The original printing has been out of print for some time now, but has remained in demand. This is a new presentation but the content has not changed. Thanks are due to Par Shortt for much effort in getting this version ready for printing.

The research project on which this report is based could not have taken place without the interest and help of a large number of people. First and foremost, we are indebted to the Department of Education for Northern Ireland who provided funding for our work. In particular, the active interest of Donald Davidson was crucial in getting this project off the ground.

We are again grateful to Pat Shortt, secretary at the Centre for the Study of Conflict, who typed large parts of the original manuscript and who lent a much-needed helping-hand in the organisation of the questionnaire. Dr. Tony Gallagher, Research and Information Officer in the Centre, also provided invaluable assistance with word-processing and publication.

Much of the laborious work of collating information from the questionnaires was undertaken by Simon Anderson and Neil Morrow. Laura McGinlay was also involved in this process. Likewise, Frank Wright and John Chilvers gave up considerable time to assist with the distribution of the questionnaire. Without their help, the project would have taken much longer to complete and we are very grateful for their assistance.

Finally, our greatest thanks go to all those who participated in this report, whether by answering the questionnaire or by allowing themselves to be interviewed. There are too many people to thank them all by name, but this report depended entirely on them. We hope that they find this report a useful contribution to their lives and work.

Centre for the Study of Conflict

This publication is one of a series of six new reports published by the Centre for the Study of Conflict in May 1994. The list is as follows:

The Company We Keep: Women, Community and Organisations by Valerie Morgan and Grace Fraser

A Welling up of Deep Unconscious Forces: Psychology and the Northern Ireland Conflict by Ed Cairns

Community Relations and Local Government by Colin Knox, Joanne Hughes, Derek Birrell and Sam McCready

Protestant Alienation in Northern Ireland: a Preliminary Survey by Seamus Dunn and Valerie Morgan

Majority Minority Review 3: Housing and Religion in Northern Ireland by Martin Melaugh

The Churches and Inter-Community Relationships by Duncan Morrow, Derek Birrell, John Greer and Terry O'Keeffe (Reprint)

For further copies of these or any other Centre publications, or for further information about the Centre, please contact Professor Seamus Dunn or:

Mrs. Pat Shortt
Centre for the Study of Conflict
The University of Ulster
Coleraine
Northern Ireland BT52 1SA

Telephone: (0265) 44141 extension 4666
Fax: (0265) 40917
E-Mail csc@ulst.ac.uk

Preface

The Centre for the Study of Conflict is a research centre based in the University of Ulster. Its main work is the promotion and encouragement of research on the community conflict and to this end it concentrates on practical issues to do with institutional and community structures and change. It publishes papers and books arising out of this work including: a series of research papers particularly designed to make available research data and reports; a series of Majority-Minority reports; and a series of occasional papers by distinguished academics in the field of conflict. It has recently published a *Register of Research on Northern Ireland* which has been widely praised, and a termly newsletter on current research called *Research Briefing.*

This new series of six research reports and papers on aspects of the Northern Ireland conflict represents the results of recent work as well as a reprint of an earlier work still much in demand.

It includes the extensive evaluation work of Colin Knox and his colleagues on the *Community Relations and Local Government* initiative, a major experiment in the promotion and encouragement of inter-community activity through the medium of district councils; a ground-breaking report by Valerie Morgan and Grace Fraser (carried out in association with the Centre for Research on Women) called *The Company We Keep: Women, Community and Organisations*, on the role and influence and cross-community activities of women in small towns and rural communities; the first in a new series of reports on the concept and experience of alienation, called *Protestant Alienation in Northern Ireland*; the most recent Majority-Minority report (joining earlier reports on education and on employment/unemployment) this one by Martin Melaugh on *Housing and Religion in Northern Ireland*; a paper by Ed Cairns on *Psychology and the Northern Ireland Conflict,* one in the series of occasional papers written by distinguished scholars . Finally, a reprint of the much discussed report by Duncan Morrow and his colleagues on *The Churches and Intercommunity Relationships* first published in 1991.

A second new series of reports will be published in July 1994 on topics such as Geographical Segregation, Education for Mutual Understanding, Disability, Community Development and Peace Education.

Seamus Dunn
May 1994

CONTENTS

SECTION ONE: INTRODUCTION

Origins

The Churches and Inter-community relationships project arose out of consultations between the Centre for the Study of Conflict in the University of Ulster at Coleraine and the Department of Education Northern Ireland (DENI). The aim of the project was to study the role of the Churches in the twenty years of violence in Northern Ireland. Three academics, Derek Birrell (Social Administration and Policy), John Greer (Education) and Terry O'Keeffe (Philosophy and Politics) became the directors of this project and negotiated with the Department. In July 1987 a Research Officer, Duncan Morrow, was appointed to research the theme.

Research

The general objective of the project was an examination of the place of the Churches in Northern Ireland society. Within this broad framework, we had a number of concrete goals. The first was to ascertain the degree to which the Churches were still important foci of personal and community life in Northern Ireland. Secondly, the nature of the connection between religion and secular aspects of life in Northern Ireland was to be examined. Thirdly, we wished to try to understand the relationship of Churches to each other and to compare inter-Church relations to other aspects of community relations and to understand the impact of the one on the other. In particular the relationship of Churches to social and political conflict was to be examined and the findings made as a contribution to our understanding of the complex dynamics and inter-relationships of society in Northern Ireland.

The research was carried out using two different approaches. The first was a questionnaire of clergy which would concentrate on the Churches and their involvement in the provision of formal community and social facilities in Northern Ireland. In this way we were able to address the breadth of church institutional and personal involvement in the minutiae of northern Irish life. The questionnaire was also intended to highlight areas of inter-community interest and activity within and between the Churches and to begin to assess the limits and possibilities of inter-community relations within Church structures.

The second part of the project was three case studies designed to reflect the range of circumstances in different parts of the province, east and west of the River Bann and in urban and rural settings. Furthermore, case studies enabled an examination of the variety of different approaches to ostensibly similar problems in different settings, of the variety of problems facing different people in different parts of the province, as well as allowing an assessment of the depth of Church involvement in community life in different places.

Through this combination we hoped to gain a more accurate picture of the breadth and depth of 'The Churches' contribution to Northern Ireland life and thereby to examine the place of organised religion in society and in inter-community relationships on an informed basis.

At an early stage we decided to restrict the survey to the four largest denominations in Northern Ireland; Roman Catholic, Presbyterian, Church of Ireland and Methodist. While we were aware that this was already restrictive, the combined membership or association with these Churches makes up over 90% of the Northern Irish population. In the case studies, we again concentrated primarily on the relationships between these denominations. Nevertheless, in each case, local circumstances meant that other denominations and groups were also considered.

We sought the agreement of the appropriate bodies in each of the four Churches to carry out this work. The various dioceses and boards were all encouraging in this matter. This made possible a research project which is firmly based in both communities in Northern Ireland and allowed for comparisons to be made and differences to be examined.

There are numerous possible approaches to the Churches and their involvement in community work. It is therefore important to acknowledge that we were unable to tackle some aspects. At one stage we intended to examine the community work of the Churches through a study of the Church institutions of each of the denominations. Examples of these include the Presbyterian Board of Social Witness, Down & Connor Family Welfare society and so on. Because of the specifically inter-community focus of this project it was thought that the Churches Central Committee for Community Work might be an appropriate body through which to examine joint approaches between the Churches. In furtherance of this and in order to establish contact and context for the research, interviews and conversations were arranged with representatives and employees of some of the appropriate organisations. Everyone was very obliging in this regard and many were very open in their comments. Eventually, however, we decided not to pursue this aspect of Church life because, although it provided valuable background, it became apparent that the central approach was too general and that the inter-Church dimension of work at this level was extremely weak. The CCCCW proved to be an organisation without teeth and with little concrete backing from the Church institutions. The staff were very open in their acknowledgement of the serious difficulties and limitations of the organisation. We decided to concentrate our research elsewhere.

The advantage of this project was that it was undertaken in an inter-community context allowing all denominations to come under one searchlight. It is hoped that the project demystifies some of the relationships between religion and secular life and the relationship of religion to community conflict.

Background

Work on the Churches and their place in Northern Irish life remains sparse. We can suggest a number of reasons for this. Secular Social Science in Britain and Ireland has tended to be dominated by an outlook in which the Churches are either small minority remnants or institutions which reflect a kind of social backwardness. At its worst religion is equivalent to obscurantism and superstition. In this context religion, particularly in its organised form, is a strange and difficult territory, easier to dismiss than to explore. The obsessive religiosity of the Irish is at best embarrassing and at worst dangerous. It is worth pointing out that in this respect England itself differs from other cultures, such as German, Polish, Italian, Russian, North and Latin American, South African, Middle Eastern and Asian political and social cultures. In these places, questions of religion and the Churches, both in general and in particular, remain central to philosophical, political and communal discourse and organisation. Even for those who are firmly outside religious bodies the debates posed by the doctrines and beliefs of these bodies are included in their frame of reference. Thus the examination of Irish religion from within an English framework is always likely to be particularly distorted, especially with regard to religion. When Steve Bruce argued that 'The Northern Ireland Conflict is a religious conflict' (l) he found himself in a minority of one among sociologists.

For us, however, the question can never be whether religion is important. Instead, the question is how and in what ways is religion important. In this respect the political debate on Northern Ireland by those who have no place for this discussion always misses a crucial dimension. Part of the task of this project was to establish the degree to which, in Northern Ireland, the boundaries between the secular and the religious are clear-cut. The extent to which Church institutions provide the context for social life and the extent to which the Churches are involved in so many aspects of life means that they cannot simply be dismissed. In our questionnaire it became apparent that the Churches are not just general labels attached inaccurately to political parties but also the context of the apparently minute aspects of cultural life. From Mother and Toddler groups to political activities, the Churches are somehow involved.

There are some problems in a simplistic secular perspective on religion, especially in the analysis of Christian religion in Western society. Often secular observers appear to begin their analyses from the premise that Churches are small subgroups which emerged within a wider society. 'The Churches' are like 'the Trade Unions' or 'the bourgeoisie' only smaller and less important.

In Ireland the first challenge to this way of looking at things is size. The Churches are not smaller than the other social bodies and by sheer weight of numbers demand a more respectful hearing. Secondly such social science is in danger of inverting the historical order of events. Modern Society retains roots in Christendom, even if the description 'post-Christian' is now more accurate for much of Britain. Of course, the Churches retain a more explicit link to that history than do other groups which dominate the modern social agenda. Nevertheless, Church members have lived through these changes simultaneously with non-Church members. As such the Churches are not a separable sub-group which have 'arisen' out of modernity, like Trade Unions. Rather, the various strands of modem secular society have 'arisen' out of a Church-based past. This means that Church people are likely also to be involved in many aspects of secular life and that they cannot be reduced to a sect with clear boundaries defined by secular categories of class or organisation or gender or age. Where the Churches are large in size, this point is obvious.

'The Churches' are not simple institutions with members whose members change their hats in other parts of life. They are also communities of people whose whole lives are lived in the light of their Church experiences and knowing. Thus when they are in the workplace, in pubs, bringing up children, or whatever they may remain partly in Church. This makes the designation of simple lines, divisions between the secular and the religious completely misleading. In Northern Ireland this is immediately clear. It is not less true in secular England. It is less obvious.

The common roots of western society in Christendom means that absolute categorisation of the Churches by social science is likely to be difficult. Furthermore, the Churches do not reflect the finality of secular categories just as secular observers reject the judgements of the Church. To examine the Churches without an acknowledgement of some common heritage will always assume that the observer can stand outside the Churches separating them as a strange sect or as a subgroup to which the observer has no relation. In a Northern Irish context the difficulties of simple division become apparent very quickly. Men on Belfast's Shankhill Road may no longer go to Church. Instead they meet in clubs and pubs and in the orange order. Despite this, they continue to live in a society that was shaped by relations between communities in which religion was crucial. 'Religious', 'Christian' or not, their predicament cannot be understood without some understanding of the relationships between the Churches.

Within their jurisdiction, States claim ultimate authority. In the final analysis, the supreme authority of the State is undermined by claims made to a higher authority. Explicitly or implicitly, the State has to make a religious claim to authority. The claim to 'divine right' is therefore not very different to a claim to the 'nation' or 'the people' except that secular language is used. In this sense, the claims of the secular State or of a particular set of humanistic ideals are just as 'religious' as the claims of Christianity. The problems arise when groups deny the authority of the State on the basis of a different but higher authority, be it God, the nation, the people or whatever.

The problem with religious wars is that they are waged in the name of an ultimate authority. The combination of violence and 'sacred cause' is therefore very potent. Again, the cause need not be explicitly 'religious' to exhibit these traits, and in our own time nationalism and the claims of a class to ultimate authority have been the most obvious such secular causes. The potential of the call of the nation has been obvious since the French Revolution and brought to an ugly nadir in the quasi-religious ideology of German Nazism.

Where a secular religion such as nationalism combines with a religion which claims universal transcendence, the potential for violence is immense. The nation is raised into a sacred cause for both man and God. A national-religious war can be pursued with ferocity by people of immensely different conscious motivations. Religion becomes a system which gives a higher justification for the national war, indeed gives it an authoritative stamp of approval. Deeply secular people find themselves following religious leaders for reasons of their own defence.

It is extremely difficult to abolish dissenting religious claims through State violence. Religious dissent in the Eastern Bloc, Jewish persecution through ten centuries, the Irish Penal laws, the Polish crisis, the rise of the Ayatollah in Iran all illustrate the difficulty of using violence to purge religious dissent. Precisely because the claims of the religious group are held to have an ultimate authority, persecution tends to reinforce the determination of the group to 'hold out'. In Ireland, the Penal Laws had the effect of binding Catholicism to the Irish experience, while attacks on Protestants from a church-dominated opponent, over which Britain has appeared to equivocate have made Protestantism important to a sense of difference in Ulster's majority.

In the modern State, the field of education has been the most obvious battleground between the State and religion. The question of 'what to teach' and how to fund it have become central. In many settings, language has been the crucial issue at stake. In other places, religion has been crucial. Multi-religious or multi-language states are faced with serious problems in this regard. Different solutions have been found in different countries. In the West, some countries, such as Germany and Holland, have allowed denominational religious education in schools while others, such as France or USA, have outlawed it, except in private, fee-paying schools. It is clear to many Muslims that secular education does not teach what they wish. Christian fundamentalists in America, Catholics in Ulster and Muslims in Bradford share the same perception. What is slower to become clear is that the curriculum of a single integrating State system is therefore 'religious' in the sense that it claims an absolute validity.

The Churches in Northern Ireland are interwoven into the social fabric of the community. Even among those who do not go to Church, the language of religious identity is not very distant. As such, religious identity has had a more consistent appeal than identities of class or gender. Indeed religious tradition remains the most consistent guide to political outlook. This is not to say that the conflict is about theology. Religion has always been more important than theology in the experience of difference in Ulster. What the Churches do in a conflict divided by religious traditions is, however, important. What is certain is that the relationship of culture, politics, society and religion cannot be simplistically resolved by ignoring the Churches on the basis that they are 'epicentral' to the main issues of the conflict.

Even in Northern Ireland, academic work on the Churches has been sporadic. Frank Wright's important work (2) established the link between Protestantism and the ideology of Unionism. John Hickey (3) tried to show that any explanation of the Northern Irish problem which did not take into account the religious dimension fell short. Although he did not provide a comprehensive theory of the nature of the relationship of religion to other aspects of Northern Ireland life he demonstrated that religion could not be bypassed. Steve Bruce (4) argued that Free Presbyterianism and its self-understanding are crucial to any understanding of the Democratic Unionist Party both in terms of ideology and in terms of practice. The political importance of Ian Paisley alone, which reached its zenith in the 1983 European Election, ensures that this phenomenon is no footnote in Northern Irish history or experience. It will be part of this study to examine this relationship of religion to politics in relation to the larger Churches in Northern Ireland. Within the Churches numerous groups have sought to outline their position. All Churches have commented through the years on aspects of the violence and their response. There have been a number of important works on the relationship of the Churches to violence (5). Bishops regularly make statements on political and social affairs while the General Assembly of the Presbyterian Church has produced annual statements (6). Recently a number of smaller unofficial groups have made headlines, particularly 'An Inter-faith Group on Faith and Politics' who have produced numerous challenging documents (7) which comment on the political, social and religious present and future.

Methods

We looked at the Churches in two specific ways. First, through a survey of clergy and secondly through a number of case studies which were to reflect some of the diverse circumstances of Church life in Northern Ireland. The methods adopted in the survey are detailed in Section Two. It is necessary, however to say a word or two about the methods adopted during the case studies.

The field studies took place during 1988 and 1989. Each of the studies lasted approximately four months, including the time necessary to record and edit material. Direct field work lasted for about three months in each case. This is, of course, an absurdly short time in which to examine the depths of Church life in any area. We were very fortunate that people were generally friendly and open to discussion in each place.

The goal of the case studies was to present a series of 'pictures of some of the dimensions of Church life. As such, the case studies were to add a qualitative rather than quantitative dimension. They were to complement the formal framework of a questionnaire and by illustrating some of the human dimensions of the Churches in Northern Ireland they were intended to 'put flesh on the bones' of other analyses. From an early stage it was clear that any study of the Churches and inter-community relationships would have to locate the Churches within the relationships of 'their own' communities first. Most of the study time was therefore taken up in identifying relationships between the Churches and other secular groups.

The bulk of the fieldwork was a combination of participant observation and in-depth interviews. Where it was appropriate or possible, written sources were also consulted. Because of the pressures of time, it was necessary to ensure that interviews with key figures in the local community took priority. These included professionals, such as clergy and school teachers, and local community activists such as those engaged in Church or secular programmes for each area, such as ACE schemes, family work or youth clubs and important social and political organisations within each area, whether official or unofficial. Broadly speaking, these people provided the main framework from which to gauge the dimensions of the Church involvement in local life. To this core, we also added discussions with people identified locally as 'authorities' on the history and development of their areas.

Secondly, we spent a long time building up relationships of trust in less formal settings such as Family Centres, Mother and Toddler Groups, Old People's entertainment's, ACE schemes, Youth clubs and so on. This provided the framework for a broad understanding of Church work within the wider local context as well as counterbalancing the reliance on professional opinion. In informal settings, people expressed a variety of views and experiences of local life. In many cases this resulted in formal interviews.

Thirdly, it was essential that people both within and outside the Churches were represented in each area. As a result, towards the end of the research in each area, spokespeople for specific views which were not yet reflected in recorded form but were everpresent in informal discussion were sought out.

Fourthly, the fieldwork had to include people from a wide variety of backgrounds. Our case studies were chosen to reflect geographical differences, rural and urban settings and wide class variations. We were careful to ensure that both women and men were properly represented, that we spoke with people of different age groups and that people of all political and religious persuasions were part of the work. In each area efforts were made to ensure that all these factors were taken into account. If there are biases in the results they are probably the result of unequal access to clergy vis a vis lay people which slant the analysis towards an over-reliance on this group.

In every case, longer individual contributions were recorded by hand and sometimes by cassette. This was always agreed in advance with each person and the rules of confidentiality clarified. The written records complemented personal observation through informal groups and Church attendance.

It was impossible to embark on a door to door approach in any area. A number of important reasons can be advanced for this. In the first place, qualitative sterility. Religion and politics are difficult subjects in Northern Ireland. We found it necessary to ensure that everybody was relaxed and free of fears before open discussion was possible. From an early stage we chose to concentrate on a smaller number of substantial discussions rather than a larger number of inflexible doorstep responses. Secondly, in the context of our work, what we were seeking from the case studies was an indication of the 'human dimension' of the Churches predicaments. It was therefore important to allow the interviewees the maximum possible freedom to describe and reflect on their life and work in their own manner. Uniformity was ensured by the consistent goals of the fieldwork. It was deliberately not imposed in the form of a semi-structured interview whose content was decided in advance, in order to discover the real diversity in each situation. Thirdly, time imposed its own constraints on the work which made any satisfactory saturation project impossible.

The case studies are suggestive rather than definitive. They do, however, claim to be a record of the broad range of discussions in which the Churches are involved in each area as related by a wide variety of people in their own words. In writing the report, we felt that it was important to begin from these views. As a result we have made widespread use of quotation from these interviews in the report.

In writing the reports, we decided on a policy of anonymity. As a result we changed most of the placenames. We have taken this decision in order that nobody should be unnecessarily exposed to difficulties.

The case studies ensure that general analyses are firmly rooted in empirical reality and allow theoretical generalisations to be clarified in concrete situations. They allowed us to examine relationships from the viewpoint and experience of those who live within them. They enabled us to assess the context in which changes might occur and discuss how any changes might occur on a better-informed basis.

Final Remarks

One of the problems of a report such as this is that it attempts to address the interests of a wide variety of people. This particular report is written with a number of different audiences in mind. In the first instance, we had to meet the contractual demands of our funders. At the same time, the report is addressed to people within the Churches in Northern Ireland, to academics interested in politics and society in Northern Ireland, to those interested in the importance of organised religion both at home and abroad and to a wider audience of Northern Irish people who are interested in learning more about the workings of their society. It is hoped that the multiplicity of audiences does not result in total confusion. For readers outside Northern Ireland, a short glossary of terms has been added to enable culturally specific usages (such as Pl, P2) to be more easily understood.

Our project focused on the Churches in relation to Catholic-Protestant, Unionist-Nationalist, divisions. In so doing, we have attempted to reflect a wide variety of circumstances throughout the province. This is not an exhaustive analysis of the Churches in Northern Ireland. Although the project raised many issues, the question of theology and politics, religion and social class and Church attendance were always subsidiary to our primary focus on inter-community relationships. There is much work to be done in these areas.

This project is a contribution to a deeper understanding of the relationship of the Churches and religion to life in Northern Ireland. As such, we hope to illustrate the breadth of Church involvement from the level of the social and political structures to the seemingly mundane. Even here it is by no means exhaustive. It is our hope that we have provided an insight into some of the difficulties in making simplistic judgements or providing easy solutions in a situation where everybody appears caught in a predicament of fear and violence, while at the same time providing examples of possible futures.

References

1. Steve Bruce: "The Northern Ireland Conflict is a religious conflict'

2. Frank Wright: "Protestant Ideology and Politics in Ulster", European Journal of Sociology, vol. xiv, no. 2 1973, pp. 213-80
   Frank Wright: "The Reconciliation of memories", in 'Northern Ireland - a challenge to theology', Centre for Theology and Public Issues, 1987, Edinburgh pp

3. John Hickey: "Religion and the Northern Ireland Problem", Gill and Macmillan, 1984

4. Steve Bruce: "God save Ulster", Oxford University Press, 1987

5. Eric Gallagher and Stanley Worrall: "Christians in Ulster 1968-82" Oxford University Press, 1982
Robin Boyd: "Ireland: Christianity discredited or Pilgrim's Progress" WCC, Risk Books Geneva 1987

6. "The Northern Ireland situation" Church Statements 1968-1986, Presbyterian Church in Ireland
Bishops Submission, New Ireland Forum Report Vol. XII, 1983

7. "Living the Kingdom", An inter-faith group on Faith and Politics, Belfast, 1988

SECTION TWO: CHURCH AND SOCIETY - A SURVEY OF CLERGY

Results of a survey among clergy of the four largest Churches in Northern Ireland.

Introduction and Rationale

During 1988 a questionnaire was sent to over 1000 clergy in parishes and congregations in Northern Ireland. The clergy were members of the Roman Catholic Church, the Church of Ireland, the Presbyterian Church in Ireland and the Methodist Church. Every Diocese of the two Episcopal Churches was covered by the survey as was every Presbytery and circuit of the two non-Episcopal Churches.

The survey had two main purposes. First, we hoped to show the degree to which the Church institutions in Northern Ireland are central to social and community organisation from the political realm to the sphere of day-to-day activities for citizens. By so doing we hoped to show that in many spheres of public and private life, the Church was present, even for those not consciously religious. Secondly, we wanted to examine attitudes among clergy to co-operation with other denominations. In particular we concentrated on the provision of social and community services but we were also interested in the limits to co-operation as envisaged by clergy. It was hoped that the survey might throw some empirical light on the degree to which Church life is central to many aspects of life in Northern Ireland which do not on the surface appear to belong to a religious sphere and on the degree to which Church attitudes to co-operation reflect, lead or contradict other impulses in community relations in Northern Ireland.

Targeting the Survey.

From the outset, we decided to restrict the survey to members of the four largest denominations in Northern Ireland; Roman Catholic, Presbyterian, Church of Ireland and Methodist. These churches still represent over 90% of all Church-goers in the province. Furthermore, there has been very little academic research on the life of these groups and their relations to one another.

At an early stage, we also decided to concentrate the survey on clergy. This has several advantages for the surveyor because clergy are easily identifiable as Church-members, professionally paid and classified. They also offer an easier mechanism for comparison, often being considered as equivalent. Clergy are also likely to be knowledgeable as to the scope and nature of activities carried out under parish or congregational auspices. Furthermore, they are generally regarded as the public face of the Churches. They are looked to for guidance on the nature of orthodoxy and for pastoral assistance in the event of personal or political difficulties.

Traditionally in Northern Ireland we avoid discussions of religion and politics when we are unsure of who is asking the questions. Questions on 'co-operation' in the realm of inter-community relationships may be perceived as threatening and responses may be defensive rather than open. Although the problem does not disappear among clergy, the relative respect for the clergy in Ulster may make such questions less threatening.

At the same time, it is important to recognise that the concentration on the clergy has several disadvantages. In the first instance clergy are to some extent a 'removed elite' within the Churches. This means that a survey of the clergy cannot be held to be a survey of 'the Churches' unless we hold that the laity are represented in their entirety by the clergy. Secondly, clergy may feel constrained by their professional and public role from expressing themselves in the same manner as other citizens. They may feel themselves to be spokespeople for others rather than as persons speaking purely for themselves. This problem may exist for some and not for others or in various degrees. There is no mechanism for separating between these responses. Thirdly the clergy remain an almost entirely male group while the majority of the active laity may well be female. Finally the most important aspect of the Churches contribution to life in Northern Ireland may be through the nature of relationships built up between people within the Church. Thus a measurement of groups which assumes all groups are of equal importance makes no allowance for the differences in the intensity and importance of each group.

In this context, the questionnaire should be seen as part of a project rather than as the whole on its own. Despite the limitations of a questionnaire to clergy, it is quite clear that the survey points to important conclusions about the breadth and depth of Church involvement in aspects of Northern Ireland life.

Methods and Response

In total, 1074 questionnaires were sent by post to clergy in each of the four largest denominations. The questionnaire involved 35 questions, often with subordinate questions. Six months later, a second copy of the questionnaire was sent to those who had not responded. The totals in this analysis are the combined totals of two send-outs. To ensure that no duplication took place, individual coding was used in the first approach. Second questionnaires were not sent to those who responded. The coding figures were deleted and nowhere recorded for reasons of privacy and security.

Questionnaires were sent to clergy in all areas of Northern Ireland, using lists of clergy names and addresses published by each of the Churches. In two cases, the Catholic diocese of Dromore and the Presbyterian Presbytery of Dromore, a number of forms were mislaid at an early stage and not sent. In this area the figures are based on reduced samples. Elsewhere, all parishes and congregations not listed as vacant were circulated.

We specifically asked clergy to record their denomination, their age and the geographical location of their parish or congregation. In the last two cases we divided age and geographical location into broad categories in order to preserve anonymity. Because of the huge imbalance between male and female clergy in Northern Ireland, we did not control for differences in the responses according to gender.

The overall response rate among all clergy was 453 of 1074 or 42.1%. In the event 172 Church of Ireland Clergy responded, 158 Presbyterians and 53 Methodists and only 69 Roman Catholics. The total is completed by one person who refused to divulge their denomination.

Nevertheless, these raw numbers mask remarkable differences between denominations. Amongst Methodists, 53 of 88 clergy contacted replied, or 60.2%. Amongst Presbyterians, 158 of 314 clergy contacted responded, or 50.3%. Some 172 Church of Ireland clergy out of a total contacted of 315 responded, making 54.60%. The overall return rate among Protestant clergy was therefore 53.4%. Among Roman Catholic clergy however the overall response rate was only 19.33% or 69 out of a total of 357 clergy contacted.

It is not immediately clear why this should have been the case. Numerous suggestions can be advanced, though none of them can be conclusive. It may be that Roman Catholic clergy are under considerable time pressure. It is possible that they regard surveys with derision, or they found this particular survey pointless. It is possible only to speculate. It is probable that there were many motives involved. It was reported to us that the involvement of the 'Centre for the Study of Conflict' with projects assessing Integrated Education had effected its perception amongst Catholic clergy.

Whatever the case, the result is that our survey while reflecting much of Protestant clerical opinion cannot be seen to have the same validity for

Roman Catholics as for Protestants.

During the collation of results, it became clear that our questionnaire sometimes imposed over-rigid assumptions. The survey was sent to clergy who live and work in a very wide variety of social settings. Responses to questions about social and community provision through Churches did not necessarily allow for the differences in context. One clergyman pointed out that in rural parishes the number of groups was relatively small while at the same time the level of personal community was very great. Indeed precisely because the community was so strong, there was no need for groups to be formed. By implication, a small number of formal groups within Church structures may sometimes illustrate a very coherent social structure and does not necessarily indicate a lack of Church involvement in local life.

The questionnaire is certainly reliable as an indicator of trends. Given the response of 42%, we cannot claim with certainty that the absolute values attached to each answer would always be valid. Despite this, the questionnaire undoubtedly achieved the main objectives set for it, by indicating the breadth of activities which can be classed as 'Church-related' and illustrating the areas of co-operation between clergy of different denominations. The results have serious practical implications for Church-people seeking to open discussion within their Churches, for people concerned about the links between religion and inter-community relationships in Northern Ireland, for those interested in the place of religion in our common life in Northern Ireland and for public policy-makers seeking to implement policy-change in Government interaction with Church bodies.

Section One: Background information

At the beginning of the questionnaire, we asked clergy to provide us with some background information. Apart from denomination, we recorded the age of each respondent and the size and geographical location of each congregation and parish.

Recording age differences allowed us to analyse differences between generations and to allow for the different age profiles of each denomination's clergy. The results do show significant variations between denominations.

In this survey, clergy of the non-Episcopal Churches who responded were concentrated into the middle three age-groups while there was a wider spread among Church of Ireland and Catholic clergy. This may have to do with different approaches to training, to the fact that Presbyterian and Methodist assistant ministers were not surveyed while curates were surveyed in both the Church of Ireland and the Roman Catholic Churches or with different average ages of entry into the ministries. It was also significant that a higher proportion of people over the normal age of retirement (65) were still active in Church of Ireland and Roman Catholic Churches. This may indicate a different approach to retirement stemming from a different understanding of vocation. Of course the response to the survey among Roman Catholics means that extreme caution must be exercised before any serious conclusions are drawn out of the numbers in the survey. Among Catholic respondents only 14.5% were aged between 46 and 55 compared to an average of 24% and nearly a third of all Methodist ministers who responded. Variations among Protestant denominations are more reliable.

Table l: Age of surveyed clergy, by denomination

	denomination				
Age of clergy	CofI. (172)	Meth (52)	Presb (158)	R.C. (69)	All (451)
25-35	19.8%	3.8%	11.0%	20.3%	14.9%
36-45	27.3%	25.0%	33.8%	14.5%	27.6%
46-SS	22.7%	32.7%	26.6%	14.5%	24.0%
56-65	18.0%	32.7%	22.7%	33.3%	23.6%
65+	12.2%	5.8%	5.8%	17.4%	10.0%

We also asked clergy to record the geographical location of their parish or congregation throughout Northern Ireland. This did not apply to Methodist clergy where location was not recorded separately because of the much smaller numbers involved. Between the other denominations the borders of Presbyteries and Dioceses are very different and no absolute comparisons can be made between denominations. In the case of the Church of Ireland, political County boundaries were used for administrative reasons. Nevertheless the divisions do allow us to ensure that the responses came from a wide variety of areas, allowing for different local conditions within Northern Ireland. They also acted as a control against biases which might emerge if the response rates had varied greatly according to geography. It enabled us to ensure that generalisations were not made using data which did not take into account variations in response between clergy in different settings.

Table 2: Survey responses by denomination and area

Church of Ireland (By county)

	replies	sent	%	rank
Belfast	41	67	61.19	3
Co. Antrim	33	71	46.48	6
Co. Down	27	55	49.09	4
Co. Armagh	17	35	48.57	5
Co. Londonderry	22	33	66.66	2
Co. Tyrone	24	35	68.57	1
Co. Fermanagh	8	19	54.60	7
TOTAL	172	315	54.6%	(4)

Presbyterian (By Presbytery)

	replies	sent	%	rank
Ards	12	26	46.2%	13=
Armagh	7	15	46.7%	11=
Ballymena	9	26	34.6%	18
North Belfast	10	27	37.0%	17
South Belfast	10	18	55.6%	6
East Belfast	12	21	57.1%	5
Carrickfergus	15	17	88.2%	1
Coleraine	12	22	54.5%	7
Derry	6	10	60.0%	3=
Down	3	5	62.5%	2
Dromore	3	5	60.0%	3=
Foyle	5	12	41.7%	15
Iveagh	8	15	53.3%	8=
Newry	6	13	46.2%	13
Omagh	8	15	53.3%	8=
Route	10	20	50.0%	10
Strabane	2	6	33.3%	19
Templepatrick	7	15	46.7%	11=
Tyrone	6	15	40.0%	16
TOTAL	158	314	50.32%	(10)

Roman Catholic (By Diocese)

	replies	sent	%	rank
Down & Connor	41	195	21.0%	1
Dromore	2	16	12.5%	5
Clogher	4	23	17.4%	3
Derry	13	65	20.0%	2
Armagh	9	58	15.52%	4
TOTAL	69	357	19.3%	(3)

Methodist

	replies	sent	%	rank
TOTAL	53	88	60.2%	n/a

	replies	sent	%	rank
All	452	1074		

As a further control, we also measured the size of congregations and numbers in each parish. This makes some allowances for the differences between clergy according to the nature of their task although without further enquiry the differences in each person's job cannot be ascribed simply to the size of the congregation. Nevertheless it also allowed for some denominational differences to emerge. In general Methodist congregations are smaller and Catholic parishes much larger in terms of numbers. Again, this figure is not precise because of the practice in non-conformist Churches (Presbyterian, Methodist) of allocating one minister to each congregation and the practice in Catholic parishes of having large parishes served by several priests, only one of which is the parish priest.

Table 3: Size of parish/congregation by denomination

	size(No. Of Families)					
	<100	-200	-300	-400	-500	-600
Denomination						
C of I	9	32	33	26	13	9
Methodist	2	16	7	4	2	7
Presbyterian	5	43	32	2	13	16
R.C.	0	5	5	6	4	4

	size(No. of Families)				
	-700	-800	-900	>900	ALL
Denomination					
C of I	7	10	8	15	168
Methodist	1	3	0	0	45
Presbyterian	10	4	3	6	156
R.C.	4	6	4	29	67
Missing	16				
TOTAL	452				

Section 2: Churches and social and recreational activities

One of the primary purposes of the questionnaire was to illustrate the variety and scope of activities in social life in Northern Ireland in which there is a significant Church component. As such, we sought to investigate the connection of the Church with the apparent 'details' of Northern Irish public life. It is our belief, that the results build up into a significant whole picture, which it is important to acknowledge.

Of course, the degree to which a particular activity is "Church-related' is not conclusively proven simply by statistical measurement. Nevertheless, the survey illustrates that there is no clean division between the Church and the non-Church aspects of Northern Irish public life. As well as housing worshipping communities, Churches are important community buildings, social centres of communities, religious institutions and parts of secular life. Without more in-depth work it is impossible to pinpoint the precise nature of these interrelationships. Nevertheless the relationships exist.

It is in the sphere of social activities that Church buildings are used by the widest sections of Northern Irish society. The long tradition especially in Protestant circles of 'organisations' attached to Churches extends the contact of the worshipping Church community to families, particularly young people who have no active worshipping connection. This tendency to set up groups active in local affairs or providing gathering points for the local community is now also widespread in Catholic circles.

Churches are integrated then into the fabric of community lives not only through the pervasive influence of Sunday attendance but through their central place as social meeting places, community centres to which wide ranges of the population have a relationship. The fusing of community political identity with religious affiliation in Northern Ireland is encapsulated in this difficult conjunction. The fact that organisations tend to be denominational means that the organisations make real social differences between each group and confirm identities. In Protestant areas this denominational exclusiveness of the organisation may be mitigated by the fact that membership of the organisations is not officially restricted to membership of the denomination. Thus the Boy's Brigade may be seen as primarily Presbyterian in character but may have non-Presbyterian Protestants as members. Mothers and Toddlers Clubs, Pensioners Clubs and Youth Clubs are other examples of this phenomenon. In such cases it is clearly the club rather than the Church which attracts the people. It may nevertheless be true that the fact that the clubs are in Churches has a pervasive influence on the sense of integration of formal religious institutions into everyday life and reinforce the denominational dimension of community identity and division.

Defining the boundaries of where Churches begin and end remains difficult. The lines between secular and Church life become very blurred, and clear-cut division is not possible. Secular life in Northern Ireland is partly lived in the vicinity of Churches and what happens in Churches is inter-related in an organic manner with events outside the buildings and communities. Moreover, even where the direct impact of Church is no longer seen as relevant, the groups which gathered around Churches have developed identities which have continued even after Church attendance has declined. The Orange Order, for example, has acted as an organisational bridge between the Church-based and those who no longer attend or feel any attraction to the Church but who share the same experiences and outlook on history and events. Thus in many urban working-class areas in particular, pubs and clubs are now the social centres for adult men, unlinked in any direct manner to Churches. Nevertheless, the clientele of drinking clubs is made up of people whose experiences and lives are shaped by the partly Church based history of their ancestors where the secular-Church divide was even less apparent. In this sense, the 'organic relationship' of Church to secular is historical. It is not for this reason any weaker especially as it is reinforced by collective experiences of violence which make escape from the separate histories of Ulster's denominations all the more difficult.

The variety of the relationships made through Churches in Northern Ireland is huge. It embraces activities for all age-groups, sexes and interests including social gatherings, sports, uniformed organisations, study and prayer groups. Of 436 replies only 15% of parishes or congregations did not have a recreational youth club of some type. The majority of these clubs were open to membership by young people who were not members of the Church concerned or whose families were not members. This open door policy to other denominations or none was stronger among Protestants than in Catholic areas. This corresponds to the residential divide between Catholics and Protestants. Different types of Protestants are residentially integrated while separate from Catholics. Thus 'open to other denominations does not mean cross-community. While on one level this is an obvious point it is important to underline that ecumenism between different groups of Protestants and between Catholics and Protestants are not the same thing precisely in the area of social implications. The difference between the two types of dialogue is not only or even primarily theological but social. Again we see the social net of Protestantism-Unionism and Catholicism-Nationalism binding together in the social fabric of life. In a sense to belong to these integrated tribes is not a matter of rational choice but of birth and growth in community.

This division becomes apparent if we look at the classical uniformed organisations in Churches in Northern Ireland: the Boy Scouts and Girl Guides and the Boys and Girls Brigades. We asked clergy to record the existence of uniformed groups within their congregations and parishes.

Table 4: Scout troops in Churches by denomination.			
Scouts	Troop	No troop	No response
C of I	71(42.5%)	74(44.0%)	23
Meth.	9 (20.0%)	21(46.7%)	15
Presb.	31(19.9%)	31(19.9%)	94
R.C.	33(49.3%)	21(31.3%)	13

Scouting is represented in all denominations in Northern Ireland. It cannot be said to belong to one group or another. It is clearly more often attached to Church of Ireland Churches than to Presbyterian or Methodist congregations but nevertheless this is far from exclusive. In Protestant circles, over 80% of clergy who responded from Churches with scout troops reported that their troops also had members who were not members of their Church. This is not the same as saying that Protestant scouts had Catholic members. In the case of Catholic parishes the proportion was reversed. Over 80% were denominationally exclusive. A further examination reveals that Scouting is divided into two separate organisations in Northern Ireland, one is expressly Catholic, the other effectively Protestant. The latter swears as part of its founding promise to be loyal to 'God and the Queen'.

If we examine the figures from the Girl's Brigade the results are even more starkly divided.

Table 5: Girl's Brigade in Churches by denomination			
Girls Brigade	Company	No Company	No response
C of I	26(15.5%)	99(58.9%)	43
Meth	24(53.3%)	9(20.0%)	12
Presb	83(53.2%)	45(28%)	28
R.C.	0(00.0%)	36(53.7%)	31(46.3%)

Immediately, it is obvious from the figures that the Girl's Brigade is largely a Presbyterian and Methodist concern. Historically, of course, this is no surprise. Nevertheless it underlines the degree to which many early experiences are separated by denomination in Northern Ireland. In

Presbyterian circles, the Girl's Brigade is part of the fabric of many Churches. In Catholic circles the organisation may not even be known. Between Protestant denominations there is considerable fluidity. Members of the Uniformed Organisations are not necessarily attached to the host Church except through the organisation. Nevertheless the barrier between Protestants and Catholics remains intact. In a society without violence and without such close Church-secular links, such observations might not be seen to have implications. In Northern Ireland the separation of youth organisations can be read as a further brick in a wall which encompasses schooling, residence, marriage and friendship.

Youth organisations without uniforms are possibly even more important. Many Churches run youth clubs with a primarily recreational thrust as well as youth groups which are primarily engaged in formal discussions and instruction on faith. This includes Sunday Schools, Youth Fellowship Groups and Prayer Groups and constitutes a system of instruction with complete geographical coverage over Northern Ireland. The involvement of Churches in schooling in Northern Ireland has been documented elsewhere. What is important here is the degree to which schooling is complemented by other voluntary possibilities specifically aimed at providing instruction for children and young people. These too are part of the fabric of life. They tend to be organised on a parish or congregational level in common with Church organisation throughout Europe. The same divisions exist for Churches everywhere. What distinguishes Northern Ireland is not so much Church structure as the human context in which Churches live.

The same divisions continue among Church Organisations for adults. Women's Organisations have a long history in Churches and groups such as the Mother's Union, The Presbyterian Woman's Association, The Legion of Mary and the Methodist Women's Association are organised throughout the province. Almost every parish and congregation in Northern Ireland has a branch of one of these organisations attached to the Church.

Table 6: Women's groups in Churches by denomination

	Women's group	no group	no response
C of I	156 (92.9%)	5	7
Meth.	50 (92.6%)	0	4
Presb.	153 (98.1%)	1	2
R C	37 (55.2%)	18	12

These too have been means of integrating secular and Church life with their combined emphases of Church work and evangelism and shared social and personal activity. They are organised within denominations with very few members coming from outside. The Church based women's groups are the largest women's organisations in Northern Ireland. Despite the recent growth of a radical women's movement, Northern Ireland women remain by and large outside this movement in it's formal sense although the thinking and actions evolving out of the more radical groups has certainly had an influence far beyond the formal structures of any 'movement'.

The older denominational groups are all losing members among younger women, even those active in Church activities. To some extent all of them, particularly on the Protestant side, share an identification with unfashionable ideas of male-female divisions and many of the members are over 50. Nevertheless, the importance of these groups for their many active members can be easily underestimated. They remain integral parts of the 'community' aspect of Church life particularly outside Belfast.

The variety of organisations within Churches for women is eye-opening. The variety reflects a concentration on the picture of the woman as child-rearers and home-makers. There were thus Coffee Mornings, Young Wives Groups, 'Women in Action', 'Mothers Together', Women's Social Committees, Women's Friendship Groups all aimed at giving possibilities of day-time community for women in the home. This illustrates the degree to which the Churches are part of the minute variations of Northern Ireland, and not just the broad sweep of generalised events. It is this, indeed which accounts for the persistent importance of the Churches in so many areas of Northern Irish experience and why it is so difficult to separate the sacred from the secular.

Adult Men do not have the same organised structures in Churches as young people and women. To a large extent this reflects the traditional divisions of labour, where women predominate in the 'private' sphere of life while men dominate in the 'public' sphere. Male involvement in Churches was through positions of authority and influence (clergy, elders, select vestry and so on) and took place outside the working day.

Table 7: Men's groups in Churches by denomination

	Men's group	no group	no response
Church of Ireland	47	94	27
Methodist	17	24	12
Presbyterian	31	100	25
Roman Catholic	20	26	19

It is interesting to note that the Catholic Church had relatively more organisations for men. The difference between the number of organisations for men and women in Protestant Churches is much starker. In Catholic circles the Knights of Columbanus, the Knights of Malta and the Men's confraternity had branches or groups in a number of parishes. In Protestant circles there were also groups (Men's Missionary Fellowship and B.B. Old Boys (Presbyterian) and Men's Clubs and Men's Fellowship (C of I)) but these were far less widespread. It is important to note that there were other social activities often mostly for men not recorded here but linked to Churches, particularly bowling.

This lack of tradition for male social groups has been a major problem in areas of high unemployment. Many people in our area studies complained that men would not get involved in any activities except work. Women could be involved in women's groups, day or evening classes, mother and toddler groups or community self-help projects. According to most local commentators, unemployed men preferred to stay in, hang around the streets or go drinking whenever feasible. For many middle class and employed men, Church activities are confined to evenings. Many congregations and parishes reported a number of groups specifically aimed at men.

All of this data illustrates the historical importance of the Churches in the social organisation of the society and of the close inter-connections between the two. As such the Churches can be seen as providing empirical evidence of the male-female divisions of secular society in considerable detail.

By recording the minutiae of Church integration into social life the range of areas in which the Churches are important becomes clear. Another ignored aspect of Church integration into the culture of Northern Ireland is provided if we look at the importance of Churches in keeping alive a non-professional tradition of formal singing. Churches have choirs in even greater numbers than they have women's organisations.

Table 8: Choirs in Churches by denomination			
	Choir	No choir	No response
Church of Ireland	151	9	32
Methodist	43	4	6
Presbyterian	146	2	8
Roman Catholic	58	1	8

This means that 90% of all Churches had choirs and less than 4% definitely did not. It illustrates the degree to which the Churches can be regarded as carriers and guardians of large parts of the formal traditions of Northern Ireland. Nearly all of the choirs are composed of members of the appropriate Churches, hardly surprising given that the primary duty of such groups is to lead the singing at Sunday worship. This underlines the interconnection between secular and church in the community. Even schools would have difficulty comparing themselves with the musical role of Churches in terms of numbers involved. It is easy to dismiss Church choirs as 'insignificant' but if we assume that each choir has an average of 25 members (almost certainly an underestimate) the numbers in the Churches which responded to the survey alone amount to almost 11,000 people. If every Church contacted also has a choir this amounts to 27,000 people.

The same can also be said for bowling clubs. It has been said that every bowling club has a Church attached to it, and certainly bowling proliferates throughout Northern Ireland within Churches. A total of 78.2% of all the Churches who responded reported bowling clubs attached to the congregation or parish. Only 15.1% reported that they had no bowling club. (6.7% no response). Unusually for Church-based clubs, the majority in all denominations reported that the membership of the clubs was open to members from other denominations.

Table 9: Does your bowling club have members of other denominations			
	yes	no	no response
Church of Ireland	103	21	44
Methodist	24	2	19
Presbyterian	86	13	57
Roman Catholic	18	11	38

Of course, inter-denominational does not mean Intercommunity. Nevertheless, there is some evidence that bowling clubs are the largest counter-example to the more general picture of denominational exclusivity, or at least an absolute division between Catholic and Protestant. The reasons for this are not immediately apparent nor does this counter-example appear to have spread beyond bowling. Probably the 'minority' membership in each case are identified as particular people rather than as representatives of a group. Alternatively, the older age-group of many Church bowlers may reflect traditions which stem from a less violent day.

The same degree of cross-community activity was not evident in badminton clubs, though over 50% of Churches also had badminton clubs. Both sports illustrate that Church halls are major facilities. Even the advent of leisure centres with entry charges has not ended the role of Church halls.

It is, of course, impossible to impute any connection between religiosity and badminton in Church halls. Nevertheless sport illustrates that Churches are central to the physical geography of communities as well as to the psychological outlooks and social networks of the community. The Churches also run numerous table tennis clubs and a variety of activities have links with particular churches. Gaelic Athletic Associations are exclusively in Roman Catholic Churches. The numbers of other clubs recorded were very small but they illustrate the width of possibilities of interfaces between Church and Society through recreational activity; 2 dog-handling clubs, 11 dancing societies, 17 football clubs, 9 keep-fit classes, 9 snooker or billiards clubs, 5 tennis clubs, a rowing club and so on. Other activities include quoits, clay pigeon shooting, martial arts, pool clubs, darts, boxing, chess, drama, golf, gardening and canoeing. In a sense the Churches input to these activities is first and foremost a building. The fact that social activities are based in Churches underlines the place of the Churches as centres of civil society in Northern Ireland.

Over 70% (71.1%) of all clergy who answered the questionnaire noted that their Church buildings were available for use of outside groups, provided that the groups were not expressly anti-Church or against Church doctrines and more importantly if they met insurance rules. Only 24.5% indicated that their buildings were not potential resources for non-Church groups. Once again the very extent of the intimate involvement of Church structures with provision of facilities normally regarded as 'secular' is indicated in the very real degree to which Churches as buildings are meeting places and physical resources in Northern Irish society.

To compound this we further asked clergy about other facilities, beyond buildings, which might be available as community resources. The most frequently mentioned resources were buses, holiday centres in seaside resorts and meeting rooms. Nevertheless only 19.3% of Churches in the survey reported the existence of such resources.

On the evidence of our questionnaire, the extension of the Churches into secular life is considerable. This is in addition to the number of more informal worship and bible study groups for adults which are now affiliated to the formal Church structures. Nearly all Churches have groups developed to extend Church worship beyond Sunday attendance. In part this may be a reaction to the flourishing house-church movement which has made inroads into formal Church attendance. It may also be due to the influence of the Charismatic Renewal Movement in the 1970s with it's emphasis on spontaneous and unstructured worship. Only 22.2% of clergy who returned the survey did not record worship groups or meetings for worship outside Sundays. The names and functions of groups vary enormously - house groups, bible study groups, good news club, Christian Endeavour, Thursday Novena to our Lady, Taize Groups, Healing Prayer Groups, Breakfast Worship for example- nevertheless they testify to the growth of active prayer groups in Northern Ireland.

These groups may be largely limited to active members of the Churches. Nevertheless, the range and scope remains remarkably large. We can also speculate that members of these groups attach considerable importance to them. The number of such groups again reflects the reality of the Churches as powerful centre's for private and public life in Northern Ireland. It is a safe assumption that the numbers are in the 10s of thousands, possibly in the hundreds of thousands. Furthermore, our survey concentrates on the four largest denominations. Even in areas where the established denominations have low attendance (e.g. Protestant inner-city Belfast) there may be a great proliferation of gospel halls and house groups unmeasured in this questionnaire.

Worship life cannot be omitted from a serious study of Northern Ireland society despite the fact that it is often ignored in academic circles. Daily Mass is celebrated in all parishes and weekly attendance remains the rule rather than the exception especially outside Belfast. Attendance at Protestant services has fallen in city areas but remains much higher than anywhere else in the U.K. Within the context of a survey to clergy, our results suggest that worship groups do tend to be denominationally specific. This may be misleading. One exception to this rule was the existence of 'charismatic prayer and bible study groups' in some places in all denominations.

The Catholic Church also has St. Vincent de Paul groups attached to most of the parishes in Ireland. This is responsible for looking after some of the needs of the poor in each parish and has no direct Protestant equivalent. Although it is officially separate from parish organisation each local group is effectively part of the parish team. It is composed of active laity in each parish who act as volunteers in their areas. The St. Vincent de Paul Groups also act as agents in special circumstances, such as the distribution of surplus E.C. agricultural products in 1987. Even the Protestant Churches were deeply involved in this activity, a reflection of their unique spread throughout Northern Ireland. Of 67 Catholic Clergy who responded to the survey, 55 parishes had St. Vincent de Paul Groups. These too act as important links between the institutional structure of the Church and the community of the parish.

Although Protestant Churches have no equivalent to St. Vincent de Paul there are numerous groups attached to Churches which undertake much of the same work. Again, the minutiae of the survey indicates an astonishing variety of groups; Social Action Groups, Parish Visiting schemes, Meals on wheels, Pensioners Lunch-clubs, Mothers and Toddlers Groups, Playgroups, Family Welfare Centres, Senior Citizens Clubs, Groups for the Disabled, Community Care group, Home Tapes Ministry, Teenage Holiday schemes, Bingo Clubs, Lunch Clubs, Hostels for the Homeless, Marriage Preparation, and so on. There were also numerous schemes for the elderly, particularly Lunch-clubs, friendship groups, parish visiting and schemes for the redecoration of houses.

One notable feature was the number of charities which had affiliates in Churches, particularly on the Protestant side; Action Cancer, Age Concern, Red Cross, St. John's Ambulance, Alcoholics Anonymous, Anorexic Support Group and so on. Here the interface between Church and non-Church in Northern Ireland is even more blurred. Even where the branches of such groups are not based in Churches some of the membership may be made up of Church activists in a secular capacity. Churches and Church members have been heavily involved with groups working on issues of economic development in Africa, Latin America and Asia. Many had 'Third World Groups' or 'Development Groups' on the basis of a perceived religious commitment. Others had small groups who worked for specific charities: Christian Aid (Protestant), Trocaire(R.C.), TEAR Fund (Protestant), Leprosy Mission. The missionary approach of the Churches has left a deeper attachment to this issue in Church circles of all denominations than elsewhere in secular society. The spectacular amounts raised in Northern Irish Churches at the time of the Ethiopian

Famine underline this. Perhaps the high overall rate of giving to charity in Northern Ireland Culture is Church-related.

Many Churches reported that some of their activities involved an inter-community dimension, although examples of this were mostly bowling and other sporting activities. Some 57.6% of all Churches who replied reported that some of their activities involved contact with other Churches of the same denomination. A surprisingly high proportion (37.6%) reported that they had no recreational activities with Churches of the same denomination. Again surprisingly the proportion of those claiming that recreational activities involved them in contact with Churches of other denominations rose to 60.1% and those reporting no contact fell to 33.9%. To some extent this can be explained by the fact that much contact is extremely local e.g. joint clubs for pensioners, bowling leagues and so on.

Respondents were then asked "Are there any Churches with which you would not undertake social and recreational activities on principle?" Only 1.8% said they would not co-operate with Church of Ireland Churches, 2.3% objected to such contact with Methodists, 2.1% with Presbyterians but 7.6% objected to even social and recreational contact with Roman Catholics. Although the figures appear low, it indicates that in some circles, antipathy to community relations extends to every sphere. Objections to social contact with Protestants appeared to be lower among Catholics than vice versa.

Despite the small percentages involved, the anti-Catholic element was nevertheless marked. While only 3 Church of Ireland clergy who responded objected to inter-Protestant contact, 15 objected to contact with Catholics. While 5 Presbyterian Ministers objected to inter-Protestant contact, 16 refused recreational or social contact with Catholics. Two Catholic priests objected to contact with Protestants while one was unhappy about any contact outside the parish boundary.

All in all, the involvement of the Churches in the social and recreational life of the community builds up into an impressive whole. Reduced in this form, it is easy to dismiss the importance of choirs and youth clubs, and nevertheless, these are the nuts and bolts of important cultural phenomena. To ignore them may have as much to do with snobbery as science.

Section Three: Churches and Social and Community Action

As we saw in section two, Churches are deeply involved with many aspects of informal social life in Northern Ireland. In this section we will be examining the Churches relationship to more of the formal aspects of community and social services. The classical expression of this in the 1980s has come to be the Churches' identification with the ACE schemes. This has led to considerable criticism in many circles of Church activities as we shall see in the case studies. The same is true of schools involvement. Due to the poor response in Catholic areas, the survey is an inadequate record of the relationship of ACE (Action for Community Employment) schemes to Churches. The spread of such schemes and the amount of money involved is nonetheless substantial. In addition Churches provide specific services from their premises for their communities: Samaritans Groups, estate management committee representatives, Summer playschemes, gardening services and parcel deliveries at Christmas. Clergy and Church people often offer Church buildings as meeting places for issues of community politics such as roadsafety campaigns, anti-hospital closure campaigns or social service groups. In one area the Churches have been involved in the setting up of a local co-operative supermarket. On a wider level, Churches, especially the Roman Catholic Church but also the Church of Ireland have been involved in the establishment and encouragement of Credit Unions while many Protestant churches make special arrangements for the security forces.

The Churches and the State also co-operate in the provision of other important services - day centres or meeting places, meals on wheels schemes, voluntary schemes, mother and toddler groups, clubs for the elderly, mothers at home, after school play groups, clubs for the disabled and social clubs. The Churches undertake by far the widest schemes of planned visitation of homes and those in hospital of any groups in Northern Irish society. Often this is in the person of the clergy and perhaps this more than any other feature leads the Churches to be identified with their clergy in their public role. It nevertheless intimates the extent to which the Churches are a personal institution, whose influence lies in the realm of personal and societal relationships rather than in access to political power. It is this involvement in the structure of daily life in the community which makes them such useful clients for the government in relation to programmes such as ACE. While attendance at Church may have fallen since World War II, Churches retain a role as 'honest broker'. It is where this relationship is in danger of breaking down that the Churches are in the most serious social difficulty e.g. ACE schemes in

West Belfast.

The clergy were asked "How important do you consider social outreach projects to be for your parish or congregation?" Only 4.4% did not respond.

Table 10: The importance of social outreach projects

	C of I	Meth	Presb	R.C.	All
very important	34.5%	51.1%	30.1%	49.3%	36.9%
important	36.9%	31.1%	39.7%	35.8%	37.2%
secondary	22.6%	15.5%	20.5%	11.9%	19.5%
not important	1.8%	0	3.8%	0	2.1%

The responses showed the Methodists to be the Church which laid the greatest emphasis on social action as part of ministry. The Methodist commitment to social action has always been central to Methodist self-perception since the days of Wesley.

The Roman Catholics who responded also saw social action as an integral part of the Churches role. It is difficult to draw any absolute conclusions about this because of the low numbers involved. Nevertheless, it does reflect the traditional Irish Catholic involvement in the social affairs of the Catholic community. It may also reflect the relatively greater level of poverty in the Catholic community.

The overall averages are heavily weighted to the Church of Ireland and Presbyterians because of their much greater numbers. On the basis of these figures alone, it is impossible to make absolute assessments of the relative importance laid on social ministry by Protestants and Catholics. Nevertheless, even in the case of Presbyterian clergy, who in this survey attached less importance to a social witness than others, over 60% regarded social ministry as central. It remains true that nearly all respondents in all Churches claimed to attach some importance to the social aspect of Church life.

Among Presbyterians, however, 3.8% of clergy who responded saw a complete separation between Church and social activism, regarding it as absolutely unimportant. It is possible that this view is current among members of some other Churches and groups, not part of the survey, who share this vision of the Church as entirely 'spiritual' in nature.

There was a broad spread of opinion among Church of Ireland clergy. Similar proportions of clergy as in the case of Presbyterians regarded social outreach as important or very important. Interestingly, very few

Church of Ireland clergy regarded social outreach as of no importance. At the same time, more Church of Ireland clergy regarded it as secondary than was the case with Presbyterians. One might wish to perceive in such nuances evidence for a distaste in official Church of Ireland circles for extreme positions.

A question of general principle is different from a question about concrete possibilities of Church involvement in local activities. We therefore asked about specific possibilities in each area.

Table 11: Do you see possibilities of developing congregational or parish community work in your area!

	C of I	Meth	Presb	R.C.	All
Yes	69.0%	77.7%	56.4%	83.6%	67.7%
No	17.8%	11.1%	35.9%	8.9%	22.2%
No response	13.1%	11.1%	7.7%	7.5%	10.1%

By far the most striking result was the very high percentage of Presbyterian clergy who saw no possibilities in comparison with clergy of other denominations. Presbyterian clergy saw no opportunities for community work from their congregations in double the proportion of Church of Ireland clergy, three times the proportions of Methodists and four times the proportions of Catholics who responded.

We can speculate as to why this might be the case. Part of the answer may lie in a relative lack of emphasis on community work in the Presbyterian tradition for which we found some, limited, evidence. Another part of the answer may lie in the relatively long-established network of organisations and structures within the Presbyterian Church in particular, although the structure of organisations in all Churches now seems very well established. The relative affluence of Presbyterians or the decline in Presbyterian attendance among the less affluent may now have resulted in an absence of pressure or urgency in Presbyterian congregations in this area.

Although we must regard figures for Catholic clergy as highly tentative, the survey indicates a strong drive for further Church involvement in community work. To some extent this may reflect a ‘catch-up’ effect, in that social groups were long seen as a ‘Protestant’ form of organisation. It may also be that changes in Northern Irish society in the late twentieth century are most apparent in the Catholic community and that the Church is anxious to be central to these developments for whatever reasons. Thirdly the relative poverty of Catholics in Northern Ireland compared statistically to Protestants may mean that the tasks to be performed are more immediately apparent to Catholic as opposed to Protestant clergy.

In order to focus our questions further, we asked clergy about unemployment schemes in their areas. The answers fell into a very similar pattern to those of the previous two questions.

Table 12: Do you see a specific need for employment schemes within your parish or congregation?

	C of I	Meth	Presb	R.C.	All
Yes	50.0%	51.1%	34.0%	76.1%	48.4%
No	39.3%	37.8%	57.7%	20.9%	42.9%
No response	10.7%	11.1%	8.3%	3.0%	8.7%

Presbyterian clergy regarded employment schemes as much less immediately pressing than clergy in the other Protestant denominations. They were less than half as likely to seek such developments as the Catholic clergy who responded. As well as reflecting theological ambiguities about Church involvement with social issues, these results probably indicate the relative wealth of many Presbyterian congregations especially given the Church's decline in working-class parts of Belfast. The fall-off in Church attendance in Protestant inner-city working class areas may mean that the bulk of Presbyterian clergy is more isolated from any sense of urgency about the economic and social problems of unemployment than the clergy of other denominations. Furthermore, there is some evidence of a residual 'work ethic' among Presbyterians which eschews state aid.

Another explanation may be that the residential segregation of Presbyterians by class is more absolute than in other denominations. If this were true, the concentration on absolute numbers in this survey might disguise the commitment of those who are committed. It is not clear that this is true for Presbyterianism any more than it is for other brands of Protestantism.

We asked clergy whether they regarded the sphere of social and community activism as appropriate for interdenominational approaches. In the first instance we asked about attitudes to inter-denominational rather than inter-community contact. It is necessary to point out that the two are not synonymous.

We asked clergy whether they participated in community projects in co-operation with local Churches of other denominations? According to those who responded, nearly half of them are involved in such projects.

Table 13:	C of I	Meth	Presb	R.C.	All
Yes	48.8%	40.0%	48.7%	41.8%	46.8%
No	41.7%	44.4%	48.1%	49.3%	45.4%
No response	7.8%				

In order to examine the limits to such co-operation, we asked clergy about the principle of participation in inter-Church projects to relieve unemployment locally. Some 89.9% of clergy who responded said that they had no objection in principle, varying between 91% of Catholic and Church of Ireland clerics to 87% among Presbyterians.

The clergy were then asked whether there were denominations with which they would not work in this sphere. While 84% of all respondents said that they would work with all denominations, 10% of our group indicated that they did have objections. In proportional terms these reservations were spread almost equally between all denominations - e.g. 8.95% among Catholics. 9.62% among Presbyterians.

We asked clergy were to indicate denominations with which they specifically would not work in this area. We offered our respondents a wide range of choices including other denominations which did not participate in the survey. If we limit responses to attitudes to other Churches involved in the survey then Protestant attitudes to Roman Catholics were notably more reserved. Some 5.13% of Presbyterians and 2.38% of Church of Ireland clergy objected to co-operation with Catholics in the sphere of unemployment. This was significant only in comparison to the willingness to work together with other clergy. Only one person (a Presbyterian) indicated an unwillingness to work in this sphere with the Church of Ireland. Two others indicated the same unwillingness to work with Methodists and Presbyterians.

However, there were some objections to co-operation with Free Presbyterians. Here 6% of Church of Ireland clergy, 5.1% of Presbyterian clergy and 7.5% of Roman Catholic clergy who answered the questionnaire registered an objection. The response of Roman Catholic clergy is clearly understandable. The response of Protestant clergy indicates a wide spread of opinion within the Protestant Churches. More Protestant clergy had objections to the involvement of Free Presbyterians than objected to co-operation with Roman Catholics. There were a number of objections to working with smaller groups; Independent Methodists, Mormons and Jehovah's Witnesses.

To complete our investigations of the Churches in this sphere, we asked about Church interaction with statutory and voluntary bodies. In this survey 40.8% of all clergy who responded had direct contact with statutory bodies in the provision of community action programmes, although 49.5% did not. Interestingly, the percentage of Catholic parishes with contact (68.7%) appeared to be higher than the percentage of Protestant parishes (C of I - 38.7%, Presbyterian - 32.1%, Methodist - 37.8%) involved. In order to be more precise, more investigation into this area might prove significant. On a general level, it indicates a close interaction between the secular and Church structures on a financial level. Furthermore, the survey did not cover schools, and it appears that the survey provides some evidence that the Catholic Church as an organised institution has come to act as a crucial bridge between the State and the Catholic population. It might also be important to analyse how easy or uneasy this relationship is.

Churches are also deeply involved in the networks of voluntary organisations. Over a quarter (25.9%) of clergy who responded reported active co-operation with non-Church voluntary agencies in the provision of social and community services. Our survey did not record the inter-relationships between the membership of voluntary organisations and their staffs and their personal belonging to and attendance at Churches. Were this to be taken into account a much richer personal picture might be built up. Involvement with external voluntary bodies was equally important in all four denominations.

Section Four: Relationships between the clergy

Although it is impossible by survey to gauge the importance of particular relationships between particular people, it was our goal to examine the existence of formal networks and their scope. We were particularly interested in the extension of formal networks between clergy of different denominations. It cannot be assumed that the lack of formal networks means that relations between clergy do not exist. In some cases the ghettoised nature of Northern Ireland living means that there are no clergy of 'the other side' in the locality. In other cases older style informal networks may exist in country areas which are of central importance to the area's stability but which are nowhere formalised.

Over 93% of clergy were in regular formal contact with other clergy of their own denomination. Each Church is differently organised. The character and importance of each structure varies. Nevertheless, such structures, particularly where they involve the government of the Church institutions are important symbols of status and place in Churches. They are also part of the acknowledgement of the 'profession' of clergy. They are opportunities for meeting with peers of the same group, the exchange of experiences and views and the consolidation of a denominational identity rather than each congregation being left isolated. They are part of the physical expression of each Church as a unitary institution.

Contact between clergy of different denominations is much less organised and varied even if the contact is local. We asked clergy whether they had regular meetings with clergy of other denominations.

Table 14: Do you have regular contact with clergy of other denominations?

	C of I	Meth	Presb	R.C.	All
Yes	62.5%	64.4%	59.6%	43.3%	58.7%
No	35.1%	22.2%	39.1%	52.2%	37.8%
No response	2.4%	13.3%	1.3%	4.5%	3.4%

The most obvious result was the much greater number of Roman Catholic clergy who had no contact with other clergy on a regular basis compared with different varieties of Protestant clergy. We must treat all figures in this survey about Roman Catholic clergy with caution. However the difference is large enough to appear significant (20%). Assuming its significance, it indicates a considerable degree of exclusion, whether imposed by Protestant clergy unwilling to meet regularly with Roman Catholic clergy or self imposed.

In total, almost two-fifths of our respondents indicated that they had no formal contact with clergy of other denominations. This indicates the degree to which clergy and parishes remain isolated within particular cultures and the degree to which denominational boundaries still define patterns of official inter-relationship. The denominational system continues to be very alive in Northern Irish Church circles. Contact within denominations in different localities is much more frequent than local formal contact between clergy of different denominations. Ongoing political violence between groups using religious labels does not seem to have led the Churches to seek any systematic inter-denominational structures.

When asked about the meetings 10.6% of all clergy who responded, and 17.97% of those who reported meetings, indicated that representatives of some denominations were specifically excluded. This was particularly true among Protestants. The survey did not record which denominations were excluded, however it is possible to surmise that Roman Catholics and Free Presbyterians were the most regularly excluded denominations. At the same time, some 81.2% of clergy reported that there were opportunities for informal contact between clergy at local level. Once more, Catholic clergy were the least likely to have such contacts (25.4%) although this is likely to reflect ghettoisation. Informal contacts require a common places, such as a common shopping area or clubs which draw on a wide area.

We then asked clergy to identify the denominations of clergy to whom they had no contact. Some 48.4% of all clergy who answered indicated that there at least one local cleric with whom they had no contact and only 43.1% who indicated that they had contact to all the clergy in their locality. The proportions varied in each denomination. Among Church of Ireland clergy 45.2% reported that there were local clergy who they never met. The figure among Methodists was 55.5%, among Presbyterians was 48.7% and among Roman Catholics was 50.7%.

Among all clergy 11.9% reported no contact with Free Presbyterian clergy and 9.2% had no contact with Roman Catholic clergy. Perhaps more surprisingly, 7.2% reported that they had no contact with local Baptist clergy. The breakdown among the denominations was also interesting.

Table 15: Inter-denominational contact of clergy

15.a. Those reporting no contact with Free Presbyterians

C of I	Meth	Presb	R.C	All
16.1%	6.7%	11.5%	6%	11.9%

15.b. Those reporting no contact with Roman Catholics

C of I	Meth	Presb	R.C.	All
8.3%	4.4%	15.4%	0.0%	9.2%

15.c. Those reporting no contact with Baptist clergy

C of I	Meth	Presb	R.C.	All
4.2%	11.1%	9.6%	6%	7.1%

Among Catholics these figures are partly distorted because for those living in entirely Catholic areas, contact with local clerics of other denominations may have little significance. Among Protestants there are significant denominational variations. Church of Ireland clergy reported no contact with Free Presbyterian clergy almost twice as frequently as they reported no contact with Roman Catholic clergy. On the other hand, among Presbyterians the proportions of those indicating no contact with Free Presbyterians was markedly less than those who indicated that they had no contact to local Catholic clergy. Methodist Ministers reported no contact to Baptist pastors more often than to any other denomination.

This already suggests that Presbyterians regard links with Catholic clergy as more problematic than do clergy of other Protestant denominations.

Many Church of Ireland clergy clearly do not enjoy open relationships with many Free Presbyterian Ministers. Given the relatively small size of the Free Presbyterian Church in Northern Ireland it is significant how often they appear in the responses. They clearly play a more important psychosocial role than their absolute size would appear to warrant for other Protestants as well as Roman Catholics.

Section Five: Inter-church ecclesiastical activity.

In this section, we focused on the attitude of clergy to the participation of people from other denominations in their Church worship activities. This is clearly the heart of the formal work of clergy within all of the denominations in our survey and indeed beyond. To participate in worship as a full and equal member or partner is to be invited into the heart of the Church's communal and spiritual life. Nevertheless there are serious difficulties in this sphere. Roman Catholic orthodoxy contends that differing doctrines of the Eucharist preclude the participation of Protestants in Roman Catholic Communion. In all of the responses in this survey, worship is clearly seen as a joint act of prayer or praise not involving communion. Very few, if any, Catholic priests would actively sanction inter-communion between denominations.

Officially, most Protestant denominations do not make absolute conditions beyond the individual conscience of the participant person on participation in communion. This does not mean, however, that their understandings of the Eucharist are identical. Many Protestants in Ulster regard the Roman Catholic Church with extreme mistrust and even total abhorrence. In this context, the claim of the Church to be the one true Church is a declaration of imperial ambition. In the context of intercommunal strife in Northern Ireland such claims can easily be seen as being put into action by attacks on 'the Protestant people'.

We asked clergy about participation in joint services of worship. The responses were as follows:

Table 16: Do you participate in joint worship with local clergy of other denominations?

	CofI	Meth	Presb	R.C.	All
Yes	73.2%	86.7%	75.0%	50.75%	71.8%
No	22.6%	8.9%	21.2%	43.3%	23.9%
no response	4.4%				

The most interesting feature was the number of Roman Catholics who were not involved in any services with other clergy. The usual precautions in interpreting this result apply, and nevertheless the notably higher proportion indicates the substantial inter-Church divide between Catholics and Protestants.

We then asked clergy to indicate the denominations with which they participated in joint worship. There were striking differences in the willingness of clergy to work with different denominations. Some 67.9% of other clergy indicated an active worshipping relationship with Church of Ireland clergy. A higher percentage of Methodist (82.2%) and Presbyterian (72.4%) clergy indicated this relationship than did Catholics (47.8%). Amongst non-Methodists, 57% indicated a working relationship with Methodist clergy. The equivalent result for Presbyterians was 65%.

By far the most striking figure was that only 34.1% of Protestant clergy indicated a working relationship with Roman Catholic clergy. While these figures must be treated with extreme caution, the trend is very stark. If we break the figures down, there are further differences amongst Protestant denominations. Only 25.6% of Presbyterian clergy appear to have active relationships with Roman Catholic clergy in the sphere of joint worship compared to 38.7% of Church of Ireland clergy or 46.7% of Methodists.

In order to clarify this position we asked a further question in a negative form: With which denominations would you not work in the area of joint worship? In this instance, less than 1% of clergy of all denominations indicated that they would not work with the Church of Ireland on principle. Some 1.1% of all clergy indicated a desire to avoid Methodists and 1.4%

an objection to Presbyterians. This would seem to indicate that lack of contact between the Catholic clergy and their Protestant counterparts is not a matter of principle. Instead it may be regarded as difficult or unimportant.

However, some 23.2% of all clergy who responded indicated an unwillingness to work with Roman Catholic clergy in the sphere of joint worship. By excluding Roman Catholics, a figure of 27.1% of all Protestant clergy appeared to hold this view. Again this figure hides very stark differences between Protestant denominations

Table 17: Proportions of Protestant clergy who would not participate in joint worship with Roman Catholic clergy

Church of Ireland	17.9%
Methodist	4.4%
Presbyterian	43.6%
All Protestant Clergy	27.1%

This indicates that by far the greatest antipathy to joint worship with the Roman Catholic clergy exists amongst Presbyterians. Whatever the statistical accuracy, the size of the difference indicates an anti-Catholic culture and theology amongst Presbyterians which is far stronger than in the other large denominations. At the same time, we should not disguise the fact that the levels of objection to Roman Catholic clergy and worship in the Church of Ireland are also strikingly high even if they are less than half that of Presbyterian clergy.

The willingness of clergy to work with Roman Catholics also varied with age. There was a tendency for younger clergy to refuse to work with Roman Catholics more often than their older colleagues. Of course there are few Presbyterian and Methodist ministers over 65 who are still active. The figures below are for all clergy who responded including Roman Catholic

Table 18: Proportion of clergy who will not work with Roman Catholics in joint worship, by age

Aged 25-35	25.4%
Aged 36-45	28.2%
Aged 46-55	24.1%
Aged 56-65	20.8%
Aged 65+	6.7%

Exclusion of non-Church members from the celebration of the Eucharist by Catholic clergy can be identified as an exclusion from the Roman Catholic Churches own understanding of the heart of the matter. A refusal on the part of Protestant and particularly many Presbyterian clergy to become involved in joint worship services with Roman Catholic clergy indicates another exclusion from a Presbyterian understanding of the heart of the matter. In both cases it appears unavoidable that a clear view of the other as lesser, not equal is being made.

The Presbyterian Church is vulnerable to attacks by more vocally anti-Catholic groups such as the Free Presbyterians who claim to be the true protectors of the Protestant heritage. In a context of violence, where Presbyterians feel under threat by people identified as Catholic, it is easy to see how a conspiracy theory can be built up around anti-Catholicism. We shall see that this is indeed the case in the case studies. As violence rises and more people start to share the fears of the religious group, so the religious fringe is transformed from being regarded as lunacy, in periods of calm, to being prophecy. 'They alone knew and understood the signs of the times'.

Mutual exclusion from acts of worship therefore becomes an act of social and theological significance simultaneously. Perhaps it is in the results of this part of the survey that the extent of the Churches involvement with the politics of conflict is most visible.

Section Six: Participation by clergy in civic activity

In order to explore the role of the clergy in Northern Ireland public life we asked clergy to record their involvement's in civic activities and positions of responsibility. Although there are a number of Protestant clergy active as councillors, and two Free Presbyterian Ministers acting as Westminster M.Ps, the tradition in the main four Churches has been to leave direct party politics to the laity. The Catholic Church frowns on the election of priests to any public office, although one priest in dispute with the Bishop of Down and Connor now sits as a councillor in Larne Borough Council. Despite this, the clergy are involved in every other area of public activity. The results illustrate how difficult it is to clearly separate the private and public role of clergy in Northern Ireland.

We asked clergy about their ex-officio participation in a number of activities. The results are listed below.

Table 19: Do you participate ex-officio in local or civic festivals?					
	C of I	Meth	Presb	R.C.	All
Yes	38.1%	48.9%	41.7%	34.3%	39.9%
No	50.6%	42.2%	54.5%	53.7%	51.6%
No response	8.5%				

Table 20: Do you participate ex-officio in remembrance day services?					
	C of I	Meth	Presb	R.C.	All
Yes	53.6%	66.7%	59.0%	11.9%	50.5%
No	38.1%	26.7%	39.1%	74.6%	42.9%
No response	6.7%				

Remembrance Sunday services in which the allied dead of the two World Wars are commemorated could be seen as symbols of the close intertwining of the Protestant Churches with the British cause. Of course, it is also a personal matter. Many of the congregations and parishes knew many who fought and died in both wars. The importance of the battle of the Somme in Protestant memory is clear evidence of this deep bond. Nevertheless the stark difference between Protestant and Catholic clergy involvement in Remembrance Sunday activities illustrates the degree to which cultural life and the nature of memory are shaped in the two communities. Ghettoisation ensures that many never experience the other's remembrance days accept as acts of violent triumphalism or strident nationalism/ imperialism. The numerous possible interpretations of Remembrance Sunday services illustrates how difficult it is to arrive at any absolute conclusions. It also illustrates the degree to which life and death, personal and cultural, national and denominational are integrated into all the Churches.

Table 21: Do you participate ex-officio on social services councils?	
	All clergy
yes	13.8%
no	71.8%
no response	14.4%

Table 22: Do you participate ex-officio on schools management boards or committees?

	C of I	Meth	Presb	R.C.	All
Yes	78.6%	62.2%	75.6%	71.6%	74.8%
No	16.7%	33.3%	22.4%	17.9%	20.6%
No response	4.6%				

Answers to this question confirm the degree to which the clergy are intimately bound up with the education system in Northern Ireland. Over 70% (nearly three-quarters of clergy) in our survey had a direct management link to schools in the province. This in itself is not a new finding. Nevertheless it indicates a degree of integration in the public fabric of life which should not be overlooked.

Table 23: Do you participate ex-officio in voluntary organisations (All clergy).

yes	40.1%
no	47.1%
no response	12.4%

Table 24: Do you participate ex officio in events organised by the Orange Order? (Protestant clergy only)

	C of I	Meth	Presb
Yes	28.6%	11.1%	18.9%
No	63.7%	77.8%	76.3%
No response	7.7%	11.1%	5.1%

The Church of Ireland clergy's links to the Orange Order appear, at least ex-officio, to be stronger than the links of clergy in other denominations. Given the opposition in Presbyterian circles to worship with Roman Catholics it is interesting to note that this is not expressed in terms of a strong clerical relationship to the Orange Order itself. Presbyterian opposition to Catholicism appears to be much more directly theological than a matter of the Orange Order as an institution. It is worth noting that only one Catholic priest in our survey indicated an ex-officio involvement with the Ancient Order of Hibernians.

In order to draw a contrast between ex-officio involvements and personal choices, we also asked clergy about their personal involvement in voluntary groups and in political parties. Some 39.4% of clergy were involved in voluntary organisations in a private capacity, spread throughout the denominations. In contrast only 2.5% of clergy in all denominations claimed to be members of political parties (91.5% recorded that they not members). The proportions were higher among Catholics and Presbyterians than among Church of Ireland clergy or Methodists, but nowhere was it more than 5%.

On the other hand, more clergy appeared to have a personal interest in the Orange Order. Among Protestant clergy, 11.9% were members of the Orange Order.

Table 25: Protestant clergy membership of the Orange Order, by denomination

Church of Ireland	12.2%
Methodist	8.9%
Presbyterian	13.5%

Interestingly, a slightly higher proportion of Presbyterian clergy in this survey were actually members of the Orange Order than Church of Ireland clergy. This reverses the ex-officio proportions which we noted above. The historic links of the Orange Order to the ascendancy may mean that ritual activities such as annual services are held in Church of Ireland Churches but that the clergy themselves are not members. It should be noted that the proportions indicated by this survey do not indicate any absolute proportions particularly given the relatively small difference between the numbers of Presbyterian and Anglican clergy involved. It also shows that although over 10% of clergy are members and the Churches are involved in the context of Orange Order ritual the vast majority are not members. Certainly it will not do to reduce the links of Churches, religion, nation and state to the Orange Order although it is no doubt extremely significant.

Conclusions

a. The survey

1. In general Protestant clergy responded much more readily than Catholic clergy. The difference between the Protestant denominations was not very significant.
2. Responses came from clergy of all ages. There was some variation

between denominations but in no case was the response so poor as to render results inadequate because of age structure. This is qualified, of course, by the poor level of response among Roman Catholic clergy.

3. The geographical spread of responses was wide. Each denomination had a slightly different regional distribution but the differences were not significant. Overall, the survey had a similar response in all areas.

4. The size of parishes and congregations varied according to denomination. Clergy ministering in the Church of Ireland and the Roman Catholic Church worked in relation to a larger number of laity. Nevertheless in such situations, and particularly in the Roman Catholic Church there was usually more than one priest. Presbyterian congregations had one minister each as assistants were not surveyed. Methodists had the smallest average size of congregation reflecting their smaller absolute size.

b. The Churches as part of Northern Ireland life

1. Churches in Northern Ireland are part of the warp and weft of society both spatially and historically. As such they cannot be expected to act as political parties nor can they be analysed simply as sub-sets of the State. They may be expected as much to reflect as to lead society, hence the present chaos. They are likely to carry the memories of community experience even for those who no longer accept the religious doctrines. Churches are central to any adequate understanding of community, social or recreational life in Northern Ireland. Nearly everybody in Northern Ireland has been in Churches in some capacity. Non-Church people come into contact with Churches through social and recreational life and through membership of outside groups together with Church people e.g. charitable activities.

2. Even in areas where Church attendance is low, communal boundaries reflect ecclesiastical boundaries. Churches are part of each community. They are places where fundamental values are passed on and which stand for specific reference-values even for people who do not attend. Churches are cultural guardians for many in Northern Ireland, with a more continuous and intimate link to the history of the peoples than any other institutions including the U.K., the Republic of Ireland or Northern Ireland Governments. More coherently than any of these they can claim to carry the memories of the peoples of Ulster. More specifically they carry, through ritual, organisations and activities much of the received culture in the community. While this is clearly breaking down in some areas, secular organisations (e.g. political parties or clubs) organise within a framework which is established in the past, a past of which the Churches

were already part. Thus secularisation does not necessarily signal an end to sectarianism. Rather it may mean the replacement of Church-based sectarianism by non-Church, and possibly less restrained, sectarianism unless it results not only in a movement away from Churches but also in a break-up of the communities in which people live.

3. The clergy are important figures in integrating private and public life in Northern Ireland. They are active at the crossroads between public life and personal concerns. Clergy are involved at every level of public life 'below' that of elected representative. On most community bodies, the clergy are or have been represented. Instead of involvement in political parties, clergy are active in the area of the pulpit proclaiming values which claim a transcendence over politicians. In this sense they are deeply involved in society's discussions at every level 'above' the practical business of public representation. In their involvement at the formal level below public representation, the Churches main function is as institutions within and beyond the State. They have formal institutional structures which take decisions and adopt official public postures. Having secured co-operation, the Churches function within the governmental structures. If, however there is a Church State clash of priorities, the other claims of the Churches become more visible. Churches may then claim a loyalty which transcends any allegiance to the State. If this loyalty holds, then, ultimately, the State cannot legislate against this level without resort to physical coercion, and even then, the impact is not clear. The claim on the members of the Church to examine their consciences in the light of teaching and events is a primary claim to consideration before any political decisions or any claims which the State might make. Hence any attempt to regard the Churches as institutions alone and disregards this dimension is fraught with difficulties, especially if there is a long history of Church-State suspicion.

4. The Orange Order while an important integrative mechanism in Protestant culture is not the sole conduit which combines culture, politics, economics and religion. Remembrance day, Church worship, the daily experience of violence and political parties which claim religious roots are all at least as important in the integration of religion, identity and politics in Northern Ireland.

c. The Churches and social and economic life in Northern Ireland

1. Churches amount to the largest voluntary and non-money economy in Northern Ireland through the vast amounts of voluntary time and money

spent in them.
2. Some formal Economic life (e.g. A.C.E., Community initiatives, Credit Unions) is also lived through Churches and Church authorities.
3. Church buildings are important community resources. Churches in Northern Ireland provide much of the non-State space for groups and social life.
4. The majority of clergy believe that a social facet to their work is important. This is true in all denominations. In relative terms, the Presbyterian clergy are the least interested in a social aspect to the Church. Presbyterian clergy appear to be markedly less concerned to develop further areas of community work in the parishes or congregations than the clergy in other denominations. Roman Catholic clergy appear to be very anxious to develop such work. Presbyterian clergy are less likely to wish to set up employment schemes in their parishes or congregation. Roman Catholic priests see numerous possibilities in their parishes.

d. The Churches and inter-community relationships
1. The majority of clergy have no objection in principle to co-operate in the sphere of community and social facilities. Objections to co-operate are strongest against Free Presbyterians. There are more Protestant clergy unwilling to co-operate with Roman Catholics in this sphere than vice versa. Catholic Church involvement with statutory bodies is if anything greater than among Protestant Churches. This may reflect the greater emphasis on employment schemes and social provision. All Churches are also linked in to the rest of the voluntary sector in the provision of community and social services in their areas.
2. Churches provide denominationally separate facilities. Amongst Protestant Churches the divide is not absolute, especially in the sphere of social services and uniformed youth organisations. Nevertheless there are few organisations which bridge this gap. Bowling appears to be something of an exception. This contrasts sharply with the apparent willingness to co-operate in principle. Most clergy who responded have no objection in principle to inter-community contact at the level of recreation. Where there are objections, the strongest trend is objections by Protestants to contact with Catholics. It should be noted that those who objected were outnumbered by 9 to 1 by those who did not.
3. Formal contacts between the clergy are stronger within denominations than within locality. The Roman Catholic clergy are the most isolated within their own denomination. Roman Catholic clergy have less formal and informal contact with other denominational clergy than Protestants

have among themselves. However nearly 40% of all clergy have no formal contacts with clergy outside their denomination. Amongst Church of Ireland clergy, contact with Free Presbyterianism would appear to be very sporadic. Among the clergy of the three largest Protestant denominations, Presbyterians would appear to be least in favour of formal or informal contacts with Roman Catholics.

4. Ecclesiastical co-operation is much more difficult between Catholics and Protestants than between different varieties of Protestant. Exclusion from worship indicates an attitude of superiority which may be difficult to keep retained within a specifically religious sphere.

  a. Presbyterian clergy are more likely to refuse to participate in worship with Roman Catholics than clergy of other Protestant denominations.

  b. Far more Church of Ireland clergy avoid joint worship contact with Roman Catholics on theological grounds than avoid Presbyterians. The Catholic-Protestant cleft appears to dominate theological life among Northern Irish Anglicans.

  c. Roman Catholics are least likely to be involved in inter-denominational services of any kind.

5. In the context of violence in which groups are religiously labelled, theological attitudes are easily translated into political responses. In the absence of other coherent defenders, the theological defenders come to be seen as the strongest card in the fight against the enemy because of their total commitment.

6. The institutional role of Churches in schools, social services and voluntary agencies make them huge structures of social organisation and integration often in the person of the clergy. It is part of their existence as integrating institutions that the clergy do not get involved directly in partisanship. Hence clergy do not join political parties in large numbers. While this has an integrating and inclusive effect when there is but one organisation, where there are two or four or many the result is integration within and serious disintegration between the groups especially if all the groups claim superiority over one another as is the case between the Churches in Northern Ireland.

Final Remarks

The questionnaire illustrates the degree to which the structures of Northern Irish Society are enmeshed with the structures of the Churches and vice versa. The Churches provide much of the framework within which apparently secular social, personal and community life is lived.

The divisions between the Churches are justified on theological grounds. These justifications have gained social significance for some, especially Protestants, and acts as an ideology of group defence. A group whose identity is forged through their common experience of a violent enemy seeks to understand the nature of that enemy and the nature of the attacks on them. The fact that theologies are used to bridge this gap underlines that for many the picture of the people under siege because of their religion is at least partly credible. The fear of an enemy combined with an actual experience of violence in turn reinforces the credibility of the theology, especially as daily experiences of violence seem to prove the theological expectations. Religions which appeared fanatical in times of tranquillity appear to have a prophetic quality under perceived violent attack.

This close linking of Church to secular culture is repeated in the organisation of society from the general use of religious labels to describe cultural groupings down to the minutiae of social organisation. The questionnaire confirms these links and confirms that Churches links, in general, are no more cross-community in orientation than links between other groups. Certainly, no clear differences can be seen between Church approaches to inter-community work and secular approaches.

While Church leaders appear anxious to mitigate the effects of division, through programmes of recreation and social activity and even through employment schemes, they also appear to want to retain their separateness in the areas which they consider most important, such as communion and joint worship. The question of schooling would also appear to fit within this context. This results in a fundamental ambiguity in even the most tentative steps to reduce inter-community conflict through Churches because all approaches are always qualified by an anxiety to ensure that the boundaries and limits to co-operation are not overstepped. Theology and the constellation of events in Northern Ireland would appear to conspire in a particularly violent way. Both Church and secular dimensions reflect each other in a symbiosis built up over years of community antagonism and repeated in a seemingly endless sequence.

The questionnaire also demonstrates that the Churches are major partners of the State. Nevertheless, as the case studies show, there is very little evidence that the State can manipulate the relationship to the Churches by financial means without the open consent of the Churches. Indeed any attempt to do so will be read as yet another attack by an enemy on the community in question. It also underlines that an understanding of the dynamics of Northern Ireland society will have to understand this inter-relationship and give adequate place to the dynamics of relationships within and between the Churches.

SECTION THREE: FAITH AND LIFE IN A SMALL RURAL TOWN

"The one place we found no difference was the graveyards"

Introduction

Ballytorlar is a small town whose shopping centre is set about half a mile from the sea. The town is dominated to the south by Ben Torlar. To the east, the area known as Glenmore stretches out. The people in this area are largely Catholic, although they have been geographically isolated from the rest of Irish Catholics in times past. To the west of Ben Torlar, the population is largely Protestant, the area being known as "Knockbeg". To the north-west the population is traditionally Church of Ireland, known locally as 'Parish'. Elsewhere, the populations become progressively more Presbyterian. Ballytorlar town stands at the meeting point of these groups. It is the largest town in the district and houses the offices of the District Council. It is the largest shopping and services centre in the district although more developed and larger facilities nearby mean that it cannot be seen as a dominant centre except in the immediate hinterland. The 'satellite' villages are Ballybeg to the east, Ballydenis to the south, both largely Catholic, Craig to the south which is a mixed community, Dunfine to the west and Torlarbeg to the northwest, both largely Protestant.

The 1981 census recorded the population of the town of Ballytorlar as between 3,000 and 4,000. The District showed a slight growth in population from 1971 to 1981. The 1981 Census recorded that over 5,000 Catholics lived in Torlar together with 3,000 Presbyterians, 2,500 members of the Church of Ireland and a handful of Methodists. In addition there were over 4000 members of other denominations and a huge increase in the numbers who did not specify any religious affiliation. In essence the statistics indicate that the population is of almost equal numbers of Catholics and Protestants.

The area has traditionally registered high levels of adult male unemployment. This may disguise a degree of informal economics which allows those with skilled trades to find occasional work. The town itself is heavily dependent on the Public Sector for employment. The District Council, the local hospital, social services and various nursing homes are all major employers. In the Private Sector the only two factories are a shirt manufacturer and a small printing company.

Three further features should be highlighted by way of introduction to the town. The first is the importance of tourism to the district. An estimated 3,000 tourists per week double the number of people in the town during the month's of July and August. While Ballytorlar is a much smaller resort than nearby Craigtown it is an important part of the regional tourist industry. The town is seen to have suffered in its development in part because of political violence in Northern Ireland. The most immediate example of this is reflected in the continual complaints of local business-people that the town lacks a centre since the bombing of the Bayview Hotel.

Secondly, the town has a boom industry in the form of retirement homes. Several new homes have opened in the last five years including one in the process of completion. Although local people have had some priority in the allocation of places in these homes many residents come from elsewhere. This must be added to the semi-permanent feature of youth emigration from the town. Together they have a significant effect on the age of the local population and on the work of the churches.

Thirdly, the townspeople distinguish as much between locals and incomers as between Catholic and Protestant. Although there is no residential division many native locals complained of the domination of public life by 'runners-in'.

The Churches in Ballytorlar: background

Ballytorlar has four Church buildings- Presbyterian, Roman Catholic and two Church of Ireland Churches. The religious division of the hinterland is well illustrated by the churches. Ballybeg has a Catholic Church with an estimated 594 Catholics in the Parish. The Church of Ireland is very small and there is no Presbyterian Church in the Glenmore area. Craig has three Church buildings, Dunfine has no Roman Catholic Church. The Catholic Parish of Torlarbeg has only 278 Catholics inside the Parish. On the other hand there are much larger Church of Ireland and Presbyterian congregations. (Dunfine - 643, Ballytorlar - 314).

In 1971 Glenmore was one of the areas with the highest concentration of Roman Catholics. Glenmore was 88% Catholic while North Torlar was 94% Catholic. In total contrast Dunfine was 70% Presbyterian, 96% Protestant. Torlarbeg was mixed with 35% Catholic, 33% Church of Ireland and 31% Presbyterian. Kindore between Ballytorlar and Torlarbeg was 37% Church of Ireland. Ballytorlar's hinterland may appear mixed but in reality this hides local polarities.

The Methodist Church is particularly weak. The 1981 census reported 36 Methodists in the entire District. This is a decline from the past when the Methodists built the first Church in Ballytorlar.

"The Methodists were the first to build a Church in the town in 1793. For some reason the Methodists declined and the Church has been closed. It closed about three years ago now. It was served from Craigtown for the last 20 years, there was no permanent clergyman here. I don't know what happened but they just dwindled, natural wastage." (Local man)

Although the Church of Ireland stands in the Centre of the town, the majority in the town are now Roman Catholic. The Diocesan Handbook estimates that there are 2,800 Catholics in the Parish. This compares with a Presbyterian estimate of 574 members and a Church of Ireland estimate of 450. The numbers do not correspond to the census record of population for the town which may be accounted for by the different boundaries of town and parish and by some people who may travel into traditional Church homes.

Churches and Personal Life.

The personal importance of faith varies from person to person. This makes it difficult to generalise about personal faith without ignoring examples which contradict the norm. Nevertheless, in our sense, we were looking for examples of people for whom faith was a central point of reference in order to establish the depth to which people are attached to their belief. Ballytorlar is not an area of overt religious display being neither a place of Pilgrimage nor a Protestant religious centre. Nevertheless, it is clear that the Churches in Ballytorlar remain important in the lives of many of the people.

People seldom volunteered information about their faith. They seemed to 'assume' Church as part and parcel of life. It was left to the clergy to sum-up their feelings about responsiveness, a sign, surely, of an older structure in which the laity deferred to the clergy and the clergy spoke for their people. The clergy spoke of others with an authority reserved for those in secure places in the community. Even in Ballytorlar this is changing.

It is always difficult in researching about people's lives to do more than listen to people talking and telling about their faith and its importance. Nevertheless there were frustrations within the churches and a sense that religious life was less important among young people.

*"For the people of Ballytorlar, God, religion and their faith would be very important. It would help them in things like honesty with money, dealing with drunkenness and things like that. On the other hand they wouldn't have that dogmatic approach to religion." (*Catholic Priest)

*"Ballytorlar is not a Church-going town in the way of Ballymena or Kilkeel would be. There is a higher proportion of lazy families.... Ballytorlar never was an area affected by 1859 Revival. I wouldn't have thought that Ballytorlar was ever a four-star religious area, though there are many fine people in the congregation." (*Presbyterian Minister)

*"We would feel that Christian education is not a matter of RE classes but permeates the whole day; assemblies, class work, reprimanding children.... Mostly the chaplain comes in and we'd have Mass in the school assembly hall about four times a year. Because its part and parcel of our lives, it has always been thus. It links us, the parents are involved and the children are involved. We don't think about it much." (*Catholic School Teacher)

*"The Churches are very important. I'm not sure if its socially. If presence at Mass and daily Mass express something then its very important. But if you talk with people about the Holy Spirit and Jesus in their lives then I'd say very few outside the Prayer Group. Two Protestant women were very important people for me. Before [I met them] I did things mechanically. Its a cultural thing, people can't talk about religion. Now I'm in Church because I want to be there." (*Catholic woman)

*"A lot of the members aren't really Churchgoing.... Its a pity. The children get confirmed and that's about the end of it.... They don't pay in but they take their use of the Church with baptisms, weddings and funerals." (*Church of Ireland, woman)

*"You have to stand for your faith, the Christian faith which they [Roman Catholics] don't believe in." (*Presbyterian, Farmer)

Nevertheless there was some significant dissent and a warning about the younger generation.

"The only thing the Church is interested in is making money. For example in this parish £20-30,000 was spent on a Church hall and it is locked. No local community groups are allowed in except for Church functions. They

[the clergy] dominate community life not for the social benefit of the community but for the advancement of the Church itself." (Catholic, Farmer)

"A lot of people listen to the Church. We have found over the years that more are choosing not to listen." (Catholic, teacher)

The first illustration of disagreements between clergy and parishioners appeared in discussions with Catholic people:

"Its very difficult to please everybody. There are people who resent change and others feel we have to change to grow. For instance, I was talking last night about the introduction of lay eucharistic ministry and my friend reacted with horror." (School-teacher)

"People will oppose the introduction of lay ministers. Some people still think that only the clergy should handle the host." (Secretary)

"If you took a consensus among them in Glenmore they'd say they're Irish first and Catholic second but it comes across as Catholic first and Irish second. There is a decline among young people because they're more enlightened now. They're beginning to see the difference between teaching and practice." (local SF Councillor)

Another example of changing attitudes to the authority of the Church was noted by a Church of Ireland parishioner.

"Our Mothers Union is small, only about 20. We tried to get more women to come, but a lot of younger women thought it was set up as too religious.... The younger end of the Parish go to the Women's Fellowship. The Women's Fellowship isn't religious, its more money-makers."

In Ballytorlar religion is ingrained in personal life and ideas of personal standards of behaviour and lifestyles. Secularisation, in the sense of a slow drift away from Churches, has taken place and yet there is little active anti-clericalism. With a single exception, nobody spoke badly of 'The Church' as an institution. For those who wish to see a more public and active personal faith this state of affairs is a source of considerable frustration and among them there would be some criticism of institutional dogma. Nevertheless, the position of the clergy in public life, seems to be rooted in many people's personal devotion which accords clergy a position of leadership. This is part of the bedrock of cultural life.

The Churches and Social Life

The Churches in Ballytorlar are very important in social life. They provide premises and focuses for groups which meet throughout the year and they are a focal point regulating life especially through weekly services, a fixed point in a moving calendar. It is important to note the degree to which the Church was and is an 'organic' part of life in the community. It is so integrated that a clear boundary line between Church and community is impossible to draw.

"The Church is the people and the people have been in the town for 100s of years. Community life has been lived in harmony. They weren't involved in anything, they just lived their daily lives, in harmony and co-operation."

Thus Church life is an intimate part of daily living. It is not seen as 'another institution' to which people relate or not, and whose members get 'involved' as representatives of that institution in aspects of life but rather is the gathering together of the people.

Church 'social life' is not limited to organisations. Any organisations in this view are gatherings of some of the people for specific tasks in and beyond the parish. Everything which occurs is understood as part of 'life' lived in a parish led by the clergy. Rural and part-rural communities such as this cannot be measured by statistical measures of membership alone nor can they be compared with the organisation of life in urban settings. Such an organic concept of Church depends on an organic reality of community. The place has to have a sense of itself as a distinct identity. Hence the importance of 'The people have been in the town for 100s of years'. This is no longer universally true and may be a root of some of the tensions in the town between 'locals' and 'incomers'. This organic history with which the entire community can identify is difficult to learn.

"The number of Ballytorlar people [as opposed to incomers] who are involved in groups in the town is very few. If there are four or five, I don't know them. I found this in the drama group and the [RC] Church choir. Ballytorlar people are very close-knit and their social contacts are within their homes. Colm's family introduced me to family, but it was through

a friend from Liverpool that I met people in the town. This dominance of runners-in probably adds to the resentment." (Catholic woman)

"I've always been surrounded by Catholic people, and we always helped each other in times of need. New people I wouldn't know as well. I wouldn't have any contact with them. I might through the Church but new Catholics I wouldn't meet." (Church of Ireland woman)

This complex reality cannot be reflected in simple statistical measures of institutions.

"Most of the people I would mix with would be of the same religion, except in the golf club. A lot of the social life of the town is run through the Churches. Even on Market Day each denomination has its own stalls and car-parks." (Catholic, schoolteacher)

Youth Organisations are particularly closely attached to Churches. This is true in all Churches. Very few of them cross the sectarian divide.

"There's a Youth Organisation, the Youth Fellowship its called. They meet every Saturday night, play games, indoor sort of games. My sons in it. Its from 11 to 18. There'd be 25 or so in it. They go to other Youth Groups and so on." (C of I, mother)

"The B.B. and the G.B. in the town are run with the Church of Ireland". Presbyterian, minister.

"The B.B. here tends to be exclusively a Protestant organisation, especially as they get older. There is a Catholic Boy Scouts again without Protestants. Rather interestingly there are Guides with integration. There is a G.B. but its mainly Protestant. The older generation was more integrated." (Protestant, schoolteacher)

"I led the Brownies for eight or nine years and we tried to make sure that it was mixed. There's no other Brownies in the town. Mind you they set up a Catholic Boy Scouts. I suppose they wouldn't swear loyalty to our Queen!" (Presbyterian woman)

"The Celtic identity is not anti-Protestant. They are not intolerant of the existing leaning of the other communities. In the Glenmore Road Hall

(C of I) there's an Irish Dancing School with a Protestant teacher." (Social Worker, Man)

The other major activities for youth in the town centre on sport. By far the largest club is the hurling club.

"Hurling would be the game of all this area. Its the social centre, the gathering point, the focal point. On summer nights all the young people head for the hurling pitch." (Catholic schoolteacher)

In reality what this means is that sporting activity is split along Catholic/ Protestant lines. There is one exception, a group of Under-16 footballers who train in the (secular) Recreation Centre.

"The under 16s is integrated, Catholic and Protestant. Its very admirable, I don't know how they did it. I'll try and get some money [for them]. They really did it out of their own pocket. Its very unusual in this town. Theres no big divide in this town........" (Recreation Centre Manager)

The Council has opened a Leisure Centre which suffers from lack of a swimming pool and lack of finance. The difficulties encountered by the Centre in attracting local custom illustrates the degree of conservatism in Ballytorlar and the degree to which new features are viewed with suspicion.

"The Centre has been opened two years and it is still getting established. When it was opened originally it wasn't well used. This is a very shy community, shy of the unfamiliar. Leisure Centres are for the city."

Both nearby Council areas have Leisure Centres which are closer to Western Torlar and are fully supported by their local councils. Both have swimming pools. Nevertheless there is a sectarian dimension even to the provision by Torlar District Council. A new Community Centre in Dunfine has been effectively deserted and heavily vandalised.

"In Dunfine there's been a lot of vandalism. I think it's political. The Unionists want to see that side joined with nearby Unionist areas. Torlar District is not popular with Unionists. They would like to see it split between other Councils." (Recreation Centre Manager)

One very important element in Protestant culture outside the town is the

Orange Lodge and the flute bands, an intimate part of the community's life together, part of 'organic life'.

"I take part in a lot of local activities belonging to the Church committees, B.B. and all the Protestant organisations. The Protestant organisations are weakest in Ballytorlar town. Probably because a lot of them aren't in any bands so they're never approached. All the lodges hold their annual services and the Churches give freely of their premises, whether Presbyterian or Parish." (Presbyterian, Farmer)

The lodge and the bands would seem to replace the hurling club as a focus of activity for Protestants. This situation was brought home to one person I spoke with when his son began travelling to Craigtown.

"I have a son who now goes to Craigtown Technical College and he finds he has absolutely nothing in common with his colleagues. Their interests and life are so different to what he has been used to here. He feels totally alien. He'd go in on Monday and talk about Gaelic Games and they'd be wearing Rangers badges and what went on at the Orange Lodge. He just feels totally outside the mainstream..... He identifies all right in Ballydenis but over there he feels out of it." (Catholic Man)

The Church organisations grow from local culture and merge into it. Thus non-Church organisations and structures are often de-facto segregated along religious lines just as Church organisations are. There is no other feature outside religious identity which divides so cleanly.

Churches are also important for the social life of adults. The Presbyterian Woman's Association is an important social meeting place for Presbyterians in the town. The same is true of the Mothers Union which is based in the Church of Ireland. The Woman's Fellowship which also meets in the Church of Ireland has one Catholic member. She is married to a member of the Church of Ireland although remaining a practising Catholic.

"I admire her. There's plenty of talkers in there and she just said, 'I don't take any notice of them'. I knew they were talking myself." (Church of Ireland Woman)

The 'secular' organisation for women in the town is the Women's Institute (W.I.). This too has more Protestant members than Catholic members although the committee is mixed. They do not use any Church premises.

The Catholic Church has a number of smaller organisations under its umbrella (e.g. Legion of Mary, Apostolic Workers). The society of St. Vincent de Paul looks after elderly people in the Parish through monthly gatherings. They also have a task of providing food and fuel for the needy for which they collect money. They are important to the Parish Priest but not uniformly respected.

"They take up the weekly collections in the Church. I would like to say that they act as ushers to welcome the flock coming into the Church but in fact stand guarding the plate." (Catholic Woman)

In addition there is the Legion of Mary the Apostolic Workers both of whom work with the parish at various tasks. All are organised as part of the Church and are pillars of Church life. As one priest said.

"Things tend to develop in each Church. They develop the Church as the body of Christ."

Implicit in such a statement is an understanding of the Church as a denomination and as an institution. Each Church has a chair and there are a number of committees. As yet the Roman Catholic Church has no Parish Council, but the Kirk Session and Select Vestry are both active.

One interesting feature is the place of Bowling Clubs. Each of the Churches has a bowling club and many people are aware that all the teams were mixed.

"The Church of Ireland have a hall with a bowling club, but again you're back to the older generation. There is also one in the Catholic Church, also mixed." (Protestant, school teacher)

The Glenmore Road Hall belongs to the Church of Ireland and is regarded by many people as a part-town hall for meetings. Much of the campaign against hospital closures and community association meetings were held there. The Catholic Church has the McAllister Hall which is also a focus of community activity.

The sense that each Church, whether understood as a building or a community, is a 'home', a base, is tinged with fears that the central place of the Church might be less than it was, especially for young people.

"I see the role of the Church as two-fold. First to care for affiliated families - pastoral care, fellowship a place of worship, spiritual encouragement. The second is an evangelistic role for people in the town with shaky faith..... The congregation is very much a home. Still, we talked about loyalty before there was the tradition of family pews. Now there's less of that. Not all the members of a family might turn out every week. One week the mother and daughter would come, the next daughter and son, the next all four and so on." (Presbyterian Minister)

"I can't speak for the Presbyterian Church or the Church of Ireland, but I think that what has happened is that the hold of the Catholic Church on their followers has slipped and I think its a good thing. The story is that a man selling a particular farm gave the Catholics who offered less money preference over a Protestant offering more after the PP intervened. Maybe the pendulum is going to swing a bit too far. I have seen a change from when I was young until now. Is the Church finished? That might be something worth thinking about." (Catholic, layman)

The Church and Public Life

The divide between public and social life is an arbitrary one. Here we shall deal with the Churches place in the provision of Welfare, in inter-community relationships, and in spheres such as schools and local politics. It will also be the place where we consider the importance attached to Church institutional involvement in public activities in the town and how this takes place.

Schools

Ballytorlar has five schools, three Primary and two Secondary. Both of the Secondary Schools are non-selective and both have sixth forms with potential for A-level study. The schools are divided on lines of religious denomination as is usual in Northern Ireland. The Catholic Primary Schools are also divided into Boys and Girls schools. Relations between the schools are cordial and at the same time important stories are told which suggests that the system is accepted because it 'is' rather than because it is desirable.

"The first thing you notice with incomers is where they send their child to school. I don't notice this kind of thing but whenever a stranger comes to town people do." (Presbyterian book-keeper)

Ballytorlar High School had a tradition as a 'soft' Protestant school with a high percentage of Catholics in attendance. This is remembered with a degree of nostalgia by some Protestants.

*"Ballytorlar High School has for a long time numbered a number of Catholics among its pupils including Bishop Donal Lamont of Umtali in Rhodesia. On old school photos there are Catholics and Protestants on the Hockey Team and so on". (*Presbyterian Minister)

*"There has been in the past a tradition of Catholic children coming to the school. We still have a few but much less than we used to. There is a degree of pressure not to come to the school coming largely from the Church. I think they've been told 'St. Mary's is 'our' school'. Having said that, we share quite a number of facilities especially the sixth form". (*Protestant teacher)

The breakdown of this system is held up by many Protestants as an example of deteriorating community relations. Schools are a major source of local Protestant suspicion of the Catholic Church (as opposed to Irish Nationalism). From the Catholic perspective the integration of the old High School was far from clear. As one parent pointed out, the integration of Ballytorlar schools was only at the level of pupil attendance:

"It was integrated in the pupils who went to it but none of the power was integrated. They did employ the odd Catholic teacher but it was never an 'integrated school'"

At the same time the power of the Church in the present structure was indicated by Catholic teachers too and often they appeared to fear for their jobs in speaking frankly.

*"Before, it was the old St. Mary's Grammar School. The thinking behind the change [to a comprehensive] was that all the children in the area would be housed and schooled under one roof. Previous to this there were two schools in the town.... On the face of it that was the reason. Ballytorlar High School had gone comprehensive before them and we were beginning to lose pupils. The Catholic Grammar School was fee-paying and the Catholic Secondary was losing pupils.... We would be concerned with the Catholic population. Not more than ten families would be sending their children out of the town." (*Catholic teacher)

"Another strong opinion I hold is that the Catholic Church is getting one hell of a deal in maintained education. Our church pays 15% of putting up a building and after that they get 100% until it falls down. In return the Catholic Church has the power to hire and fire the teachers and they are legally my employers." (Catholic teacher)

The philosophy of the interrelationship between Church and School was spelt out by another teacher.

"In this school we have very close links with the parish. We see it [the school] as an extension of the home. We would look at the community the parish and the school as part of the same, home outside the home."

The Protestant Churches are also involved on the Board of Ballytorlar High School.

"The Church of Ireland rector is chairman of the Board of Governors. The Presbyterian minister was a member of the board then he did some part-time teaching and he had to leave the Board. We now hold our annual carol service alternatively in the Church of Ireland and the Presbyterian Church. Its a much better atmosphere than the Assembly Hall." (Protestant teacher)

Everyone seems to assume the intimate involvement of Churches with schools. The school is one of the most tangible institutional devices by which the Churches integrate Sunday and weekday life. Nevertheless the umbrella over the whole of public life happens on a strict Catholic/ Protestant basis. There appears to be a desire on the part of some teachers to see greater integration at secondary level. One of the powers they see ranged against this is the influence of the parish priests.

"My own feelings would be that our Board of Governors would like this co-operation to go on as long as it doesn't rock the boat too much. They seem to be happy to let it go on informally but they don't want to grasp it formally. I think its a fact of life but its an opportunity missed for me. But the Church would still have considerable influence would still be against. Its not that they're actively against, its just that they're passive." (Catholic teacher)

The Primary schools in Ballytorlar provide only part of the secondary intake. Ballytorlar is the regional town and there is a wide network of bus services from outlying towns and villages. Protestants in the area also send their children to Grammar Schools in Knockbeg and Craigtown. Catholics in the area tend to use St. Mary's

"Less than half of our children come from St. Patrick's or St. Brigid's. [town local primary schools] We have 140 children coming from Ballydenis. We have children coming from Glenmore, Torlarbeg, Ballybeg, Magheramore, Craig, Tobarglan and even a small number from Dunfine." (Catholic teacher)

"The bulk of children in the school come from outside the town. Probably because of declining Protestant population and the fact that they go to other schools." (Protestant teacher)

The Catholic Primary Schools together are almost three times bigger than the State Primary. The schools have only been established in their present form since 1969. There is very little class-room co-operation between the schools although there are good relations between staff members on a personal level. The cultural divide begins early. The Girls Roman Catholic Primary School now plays camogie and has closer contacts through sport with other local Catholic schools.

"We wouldn't have much contact with the County Primary. We used to have Christian Aid concerts in the Glenmore Road Hall. We can't have inter-schools games, as the games we play aren't the same. The main game is camogie." (Catholic teacher)

Sporting relations between the County Primary and St. Patrick's Boys Primary are somewhat closer.

"We practice football together. They've visited our place for films and things. The schools get on well even in troubled times." (Protestant teacher)

The relationship between the two schools is cemented by some strong personal relationships between teachers.

*" ** comes down to help me with supervising the selection tests. The Roman Catholic Primaries don't have many for the selection test. They*

practically force them to go to St. Mary's. They've put so much money into it. St. Mary's cost over £1 million." (Protestant teacher)

"I'm a personal friend of (Protestant Teacher). Whenever I'd find our head difficult I'd go and speak to him and that'd put me on an even keel." (Roman Catholic teacher)

In the last two years the Catholic schools have appointed lay head teachers for the first time. Church influence in school activities is a controversial issue in the town, especially in the question of whether and how to undertake joint activities with other schools. Unlike the High School, the Protestant Primary has no Catholic pupils except in extraordinary circumstances.

"Occasionally there's parents trying to play off one school against another. That was ever so. I don't want to be taking Roman Catholic children from their schools. They have a different religion and they want to look after their own children. I have one Roman Catholic child and I've said he can stay but only for two years. In P3 they have first communion up there, so he'll have to go and I've made it clear. If people ring and ask about transferring I tell them no and that they'll have to make peace with their head. Given the situation in Ulster I have to accept that." (Protestant headteacher)

The situation seems to be one of peaceful co-existence rather than integration. There is opposition if only quietly, to any attempt to blur the divide. The opposition appears to stem from local diplomatic considerations, often because of a desire not to be seen to be poaching.

"Relations between the Churches are good. I know the clergy are very friendly. But having said that, our PP wasn't too happy when I was mixing with the Protestant Primary. He kept saying 'make sure you keep clear that we're the right one'. Surprisingly enough it was the one time I got no criticism from parents. I took a P5 class and joined with a P5 class in the County Primary. It was spearheaded by a Jesuit trainee and a Presbyterian Ministry student both working nearby. We took the kids to all the churches. We checked that the readings were the same in all the churches. Our kids noticed the plaques, theirs our statues. They found them beautiful. Funny enough the one place we found no difference was the graveyards. I found it very interesting. I didn't repeat it because I got the

feeling the Parish Priest didn't like it and I was going for promotion. Then I had a P6 class and I got the feeling the P6 teacher in the County Primary wasn't so interested." (Catholic teacher)

The attitude to formally integrated schooling within the schools was instructive. Many people supported it in principle but opposed it at present.

"Protestant children end up knowing other Protestant children. I'm not really into integration as it exists at the moment. I think its mostly English people. Its just taking people away from the existing schools. The Roman Catholic Church is opposed to it of course, .. I would like to see the government change everything overnight but I can't see it in my lifetime." (Protestant parent)

"This area really needs an integrated school. It won't happen though. This place is too steeped in tradition. An awful lot of money goes into the upkeep of the school. There's a kind of 'we built it' mentality. But best friends can't go to the same school." (Catholic parent)

In the meantime, the Catholic schools remain deeply attached to the parish and to the faith while the Protestant school displays the Union Jack. The proximity of the two Secondary Schools (directly opposite one another) illustrates at one and the same time the intrinsic division in Ballytorlar and the local acceptance of this fact allowing both to exist without real opposition. As we shall see there is considerable concern that the underlying trends are against this stable structure. The divide in the schools is the same as that elsewhere in Northern Ireland, along religious lines, with serious ethnic and cultural implications e.g. in the sphere of games.

The Churches and Inter-community relations.

Many people in Ballytorlar are at pains to emphasise that community relations in the town are good. This is confirmed for most people by the relative lack of overt sectarian violence, the fact that even now Ballytorlar town has no residential ghettos and the fact that the town is considered tolerant in comparison to all the surrounding areas. In many ways Ballytorlar represents a truly neutral territory. Many of the people of the town sympathise with groups at war or on defensive footing outside the town but are aware that to date the town has been spared the worst aspects of the violence and its impingement on private life. They are anxious in varying degrees to keep the situation calm although there are people in local politics, schools, social services and police who identify particular elements which endanger tranquillity. The Churches, and in particular the relationship of the clergy to one another was a feature noted by many. It is important when dealing with this to underline the degree to which clergy activities were held to personify the Church as a whole. This is in sharp contrast to the expressed self-understanding of clergymen that Churches were a community. This permanent interchangeability in conception is a matter of some confusion. The Church institution is represented in the popular mind with a power-network headed by the clergy. The Church community of people living their lives is seldom counted as 'Church', rather as private. In Ballytorlar at least, the clergy is held to represent orthodoxy.

"There's no big divide in this town. Now at school age the Prod/Taig thing develops. The schools literally face each other across the road. I'm a near-local. My relations all come from here. Ballytorlar's a nice place to live, very little hassle.... I don't think there's trouble but at certain age groups there's trouble. My kids came from Andersonstown and though they're Catholic they got called 'Orange B's'. As far as I can make out its the same in the other school. Its developed a lot earlier but its not as bitter." (Catholic man)

"Things can happen here quite naturally that wouldn't happen elsewhere. Ballytorlar has always been characterised by fair-mindedness in giving out positions. For example in the Golf Club and the Bowling Club or in the communities for various churches. I think if you move a few miles out of the town you'll find the tribal thing. But again its a working-class thing." (Presbyterian Man)

"There is a welcome, but it stays very superficial. They're very different with strangers than they are at home. By that I mean their duty reaction to political situations. There's a very sociable thing. They would say things about how good this place is. I suppose it depends on what you compare it to." (Catholic Woman)

"Ballytorlar is not a Catholic town, probably two-thirds Catholic. It's a mixed community.. There's never been any trouble between the communities even at the time of partition. There's never been any in my

lifetime." (Catholic Man)

"I like living in Ballytorlar. We haven't faced any problems since we moved. I couldn't say which was a Catholic area and which was a Protestant one." (Presbyterian Woman)

"Policing-wise this town's not too bad. There's nice people on both sides. Crime's not too bad. There's a criminal element the same as any other town. There's some assaults in the summer between the natives and outsiders. Most of the gangs have been split up. There's some conflict between Belfast and Ballytorlar ones." (Ballytorlar Policeman)

Ballytorlar is thus proud of the relative tranquillity of the town. There are no segregated areas nor any apparent demand for them. This contrasts sharply with nearby Craig. Size is therefore not the crucial element.

"Ballytorlar used to be known as a Nationalist town but you couldn't say that any more. People here are loyal to each other and politics might take second place. I've talked to people who've moved here who say they've been made very welcome. We meet the public in my business. We're Catholic, nobody cares about that, everybody comes here. Twenty five years ago people said to me 'You'll have to put a so and so into this house or that house'. But I always ignored that. I always said that it was their cheque-book not their politics that mattered." (Local Businessman)

The profit motive seems to be one way to escape sectarian thinking. Sectarianism was also absent in Public Housing policy.

"Sectarianism doesn't appear to manifest itself in the division of properties. In a sense the wider boundaries between Glenmore and North Antrim is perceived as a divide. It doesn't appear to affect allocation. Intimidation is certainly not a big problem here.. There is some graffiti and in most instances we will remove it. You have to be sensitive. Any graffiti in Ballytorlar we will remove.. When a house comes free in Ballytorlar I don't have to look at whether Sean O'Brien or Billy McCusker want the house." (Housing Executive)

This accounts for the absence of large scale symbolism in the town. Ballytorlar has no painted pavements nor are there many flags. The Irish tricolour flies at hurling matches while the Union Jack flies over the State school. The Youth Organisations parade using flags in Churches. This is normally inside the Church. This contrasts very sharply with the situation in surrounding settlements. Dunfine is literally festooned all-year round in red, white and blue. In Ballydenis the green, white and orange colours are on pavements and lamp-posts. During the summer, Ballytorlar town was covered in multi-coloured bunting. Many speculated that this was to pre-empt the Orange Order from hanging Red, White and Blue flags everywhere. The Chamber of Commerce were sure that this was not their intention.

"We couldn't afford lights for the town this summer. We'd bought lights for Christmas but a lot of the bulbs stopped working. So we bought bunting, it's better than having a bare town. We said we'd leave the Glenmore Road free for the [Orange] March but they didn't put up their bunting. Some people thought we put it up for the 12th, but that wasn't the case. Actually most of it was borrowed from the Fleadh Committee." (Chairman, Chamber of Commerce)

The tranquillity of inter-community relationships is reflected in the continuing co-operation of the town's middle-class on public committees. The Chamber of Commerce has the membership of around three-quarters of the business people in the town. The main function of the committee is to co-ordinate business communication and to act as a channelling agency to channel information about financial assistance, grants and other political developments. Of late they have also employed a number of ACE workers.

"There's an ACE-scheme going through the Chamber with 41 jobs; clearing up old people's houses, graveyards, Church yards and company for the elderly, things like that. We try not to tramp on Union toes. They get £72 per week. All their equipment is bought in the town. In the Chamber's office there are four full-time staff. The co-ordinator gets £90 a week. Its a fair bit of help for the town. We've only had to pay one man off... Religion doesn't matter if someone wants to work. The members of the Chamber are of all denominations, a mixed bunch. The fights are about money and about schemes." (Local man)

There is no tradition of exclusive shops or pubs. Employment is also not an object of particular outrage.

"The fact of people being Protestant or Catholic doesn't matter. There's no tradition of not shopping in certain shops because of religion." (Roman Catholic clergy)

Pubs are mostly Catholic-owned though the Pub with weekly Irish traditional music is owned by a Protestant. In some ways the objection is much more to incomers than it is to people of another religion, and newcomers tend to dominate on many of the committees in the town.

"People look to incomers for leadership and at the same time they resent it if incomes lead too obviously." (Presbyterian minister)

"There'll be those who want to get the thing moving. The tendency would be to say 'who the hell do they think they are, they're only runners. Its the 'topping off of emerging heads'." (Social Worker)

"I was chairman of the local community association. A friend told me that my predecessor was annoyed because it was a Catholic the last time. But to my mind people in the Community Association shouldn't be thinking in that way. Its for all. Maybe after twenty years if there's been no change you can ask yourself 'are we following the aims of this thing?' To me it seemed so petty." (Catholic Man)

Other mixed activities include the Golf Club, which is seen as the middle-class element in the town and local charities. Class division is apparent in housing, where public and private housing exist in separate areas. Nevertheless the schools and Churches tend to blur these distinctions. The best organised charities in the town are Concern and Save the Children Fund.

"There's a social classification between the estates and private. Then there's the Golf Club set of better off" (Social Worker)

"Golf is cross-community...." (Presbyterian Minister)

"The Golf Club is mixed.. It might be considered elitist but in actual fact it isn't." (Catholic woman, Club member)

The Golf Club is nonetheless one of the places in the town where some Protestants and Catholics mix freely. To some extent this is true of

Concern, although the fact that it is Irish-based and has offices on Roman Catholic parish property has identified it most closely with the Catholic Church. Nevertheless, the clergy in the area have supported it jointly.

"There's support for cross-religious things such as Concern. There's a fast around Christmas time and a fair. It started off cross-community. The Catholic Priest and the Presbyterian and Church of Ireland clergy have all taken part in that together and a considerable amount was raised. Concern had its birth in the South of Ireland and the organisers were a bit worried. Fortunately the ministers led the people over that hurdle. Concern now has a Northern Ireland section based in Belfast. That has been successful. The membership of the committee went across the sectarian divide. That would have dwindled to some extent and the Catholic members have stayed on though Protestants would still support. On the other side there is Save the Children Fund. That's nearly more class-based than sectarian based. More the well-to-do." (Concern member, man)

The town has also found strong local identity in the campaign against closure or cuts at the local hospital. This united the town, although its political success was dubious.

"There are examples of when they can come together. Recently in the attack on the Dalriada Hospital. There's much less coming together than in the past. I don't know if its because the Trade Unions have lost their teeth. I was told that in the past, in the forties, when there was an attack on the hospital people went and lay on the roads. They might argue that since then the place has been diluted by runners." (Social Worker)

"I mean the hospital campaign set things going a bit. It was cross-community" (Protestant teacher)

"We've come together over the Hospital Action Committee. The Glenmore Road Hall is nearly a town hall. It's still used, by the hospital action committee." (Protestant teacher)

"We've probably the most modern hospital in the Health Board Area but the beds are being closed down.. Due to a certain pressure from Medical Consultants in Knockbeg that they wouldn't be willing to come to

Ballytorlar there was resentment in both communities at the time." (Catholic Councillor)

Often the strongest identity to which both Catholics and Protestants can appeal is an appeal to an identity as Ballytorlar people separated from the rest of the world. In Ballytorlar the local 'place apart' identity is most often the alternative to sectarian division. Sectarianism is most effectively countered by the actual friendships across religion barriers and by the fact that these friendships take place at all levels of the towns life. One of the most significant indicators in the community as regards its stability is the ability of the police to move freely and work.

Although Ballytorlar has a Catholic majority the RUC have been able to continue working in the town on an agenda dominated by assault and petty crime rather than sectarianism. In this they seem to have earned a degree of respect from the Catholic establishment. The UDR does not patrol the area regularly and is not seen as part of the local furniture. Overall the security presence in the town is almost non-existent. The only exception to this rule is the netting around the police station itself which gives the impression of being a fortress.

"The police are fairly well-respected in the town - by 80% I'd say. They have been even-handed to give them their due. Even as regards dealing with pubs they haven't come down heavy. They usually ring up before they come. Generally the police have been very good." (Catholic, local councillor)

"Intimidation is certainly not a big problem here. Any instances can be dealt with by the police. The police have always been very co-operative and very level-headed. The most common form of complaint would be by Protestants. If I feel its sectarian I would feel obliged to apply to the police in writing. They've been very straightforward and we've very good relations." (Housing Executive)

"For RUC and UDR men this is a relatively safe area because those kind of things don't happen here, but why?" (Catholic teacher)

"The attitude to the RUC would be ambivalent. I remember the hunger strike, a highly emotive time. I was on holiday but I was told that you'd be surprised how many came out with black flags that night. They'd be against the police on issues like that. Some would prefer to use their own

forms of social control and others would use the police. On the other side there is a good number of solid lads over there who know when to act and when to close their eyes. They'd be respected in the town. Then there's the hotheads who'd act first and think second. It's not wildly different from England or the South in general. There's a lot of hooliganism on a Saturday night. Some group tried to ask the police to clear the town at 2 or 2.30 a.m. To my amazement some businessmen were raging. Whether that's because they think it'll make things worse or whether its ideological I don't know. Another example, there were bands at the Republican Memorial in Glenmore and they came to Ballytorlar and sat in the Square waiting on the police. They blocked the traffic through the town. I had to reverse back. The police said we'll just sit them out and didn't go near them. The bands left because there was no crack. This is an example of good policing." (Social Worker)

The police themselves, they were at pains to emphasise the degree of normality in the town. Nevertheless, the extent of pressure felt by the police is reflected in their defensiveness in the face of interviews which might be quoted publicly. One indicator of police security was that some felt secure enough to live locally, although none lived in Glenmore.

"It's general common knowledge that police live in the area and there's no problems. Its not an area where you wouldn't live. We've no objections at all. I would say that relations aren't too bad. You have your conscientious objections, you have that everywhere. There's no trouble with the Churches. I wouldn't say there's an anti-police feeling in the town." (R.U.C. Officer)

That community relations between police and policed continue more or less intact is remarkable given the degree of bitterness in other nearby settlements. As well as a recognition of the relatively tranquil state of affairs many people expressed reservations. Everyone was aware that inter-communal violence had become 'normal' in other parts of Northern Ireland. Many also spoke of their fears that this might spread.

One major area of concern is with young people. This is expressed in several ways. For some it was a matter of increased rowdiness due to drink, for others a matter of a break down in family discipline. For others it is a matter of increasing distance between young people of different denominations.

"We have found in recent years among children that there is a growing lack of integration. I would say that among the rural children there is an increasingly right-wing attitude. In the Roman Catholic children there is a growing anti-Protestant feeling. This manifests itself at times of high political tension - there might be a scrap on the bus. This tends to happen with lower and middle ability children." (Protestant teacher)

"The increased tension passes over in a physical way. For example if Protestant children are coming home from B.B. they would be jostled in the street by Catholics. The Protestants are in a minority and they know it. The Catholics are in a majority and an element of them are very aggressive." (Protestant teacher)

"I would always have a fear that incomers, people who have moved from Belfast where things like this are endemic, would spread their activities here. We have a lot of young fellas who are unemployed. If you got a few bad pills in who teach them 'what we are up to in Belfast'... There is a residual republicanism in the town. It's not the Belfast republicanism more a harking after the Celtic twilight. But the residual republicanism could always be set alight." (Social worker)

Despite the sense that events were causing division the peace of Ballytorlar had not been disturbed. Many people seemed to acknowledge two levels of living: a community or public level and a much more suspicious internal viewpoint only ever confided to close friends and family.

"On the surface everything seems fine, nobody bothers. Whether there's any commitment to hands across the divide...? Most of the people I would mix with would be of the same religion, except in the Golf Club." (Local Woman)

"Every time the IRA do something Protestants bring it up almost triumphantly. Very rarely do Protestants come out and condemn the UDA and UVF and Catholics don't feel they can bring it up in case they [prods] feel personally attacked." (Local Catholic woman)

"There are a lot of people in the town who would not wish any break-up, who would deplore the breakdown of community relations elsewhere in Northern Ireland. The past historical record of the town and these people would be a restraining influence. There is an increasing tension in young

people. Community divisions are more marked. The Protestant community is decreasing and the town is becoming more nationalist. I would compare this area with the border in the sense that like the border we have our back up against is the sea and the mountains. Increasingly the Protestant community is in a similar situation without the violent incidents. To a degree it produces a close-knitting in the community in terms of Church-groups clinging together. At the same time there are people who make efforts to integrate. These are deep underlying things. People are aware of them but any debate would go on within the groups rather than across." (Protestant teacher)

One of the biggest changes in recent years was the gradual disappearance of independents from the local council and their replacement by representatives of political parties. This included after 1984, representatives of Sinn Fein. The political balance in Torlar is neatly balanced. In theory there are eight Nationalists and seven Unionists. Nevertheless, the Unionists hold both Chairmanship and Vice-Chairmanship of the Council because of rifts between SDLP and the two Sinn Fein councillors. The balance of the council is in itself deceptive. The District is divided into three constituencies each with five members elected by Single Transferable Vote. The Knockbeg constituency to the west of the town returned five Unionists, while Glenmore constituency to the South and east of the town returned five Nationalists including one from Sinn Fein. The third constituency consists of Ballytorlar town and the area around Torlarbeg. This area returns councillors from the DUP and the OUP, from the SDLP and Republican Sinn Fein and an independent Nationalist. This illustrates neatly the situation in which Ballytorlar politics takes place.

The election of a Sinn Fein councillor for the town is regarded with horror by many Protestants and considered a major new imposition by the Protestants.

"I remember we [TDC] appeared on television, set up as an example of a working council when others had trouble. We had a Unionist chairman and a Nationalist vice-chairman one year and then the next year the other way about. Trouble began when Sinn Fein came into the Council. Since then we've had hymn singing in the Chamber, talking through speeches, loud whispers and shouting. The Council has never gone out of business though." (Town Clerk)

"I've lived here since I was born. There's been political changes. Sinn

Fein has got in now to make their point. It doesn't go down too well. I don't agree with them. In the past I knew a lot of the ones that were in the Sinn Fein party. They've got into the Council and they're doing no good for the community and its why I feel they shouldn't be there at all. They should be given no credibility in the running of any community. If they're not terrorists then they support terror.... I ignore Sinn Fein as if they weren't there, ignoring terrorism... [The Sinn Fein Councillor] is an evil man. Sinn Fein is out to destroy everything for their own gain. They could sit back at Council meetings and say nothing but they're always taking notes, anything to discredit the Protestant population. At the majority of Council meetings they don't get doing it." (DUP Councillor)

Non-Sinn Fein nationalists regard the Sinn Fein vote as a latent vote which had not previously appeared because Sinn Fein had not stood in elections.

"It could be said that a lot of people voted Sinn Fein who'd never bothered before. There's a feeling that some people would vote for a dog if you put a Sinn Fein label onto it." (SDLP Councillor)

Among Nationalists the strongest political feeling was expressed against the UDR. There was a distinction made between the UDR and the RUC.

"The UDR is not trusted at all by Nationalist people. I met an old teacher who was very antagonistic to the UDR. But fortunately the UDR takes a very low profile. There hasn't been any incidents involving them. When they did a few years ago it did cause agro." (SDLP Councillor)

"It could be that we haven't suffered as much as other places have. We haven't had the UDR or British Army here who might harass or pick up the young fellas." (Catholic teacher)

The extent to which the Sinn Fein vote is personal and the extent to which it reflects deep support for Sinn Fein is difficult to ascertain. What is certain is that it reflects an uncompromising nationalism.

"This two-state Ireland has to disappear. They [Protestants] won't talk until the Brits withdraw. You've arrived at a situation where they've got to be told. They've got to come to terms with the Irish people not we with them. They're defending the right of conquest, then we have the right of reconquest. If that means war..... But there's an end to war. There's no

question of surrendering our Nationality ever. This is my home and I'm entitled to defend that against any invader." (SF Councillor)

The Protestant assumption that Sinn Fein could be stopped by excommunication is questionable given the outspoken anti-clericalism of many supporting Sinn Fein.

"I tried to figure out the Catholic Churches relations to the Irish State. The Catholic Church is directly responsible for the slaughter of the Irish Language through the building of Maynooth. It was a condition of the building of Maynooth. They went about it deliberately too. You've heard of the tally-stick...? Every time the child used Irish a notch was put in the tally stick and corporal punishment was administered one blow for each notch. If that's Christianity... - the Gas Chamber would be too good for them." (SF Councillor)

"The Catholic Church rules Ireland in the interest of the British. I can't think of any other logical explanation for the attitude of the Catholic Church towards nationalism. They see Ireland as part of the UK and as a stepping-stone back to Britain." (local man)

The roots of the antagonisms to all British authorities are as deep as the defence of them on the Protestant side. The Sinn Fein Councillor explained the roots of his own attitudes.

"The clergy are finding it difficult to see how their authority is flaunted. The priests in those days were held in awe. To be a good Catholic was to be a good Irishman. We learnt the bitter truth that it wasn't what mattered.... What matters is the social and economics.

My roots are here. I look on this as my country with a territorial aspect. I remember as a youngster in Glenmore where we were told of Roger Casement. He was a friend of our family's. Then an uncle of mine was shot by the RUC in Ballytorlar in 1922 and I began to ask myself why all these things happened. I was born in 1929. I started to read Irish history and I discovered that we hadn't got a country. We were governed from London. The Government was exercised in favour of the Protestant community and the Catholic community was barely tolerated. The common phrase was 'second class citizens', but I would think that was liberal terminology." (local Sinn Fein supporter, man)

On one level there is a recognition that the town has not disintegrated to the extent of communities elsewhere and that good cross-community communication can take place in personal relationships and in aspects of social life. Outside the town the polarised nature of the residential pattern means that there is only limited scope for Catholics to meet Protestants as part of daily life and vice versa. This is not necessarily true in the town.

A second level is a sense that the superficial calm is in fact unstable. Many people seem anxious to accentuate the positive aspects of inter-communal living while others seem anxious to open up the seeming contradiction. There is general consensus that life is relatively easy compared to other areas of Northern Ireland and this contributed to a sense of local pride. This pride in itself provides a local identity to which all can appeal and which in Northern Ireland terms was very tolerant of the other community. In the town itself both seem to desire that both communities could continue to live together in the town. This might have to do with the existence of a comfortable and established Catholic middle class who emphasise prosperity before national claims. At the same time community leaders are all aware of the implications of their behaviour. The most important symbols of this are the clergy.

Tremendous importance is attached by many people to the fact that the clergy get on well as people. Everybody appears to know that this is the case and many held it up to me as an example of the state of good community relations. This fact seemed to create a general sense that tolerance was officially sanctioned.

"The Churches do a good job. The old Parish Priest would have visited the other clergy, nice and quietly. In his own quiet way he went on. And we're very fortunate to have the Presbyterian moderator from the town. It's done a lot for the atmosphere in this town." (Catholic businessman)

"I would say the Churches would still carry some weight among a certain section of the population. There might be some stratification by age. If all the three Churches got together and gave the line the vast majority would adhere to it. The relations between the clergymen have always been good and helpful. In a sense they give the right cues even if they are ahead of their people.... By and large the Churches carry some weight due to the behaviour of the clergy giving examples to the people." (Social Worker).

"We have very good relations with the Churches here. The Protestant churches interchange ministers. They're in close contact with the Roman

Catholic ministers. They're all ex-officio on the hospital committee." (Protestant teacher)

"The churches are the focal point for the various clubs. They provide the premises for these things to happen. In bowling if there's a photo of Ballytorlar Bowling Club you'll probably find the Parish Priest alongside the Church of Ireland Rector." (Catholic layman)

"Relations between the Churches are good. I know the clergy are very friendly." (Roman Catholic teacher)

For the clergy themselves this gives rise to a number of issues. In the first place, they are keen to avoid tokenism. Unlike in some other places there were no monthly or weekly prayer meetings for clergy. Indeed on this level of 'organised symbolism' Ballytorlar is almost 'organised against'. The spirit which came across was a sense of resentment that such symbolism should be necessary.

"We live our lives, its an intimate matter. They look after their own flocks, the good and the bad. Its not my business what (Church of Ireland clergy) or (Presbyterian clergy) does, what backsliders he has. There's no question of involvement: We don't publicise meetings. We don't say 'Oh look at Father X talking to the Protestants isn't it wonderful'. Its just life. These aberrations, like offence given, attacking each other's premises are extraordinary. I don't believe in highlighting things - like there was a school meeting with all the clergy on the platform. We just get on. You don't make a big thing about it. Its the same as farmers." (local Priest)

While this may once have been true and may be again, it is not now the case that interdenominational meetings of clergy are considered of the same significance as meetings between farmers. The wider importance of inter-community relationships are focused at these meetings. Although the power of clergy has diminished, the symbolism of private goodwill does not pass unnoticed in Ballytorlar. The clergy, as moral guardians and authority in the community bring these aspects of their relationship to their congregations into the meetings on the town's streets.

"There's no big deal made about working together. I see this as a sign of the security of people in Ballytorlar. In Ballytorlar meetings just happen in shops or on the streets. There's no monthly meetings of clergy and no

felt need for symbolic gestures. In my opinion there could be more." (Roman Catholic curate)

The Protestant churches were clear in their delineation between the inter-relationship they had with each other and the relationship each had with the Roman Catholics. In general the difference was that the latter was largely social and had only a limited theological dimension. The Church of Ireland and Presbyterians do have some joint services.

"When I came and started a few joint services with the Church of Ireland there were a few people who objected. Now I don't hear any murmuring. People still don't maybe feel at home with Church of Ireland services but they don't seem to object. With the Catholics there are good community relations but we don't attempt any services. We do get together and drink coffee and work on specific things... There is a measure of religious common ground. We don't have big services but I think this is wise. In that way we would get backs up." (Presbyterian Minister)

"As far as the Churches are concerned there's a very good relationship. Between ourselves and the Presbyterian Church there's a very good relationship. The Presbyterian Minister has been very co-operative to work with. We share some services, youth organisations and epilogues in the summer. With the local Roman Catholics there's a very good relationship really. We don't have any united services yet I don't know how people would take that. Sometimes I think we ought to but some of our people might not like it. More of the Presbyterians might object." (Church of Ireland Rector)

The first service to involve all the clergy in Ballytorlar in the worship took place this year (1989) during the Octave of Prayer for Christian Unity. This was an item noted by many people as an important break with the past.

The most profound moments of inter-denominational coming together took place at the time of Ballytorlar's largest bomb. The bomb exploded in 1973 outside the Catholic Church, 'the Chapel', timed to coincide with the exit of people at the end of Sunday mass. The priest who was saying Mass that day took up the story.

"It was a six-hundred pound bomb and fortunately I couldn't find a piece of paper and the people weren't released. The first person to come up and

see me was the Presbyterian Minister."

All who spoke about the bomb remember it as an event which united the town. This is true of Catholics who were there at the time.

"We had a bomb at the chapel and everybody helped." (Catholic businessman)

A social workers recalled how the Roman Catholic Church intervened to put a stop to rumours about who was responsible for the incident which began to fly around the town.

"It was very interesting to note that Catholics in the town started to ask 'who did it?' and a name was given, that of a prominent [Protestant] businessman in the town. He would have been ruined. The next week at Mass the Parish Priest took up the issue and castigated the rumours. That stopped it."

The bomb itself was a huge shock to the town and is one of only two major explosions in the town over the last 20 years. The realisation that it was intended to kill 50-60 people leaving Mass caused great trauma. The other explosion which destroyed the town's only medium-sized hotel is bemoaned by the business establishment, but the fact that it was aimed at property not people means that it does not have the same traumatic resonance as the Chapel explosion.

The Church of Ireland has suffered from vandalism over the years. At one stage the Glenmore Road Hall was burnt down. The town again rallied round. More recently, all the windows of one of the Church of Ireland Churches were smashed.

"We had a very traumatic event two-years ago. On a Good Friday night all our stained-glass windows were smashed. At that time Roman Catholics and Protestants were outraged in the town. The telephone was red-hot here with Catholics expressing their horror. This did something though, it helped to express a solidarity in the town here." (Church of Ireland rector)

Events of naked violence have the effect of strengthening town unity. Having escaped the worst of the violence in Northern Ireland. Ballytorlar has developed on identity in relation to this outstanding fact. The protection of this situation has become part of the local identity and the interest of Protestant and Catholic Middle Class. The role of the clergy in this is leadership.

"There's no consistent violence here and it gives people time to forget it. The clergy have to keep on trying to foster this stability by personal contact with people, not just your own people. I remember one of my old parishioners saying. 'Its most important for you to be seen talking to Father O'Hare in the Square'. He seemed to think that was one-up for community relations. A few year ago there was a visit by a Roman Catholic Auxiliary Bishop. The Parish Priest invited the Presbyterian Minister and I up and we had tea with him." (Church of Ireland Rector)

The Presbyterian Minister had recently been elected to high office in his Church, and this too had been seen as a time of local celebration.

"A number of Catholics in town asked if they could come to my installation.. and they were introduced to great applause at the General Assembly. The Parish Priest came to our Church after I was elected and spoke from the pulpit. He got thunderous applause. I was prayed for in all the Churches of the town."

"I don't think the troubles have had any effect on Ballytorlar. For instance on the night of the election of the Presbyterian Minister I would say at least a third of the congregation were Catholic. The community was there to say "well done, you're a member of our community, we're delighted. As well, at the ceremony in Belfast there were Ballytorlar Catholics which I think is a pointer to the situation here." (Catholic layman)

The townspeople were keen to acknowledge their happiness at this event and yet the same 'duality' seems to exist in Church relations as in community relations in the town. In public the churches have reached an equilibrium with one another which allows co-operation on areas in which they do not compete. In Ballytorlar this extends to conversion, where no Church is seriously attempting to win over members of one to another. Nevertheless, there is an underlying sense that ultimately they are institutional competitors rivalling over theology and doctrine, and claiming each to have if not a monopoly, then a greater insight into 'truth'. This balance and it's limits seem to be defined by the clergy whose social unity and theological difference exist side by side.

"They [the clergy] are all ex-officio on the hospital committee. The Parish Priest was one of our most stalwart supporters." (Protestant layman)

"People look to the clergy. I think they probably look for too much to the clergy. They feel you should be on every committee under the sun. Sometimes the committees can be very time-consuming. You do play a pretty prominent role in the town in the sense that you're asked to be at all these things. I suppose as a clergyman that to be happy in this place you'd have to be of a co-operative disposition. I'd hate to think what would happen if some of us would go and somebody was appointed who didn't have a bit of give and take and come and go." (Church of Ireland Rector)

The public life of the community is also expressed through private acts such as marriage and funerals. Marriage is a particularly important area as it is a particularly personal way by which institutional divisions can be ignored. The attitude of the Churches to mixed marriage is, like schools, an area where institutional power is very important. Most marriages are not 'mixed'. They remain a matter of comment, a disorder which challenges or upsets the institutional order of things. On the Protestant side it is an issue often held to illustrate the inflexibility of the Roman Catholic Church. In Ballytorlar however, mixed marriage has a longer tradition. It is seen in part as a binding force in the community acting as a link between families rather than a divide.

"This being a predominantly Roman Catholic town, at least in the town, there are more mixed marriages. Sometimes that creates a bit of tension. From a denominational point of view it's tricky. Being a clergyman of one denomination one wants to see that they're doing the right thing. On the other hand you find in Ballytorlar that a lot of their parishioners have Roman Catholic relations and that tempers you a bit. That keeps things together a bit. I'm not advocating that mixed marriage is totally accepted but its a fact and people have learned to live with it." (Church of Ireland rector)

It certainly appeared to be a more contentious issue among Protestants, especially given the resentment that the children would almost always be brought up Catholic. Nevertheless, for at least one lay woman it was an important part of her understanding of inter-Church relations.

"I suppose there was a bit of feeling about it at the time. There was a feeling 'It would be nice if he married one of his own'. Everybody went to the wedding. The children were brought up Catholic. It was their agreement and they're very happy. To me they're all Church though I do like my own Church of Ireland."

Others often saw mixed-marriage as an excuse for non-attendance on behalf of both, including under 'mixed marriage between Presbyterians and members of the Church of Ireland.

*"There's no established tradition of what is expected in cases of inter-Church marriage. In the better families people join their partner but in fringe families people keep with their own Churches and use it as an excuse to get involved in none." (*Presbyterian minister)

Another area of Public life where the Churches are deeply involved is funerals. In Ballytorlar there is a tradition of attendance at one another's funerals. This is a feature which is fully reciprocal. It may be illustrative of a deep sense of local identity reflected in funeral attendance and a common sense of loss. The fact that it takes place in such an unselfconscious manner in itself contributes to continuity and stability at a local level.

"We go to one another's funerals quite readily." (Presbyterian Minister)

"If somebody from the Church of Ireland dies there might be more Catholics at their funeral than Church of Irelands. Its not a thing to be wondered at here, it's something we just accept." (Catholic layman)

"I've been to some of the services in the Chapel. They've been funeral service's and it causes no eyebrows to be raised even among my own people. If I'd done that in my last parish...." (Church of Ireland Rector)

In this context, the Churches as a whole act as central institutions in the midst of life and death, and in Ballytorlar at the point of death political rivalry between Church Institutions hardly seems to exist.

This reflects itself too in the attitudes of the churches towards conversion. Most of them are internally orientated and do not attempt to upset the existing balance.

*"There is no competition between Churches as people just stay as they are. You have to be a brave man to change from being a Presbyterian to a Roman Catholic or the other way around in Northern Ireland." (*Roman Catholic Priest)

"The Churches in Ballytorlar do not proselytise each other's members. Sheep-stealing is not a policy of any responsible Church. I see the role of the Church as two-fold. First to care for affiliated families, pastoral care, a place of worship, fellowship, spiritual encouragement. The second thing is an evangelistic role for people in the town with shaky faith. We also have an outreach to people with no faith." (Presbyterian Minister)

Nevertheless their institutional division may effect their moral impact, especially with the young in that their individual power may not create sufficient support.

"I would say the Churches would still carry some weight among a certain section of the population. There might be some stratification by age. If all the three Churches got together and gave the line, the vast majority would adhere to it." (Social Worker)

The Churches in Ballytorlar have settled for an equilibrium of institutional separation. Contact at the level of Clergy, representation on public bodies and at funerals have become 'normal' and are expectations. Nevertheless in the area of schools, mixed marriage and social clubs divisions exist and no attempt is made to challenge these. That is not to say that such divisions are considered desirable. Rather they are accommodated as part of life. Politics and theology are privatised and public gestures are in the direction of minimising the effects of division whose private existence can only be acknowledged. Much effort goes into ensuring that no excuse is given to escalate tension.

Tensions can be worsened but the result has usually been smoothed over. Usually the causes of upset are found outside the town itself- e.g. political events, marches by bands outside, Church politics. Distinctions are made between opposition in general and action against local representatives. The Churches reflect and direct the 'Janus' approach.

They do make gestures to unity of purpose and live within the context of division. These apparently contradictory signals are based on a fear of what naked division can mean. Such signals are open to the charge of hypocrisy. The alternative appears to be open hostility and violence.

Public gestures of unity are not simply appearance. Mixed up with appearances are genuine desires to take every opportunity for local signs of friendship. Without this real basis it is unlikely that the town could have remained stable for such a length of time. Examples are found in town co-operation over public appeals for help.

"One example of this local sense of belonging was Ballytorlar reaction to the Johnstone twins. It was completely unimportant that they were Presbyterian, the fact of their need was the most important thing." (Catholic Priest)

The Johnstone twins are local children born blind. An appeal was made to raise £50,000 for an operation in America which might reverse their blindness. After a huge community effort, £100,000 was raised in a very short time.

"A nephew of mine with Down Syndrome went missing four years ago and this whole town to a man and woman left their work to search this area for him. This went on for three days and three nights. Then it went on for three weeks in rotas. They're not shut up in their enclaves -its a community." (Local man)

Another example was over the question of a presentation of a gift to the retiring Roman Catholic Parish Priest by the Protestant congregations. The Catholic Church responded by changing their plans to accommodate this wish.

"The Parish Priest in Ballytorlar has just retired and there's a presentation to him. Because the other Churches want to be involved it won't be on Sunday Night but on a week night. That's a real evidence of what I'm trying to say. I think this spirit spreads through this area." (Catholic layman)

"A collection was lifted to make a presentation to the Parish Priest. The Church of Ireland made it known that they wanted to be involved as they've bought him a painting." (Catholic layman)

One further agent of unity in the community was the presence of a Catholic/Protestant centre nearby. This had initiated a joint carol service in the town and was an important employer in the area. In addition the ecumenical prayer group in the area had links through people who were involved in both. Nevertheless its existence as such was held also to be having an effect on some.

"I think the centre has had a bit to play a bit of a leavening effect here. People have seen that Roman Catholics and Protestants do meet there. They've had their bit to play. For example in the local carol service. Even like last Friday inviting the local clergy up to lunch. Once a year during the week of Prayer for Christian Unity they have a do up there." (Church of Ireland rector)

The extent of joint-services illustrates the limits of Church unity. In 1987 the Chamber of Commerce and local groups organised a joint Carol Service in the Square to which many people came. This was the first time that such an event was held. There are ecumenical groups in the town, in the form of a Charismatic Prayer Group and two Bible Study Groups. Even here there has been suspicion and a degree of cynicism.

"There has been the recent addition of the town Carol Service in the Square. We go to one another's funerals quite readily. We have a Bible Study Group in the Presbyterian Church and there is also one in the Convent. The one in the Convent is officially ecumenical but it is 90% Catholic. There are occasional joint meetings one or two times a year. There's a mixed children's carol service and we go to it. There is a measure of religious common ground. We don't have big services but I think this is wise. In that way we would get backs up." (Presbyterian Minister)

"In the Church unity octave in January normally the Protestant ministers would get together. There's a communal service, quite well attended by Catholics though how many are native? I would say that the bulk were runners and often those interested in Church politics. The Joint Carol Service was well attended at Christmas time." (Catholic Social Worker).

"Even on Market day each denomination has its own stalls and car-parks." (Catholic lay woman)

"The Parish Priest was opposed to the Prayer Group because it wasn't started by him. Lay people started it. With the Parish Priest I found it difficult to celebrate the liturgy. We [he and I] were different. He firmly believed what he said and did. The Prayer Group was too emotional, all this hallelujah stuff. Certainly we've always been lucky and had support from one of the curates. The Prayer Group has been on the go for 10 years now. For us, its the only opportunity to talk about religious things." (Catholic Prayer Group Member)

"As an official group of parishioners Inter-Church contact is nil. Individuals however have attended services in the Church of Ireland and Presbyterian Church such as the Church Unity Octave, Christian Aid Services or the Woman's World Day of Prayer. Some have taken part in readings at these services. The Parish Priest himself would occasionally present himself at invited gatherings but the invitation if mentioned in the weekly Parish Bulletin was nearly always played down or not extended to parishioners at all. However some personal contacts always spread the word through a small group of people and a small number crossed the divide." (Catholic lay woman)

"It's very difficult to know what the Churches can do more than at the moment. If they could have worship together that might show that we're Christians. There's just a bit of fear in some people, and I suppose its in me too that some of the important things we stand for might get lost. We have a service for the week of Prayer for Christian Unity, once in the Church of Ireland, once in the Presbyterian Church. Sometimes I wonder if we should go on if we can't get the Roman Catholics. It's just a wee niggle in my mind - what is the next step? There's a bit of unreality. In the Woman's World Day of Prayer there is now Roman Catholic participation. There is a prayer group in the town. It's lay and in the Convent. They have sponsored an inter-denominational prayer service in the Glenmore Road Hall. I have recently came across a person in the parish whose been greatly helped by this." (Church of Ireland Rector)

In recent months the Catholic Church has begun to participate active in the joint-services during the Week of Prayer for Christian Unity. This is seen as a major change in inter-Church relations.

Nevertheless, the impression left is that the Protestant Churches have regular interchange with one another but that the contact with the Roman Catholic Church extends to the door of the Church buildings but no further except for funerals. In a social sense this may appear relatively insignificant, but given that community worship and mass are the centre of the Churches life as understood by the Churches themselves, it is an exclusion from the heart of matters. In Ballytorlar there has been a willingness to explore all avenues except where central interests are concerned. A very large crack is thus papered over, though the job has been well done given the nature of the division. There is nonetheless an uneasy sense that the social equilibrium made possible is an unstable one and that this is interrelated with the 'ethnic' and 'political' tensions which have the same structure of papered over division. Ballytorlar has strong if non-violent Unionism and Nationalism. It has never been a stronghold of the Alliance Party.

The theologies which contribute to and derive from this situation were only referred to in passing. Nevertheless they provide an interesting insight.

"On the other hand the Catholic people of Ballytorlar wouldn't have that dogmatic approach to religion. This is not characteristic of Catholicism or of Irish Catholicism in any case." (Catholic Priest)

"There are major theological differences between Catholics and Protestants. Anglicans and Presbyterians are much closer. The common ground is much more than what divides us including the sacraments. There are two main views of the Catholic Church in the Presbyterian Church. One views it as a Church which has lost its way, verging on apostasy. Another sees it as a true Christian Church in serious error on major points off doctrine. Many of us would feel that there are many points of agreement. I have always maintained that we can disagree without being disagreeable.. Ballytorlar has no deep tradition of viewing the Roman Catholic Church as apostate. In the wider Presbyterian Church this view is more widely held, especially among younger ministers. There is a deep suspicion of anything ecumenical and a fear that it will lead to a union with Rome." (Presbyterian Minister)

"The task of the parish priest is enshrined from earlier times in Canon Law. We have authority within the boundaries of the parish. We don't overstep. The task is the saving of these souls, to be a father and a guide like your own family. He acts with authority and is responsible to his bishop. I can't overstep my boundaries, we've enough to do. Each man has to see his flock from birth to the grave." (Catholic Priest)

It would be possible on the basis of these contributions to show how each of these theological and doctrinal positions is connected to divisions in the community. Each can also be challenged as a picture of theological or actual truth. Nevertheless all of these comments must be read in the light of a remark made by the Presbyterian minister.

"People in Ballytorlar are mostly not deeply aware of doctrinal differences. Many are stumped for theological reasons. They rest in the simple fact that they know we are different and leave it at that. I would say that older members are more aware of doctrinal points and perhaps now the very young members who are learning them again." (Presbyterian minister)

One further feature remains. One of the most regular features of Northern Irish life is the Protestant parade. They have often been the focus of tension.

"Relations between the two communities are fairly good. It heightens up occasionally when you have a provocative parade from either side. The Hibernians haven't been in a few years. The Orange have had a few. The last time they were here in 1986. They were very well behaved. It had been looked forward to with trepidation. Riots were expected. I made it my business to go down and nothing happened. A couple of months ago there were a few provocative people on a march. There's a vague resentment that the Orange Order comes so often to Ballytorlar as its a Nationalist town." (SDLP Councillor)

"Occasionally there is tension in the town. Last year, Paisley brought bands and people couldn't get to their business. Paisley would come to speak. It is generally known as a Nationalist town and he come to show that he can walk through." (Catholic teacher)

The majority of Ballytorlar Protestants are not members of the Orange Order. The Order has little influence on the Churches or communities in the town. The Orange Hall is usually closed and used as a weekly office for the Department of Employment to allow people to sign on for benefit. This is a marked contrast to the Protestant areas to the west of the town where the lodges are large and significant. The Independent Orange Lodge often march through Ballytorlar on the Twelfth. Until now this march passed off peacefully. Recently in September, local bands marched through the town on a Saturday night. That same night someone was seriously injured in the Square. This was linked by many people in the town to the march. The march was resented also because it was unexpected although notice had been given in the local newspaper. The increase in tension locally as a result of these incidents was marked.

"In my last parish one wouldn't have met many Roman Catholics. It was very Orange. Most of my good Church workers were Orangemen, in many ways the salt of the earth. Personally I found this very interesting because I am not Orange Orientated. When I came to Ballytorlar there was an entirely different atmosphere.... Certainly the Orange Order doesn't count for very much. I think its because the town is a bit of a mixture or at least it was. I think it's changing now. There's a lot of imports who weren't of the Orange Order type.... People have been tempered by living cheek-by-jowl with people of another tradition." (Church of Ireland rector)

"As far as our Church is concerned, they're probably Unionist to a man. This is not a strongly Orange Area and its not very politically active. I have very few card-carrying party members. I would have thought that on the whole there is a less clear identity of Protestantism and Unionism here than elsewhere.... I think if you move a few miles out of the town you'll find the tribal thing. But again its a working-class thing. They see Paisley as a man who speaks the truth. 'It's a good thing somebody speaks out' sort of thing. He articulates their fears. But they don't want his Church." (Presbyterian minister)

Once again this is evidence of the stark division perceptible in Ballytorlar between public behaviour and private opinion. The Catholics of the town have traditionally ignored Orange Parades, and adopted an attitude of indifference which has meant that the parades are not associated with violence.

"How would you measure a religious divide? On the twelfth this year the town decorated itself. They came, they marched, nobody said anything. There was no trouble from the bands no damage done in the town. The independent Orange Lodge comes here. There's a certain provocation that is not responded to. People just keep their heads down... They're all aware that the town they love so well could be smashed if anybody got control. That's why they react like that to the Twelfth. It's organised from outside and they let it go." (Social Worker)

Nevertheless the incident in September did make waves.

"I remember when I used to run behind the bands on the Twelfth as a wee boy. The other night I spoke to a few Protestants at the bands and they didn't speak back." (Catholic tradesman)

"Trouble can be provoked here like anywhere in Northern Ireland. The march of the bands through here last Saturday has made waves. Incidents like that make it much more difficult for me to preach Christian responses. Such things cause a lot of reverberations. If it happens again it could cause reverberations. They could cause escalations." (Catholic priest)

The Police officially said that they had no trouble with Orange demonstrations.

"We'd bring in extra police on these days, we've had no real problems so far."

Talking privately with some policemen some admitted that it was awkward.

"I hate to see it but what can you do?"

Another also pointed out how communal violence caused every incident to be read in a sectarian light. The police were sure that there was no direct connection between the march of the band and the beating in the Square. Nevertheless many people insisted on establishing such a connection. This always raises the problem of revenge.

"The doing in the Square had nothing to do with the Orange Parade but in the town that's the way it's picked up."

Nevertheless many Catholics maintained that the Protestants were the more embittered group. This reflects the sense of beleagueredness mentioned above.

"Ballytorlar is now more a town attached to Glenmore [RC] rather than to Knockbeg [Protestant]." (Presbyterian Minister)

"The Catholic people in the town are more tolerant than the Protestants." (Catholic Secretary)

"Within Torlar, the Orange Tradition is more bitter. Orangemen can march in Ballytorlar and people don't bother. There are towns with similar population structures where that couldn't happen. The Dunfiners really love to march through Ballytorlar. There are no flags in the town on the 12th or at Easter. I can think of two Union Jacks that go up and no tricolours. The only reason for emblems in Northern Ireland is to rule someone else." (Catholic Sports Officer)

The 'intolerance' or 'tolerance' of a group is almost certainly dependent on which side the observer stands on. Nevertheless on one thing the townspeople concerned with the maintenance of order agree: Trouble comes from outside.

"Over the last five or six years people have come in from outside and tried to stir the pot, but in a small town we have to work together." (Businessman)

Conclusions

People in Ballytorlar were all aware that their town had not faced the violence experienced in other parts of Northern Ireland. By and large they were anxious to keep it that way. Partly as a result, however, there is a sharp division between public and private opinions in order to protect this stability.

People are anxious to convey the impression of a peaceful settlement where community relations are harmonious. There was no immediate public evidence of a rift or of an uncrossable divide that can be found elsewhere in Northern Ireland. This no doubt contributes to and results from the relative lack of sectarian violence. Matters have not escalated in Ballytorlar as in some other towns. The relative geographical isolation of Ballytorlar from other areas of trouble, the distinct identity of Glenmore and the behaviour of leading figures and institutions in the town may all have contributed to this stability. Central to these stabilising influences have been the clergy and the Churches. This is one aspect of town life.

This must be set alongside a parallel strand which can be identified. Ballytorlar has echoes of all the main religious and political quarrels in Ulster. They stem from locals as much as outsiders although the common myth is that it comes from outside. This too acts as a political brake by concentrating public antagonism on less dangerous people. Ballytorlar has not been the scene of any experiments. Apparently conflicts have to lead to dramatic deterioration before attempts are made at radical change. The Churches, the Schools, most social life and much private life continues in tranquil exclusiveness. The Churches are not competing for each others members nor are they seeking ways over theological division. The same is true of schools, social life and private life. The mixed communities in the town or experiments which might blur lines are regarded with suspicion and fear of the consequences. The Churches have indeed reached an agreed equilibrium and nevertheless appear unsure about whether they are rivals or fellow-travellers.

The result is a conservatism of response extended to all change. This protects against radical violence and hinders change in community relations at one and the same time. There are of course people who attempt different relationships - the local prayer groups, Chamber of Commerce, Torlar Recreation Centre, etc. Their continuing life has had an important impact in the town, though often they are regarded with suspicion.

Ballytorlar retains through its ‘order’ the possibility of meeting across divides. This is an important factor. The schools, the Churches and private people can meet and learn together in safety. This is an achievement in Northern Ireland. Ballytorlar remains a pleasant town, and the duality of its nature means that the atmosphere in the town has not shifted to one of community antagonism. The Churches have fostered some of this, unanimous in their opposition to violence. At the same time the institutional Churches remain as obstacles to more radical change which might threaten the institutional separateness of each group. This is not unique to Ballytorlar.

The Churches in Ballytorlar are therefore important as part of the cultural and social organisation of the town. The town, as such, cannot be seen without an adequate understanding of the Churches. Moral leadership is still sought in the Churches and most particularly from the clergy. Their impact on violence stems mostly from their importance as keepers of the local conscience and models of good behaviour rather than from their radical initiatives.

SECTION FOUR: HOLY WAR IN THE BELFAST AREA

"You might as well have holy gangsters"

Introduction

Walkerstown is an old settlement with roots which pre-date its incorporation into the Belfast area. Major new by-pass roads loop the area and cross the main Walkerstown High Street at the northern edge of the area. This provided the northern boundary of the study. The Walkerstown High Street acts as the main shopping area and the traffic thoroughfare for Walkerstown. As the road leaves Walkerstown, Rathcrone Housing Estate comes into view. At the southern edge of the Estate the by-pass joins the High Street again, acting as the southern boundary to the study.

Rathcrone consists mostly of low-rise accommodation although there are five multi-storey flat blocks on the estate. In total there are 1526 dwellings. The estate was built in the 1950's and 60's by the Housing Trust, now the Northern Ireland Housing Executive (N.I.H.E.). The eastern edge of the estate also acted as the Eastern boundary of this study.

Glenfoot Road crosses Walkerstown High Street in the middle of the shopping area. Lower Glenfoot Road to the west rises through an area of private housing to the Clonderg Estate. To the south of Clonderg lies Drumglass, a large housing estate built in the 1960s and 70s with 1,600 dwellings. This estate extends to the Drumglass Road. This road was the westernmost extension of our study. Rathcrone and Drumglass can both be said to belong to the 'Greater Walkerstown area'. A stylised map indicates the relation of the areas to one another.

Walkerstown was once a separate from Belfast. Today it is indistinguishable from much of suburban Belfast. Undoubtedly the vast majority of the present-day residents in all of our study area now feel part of the city.

In Rathcrone and Drumglass this may be explained by the history of the estates. Rathcrone is made up of families originally from inner-Belfast, often Sandy Row or Shankill Road. The population is very settled and the NIHE has no difficulty in finding people to move into the estate. In Drumglass many of the people arrived as the result of intimidation in other parts of Belfast. The estate is virtually entirely Catholic. The facilities on the estate are very limited and it is generally regarded as an area of serious deprivation.

At the entrance to Rathcrone stand two permanent signs with the script "Rathcrone Says NO". These are clearly intended as territorial markers.

On the first tree visible from the main road hangs a large Union Flag and on many lampposts around the estate there are posters urging "Join the UDA". Grafitti on the estate is limited. Nevertheless the condition of the estate deteriorates markedly as one moves away from the main entrance. This is noticeable in graffiti and an unkempt appearance and in a reduction in the number of houses now privately owned. The graffiti is largely political: e.g. "Three Provies - One Stone" or UDA badges. The kerbs of pavements are painted red, white and blue.

Drumglass has paving stones of green, white and orange. Grafitti is widespread and includes murals on the gable ends of houses. Slogans include "Beware a risen people." This gives the estate an entirely different atmosphere. The local paper is largely identified as being Unionist and is not stocked in local shops. Many people expect to be neglected and treated with contempt by the local Council.

The towers of Rathcrone are clearly visible all over Drumglass. However, the physical contact between the two is effectively non-existent. The one exception to this rule is contact made in the workplace. Walkerstown Industrial Estate effectively separates the two estates. It has nevertheless provided some employment for some people on both estates. This was particularly true before the collapse of multinational and State-subsidised investments in the industrial estate. It was notable how cynical local people were about new developments following the collapse of the well-publicised large investment programmes for the area..

Walkerstown itself is largely middle-class. The houses are mostly owner occupied and the area has an atmosphere of relative affluence. There are very few wall-slogans to be seen. This is not to say that the area exudes wealth. Much of the housing on the western side of Walkerstown High Street is modest, although the housing on the eastern side is more mixed, including larger, Villa-type detached houses. Many people in the area travel to work in Belfast or outside the city in nearby towns. Much of the original coherence of the area has been lost, and the High Street is often filled with through-traffic. There has been some decline in the area as a shopping centre in recent years.

As we shall see, by far the most controversial issue in the area at present is the movement of Protestant families out of the area and of Catholic families into the area. Traditionally Walkerstown was a Protestant area. It is now clearly mixed with a Catholic majority on the western side of Walkerstown High Street. The exception to this is the Clonderg estate which retains its Protestant majority. Nevertheless there appears to be very little real contact between Clonderg and neighbouring Drumglass.

The neighbouring districts mentioned in our text are Ballyray, which begins on the northern side of the by-pass, Dunroe, which borders on our study area to the south. Both of these areas are similar to Walkerstown, although Dunroe remains predominantly Protestant. Ardbann, a newer Catholic housing estate borders on our study area to the to the west.

The Churches in the District

There are no Protestant Churches in Drumglass and no Catholic Churches in Rathcrone. Walkerstown has numerous Churches of all denominations.

The Roman Catholic Church in the area studied is divided into two parishes. Drumglass (St. Brigid's) Parish covers the area of the estate. The Church, Parochial House, Convent of the Sisters of Mercy, Family Centre, A.C.E. Scheme and St. Brigid's Primary School are found together at the main entrance to the estate. The second Parish is Old Walkerstown centred on St. John's. The Parish covers a huge area including Dunroe, Ballyray and Walkerstown. Originally Drumglass was part of this Parish.

Old Walkerstown Parish now serves an estimated 10,000 Catholics. It is de facto split into two main centres; St. John's between Walkerstown and Ballyray (to the North of our area) and St. Peter's in Dunroe (to the south of our area). Most of the Catholics in Walkerstown attend St. John's. The St. John's complex includes the Church, the Parochial House, St. John's Primary School and St. Joseph's Grammar School.

The Presbyterian Church has two congregations in the area of study. One covers the Rathcrone estate, while the other covers Central Walkerstown. Walkerstown was a major centre of Presbyterian revolt in the nineteenth century. The minister in Walkerstown was a leading non-subscriber. As a result, the original Presbyterian Church Building belongs to the Non-subscribing Presbyterian Church. The Church of Ireland also has two parishes. St. Dorothea's serves the Rathcrone area while St. Peter's covers Walkerstown. The Methodists have one Church in the area on the edge of the Rathcrone Estate. This covers Dunroe and Walkerstown.

There are also smaller Churches in the area. There are two Gospel Halls in Walkerstown, a Free Presbyterian Church in Rathcrone and a Christian Fellowship linked to the Bible College in Walkerstown. These smaller groups have not always been insignificant, especially in political terms.

The Churches and Personal Life.

In a survey conducted by Rathcrone Council of Churches in April 1987,

73% of homes who completed the survey (50% of total on the estate) claimed some attachment to a Church. The survey does not record how deeply people valued this attachment. Nevertheless it indicates at least two features worthy of comment. Even where Church attendance is falling large numbers feel an attachment to a Church in proportions far larger than might be expected in England and Wales. However, attachment itself is not sufficient to allow us to speak of Church as central to personal life. Some 27% of the estate did not claim any allegiance to a Church. In such an area we can talk of the Churches as significant though not as holding a monopoly. The Churches are part of the fabric of the area, although it can no longer be said that everybody has some links with the Church. Nevertheless they clearly belong as part of the community and can probably claim a wider acceptability than other groups or institutions in the area.

Among those involved in the Churches, there were many who were very dedicated to them:

"I think that I only realised my own need to be saved when I was here in Rathcrone. I see this as part of my Christian life. I knew that it was God calling me." (Presbyterian, Rathcrone, Woman)

"For me the kingdom of God is righteousness, peace and joy. It's within me. With all that we do we have to see that in all things Christ has first place. It would be so easy to get away from that through busyness." (Man, Walkerstown, Christian Fellowship)

"We'd be quite involved with the sacramental work of the Church. We have a pre-baptismal course and that's very popular. We've three or four babies every week." (Catholic Nun, Drumglass)

"About five months after I'd been attending the Free Presbyterian Church I was laughing and then all of a sudden a cloud of doubt attacked me. All these things happened. My husband asked me what was wrong, everybody noticed. By this time I was totally gripped with fear. My mind went berserk. My friend came to visit me and I thought it was Satan to take me away. They took me to all these Churches. The only person I wouldn't go to was the Presbyterian Minister. Nothing worked. Then one day I was watching TV. It ended up that it was a Catholic on it. I thought "he loves the lord!" On the next day I saw the Presbyterian Minister just walking around the estate. I just ran over and the love started coming, the deep

love. From then on its just been each day." (Woman, Rathcrone)

"We pray with and for one another all the time. We have groups who meet, or if people have special needs. Its a very real ministry. I'd say many of us were Presbyterians first and have become Christians first." (Presbyterian Minister)

"We've found a lot of encouragement in the Church. Many of those people from the earliest days are still with it and are now beginning to minister to people. Whenever I tear myself apart I do so for not going fast enough." (Church of Ireland Rector, Rathcrone)

At the same time there were dissenting voices:

"I would be very worried at times about my Church, the Presbyterians. They want to close down all the old organisations like the Boys Brigade and there can be a terrible amount focussed on the Minister." (Presbyterian man)

There is a sense that the Churches in decline as a focus of moral teaching. It is no longer seen as a necessary social duty to attend Church. This is true in all areas, and was often mentioned.

"My main worry is that while a lot of people are connected to the Church they are not committed..... People have the attitude "The Church should be there" but aren't prepared to take the initiative. My Choir's down from 30 to 15. People still look to the Church for spiritual guidance. Certainly in times of death or sickness they want you there. Surprisingly so." (Church of Ireland Rector, Walkerstown)

"I think the Church has lost a certain amount of influence. You always hope something rubs off. All Churches find this. The numbers regularly attending Church have fallen. Things of God aren't as central as they ought to be." (Presbyterian Minister, Walkerstown)

"The majority on the estate wouldn't go to Church on Sunday. On Sunday mornings the Church is full, mostly people from the estate. In the evening it's just the stalwarts. There's much more women than men. The Kirk Session is equal numbers." (Presbyterian Woman, Rathcrone)

"I suppose there's Paramilitaries in Rathcrone and Drumglass but they've long since left the Churches. There's a task of evangelisation of the Gospels. The Church can just talk, we can't force people." (Catholic Priest, Walkerstown)

The Churches and Social Life

In the Walkerstown area the nature of community resources was very variable in different areas. In Rathcrone the Churches were central to the provision of facilities for social life. Nevertheless it is a complex picture. The estate has a recreation centre run by the Recreation Department of the Council. There is also an Orange Hall which is used for meetings of the Lodge but is mostly closed during the day time. There are no pubs or clubs on the estate. The local drinking club is in Walkerstown. During the period of study the club was the scene of an armed robbery. In the course of leaving the scene, one of the robbers was seriously injured by the police. This was a matter of some controversy in Rathcrone.

There is no Community Centre on the estate with the effect that there is no single meeting place for the whole population. The 'estate' has a geographical existence but it is doubtful whether one can talk of a united community. In this context the three Churches provide many of the meeting points through the week.

The Activity Centre is deemed by the Council as the Centre for Rathcrone and Walkerstown. It has recently reopened having been closed following allegations of misappropriation of funds by the committee. The Centre operates as an agency which provides facilities. It has no membership. Outside the Churches it is the main focus of activity on the estate. The programme includes football Volleyball, Gymnastics, Men's and Ladies Keep Fit, Snooker and Old Time Dancing. It is also the venue for the playgroup run every weekday and a Senior Citizens Group. In addition the Estate Flute Band uses the centre on one evening each week.

"The centre operates for Rathcrone and Walkerstown. Its one of three run in the area. The main Leisure Centre for the area is some distance away. Casual users at this centre can play table tennis, volleyball and snooker." (Rathcrone Leisure Centre Attendant)

A Boy's Brigade and a Girl's Brigade are attached jointly to the Presbyterian and Methodist Churches. Although no longer as large as they were, they remain large organisations. In the Church of Ireland there is a Church Lad's Brigade and troops of Guides, Brownies and Bunnies.

There are also two Youth Clubs on the estate run in the Presbyterian and Church of Ireland Halls. The larger of the two meets in the Presbyterian Hall on Tuesdays. Wednesday is used as a night for trips e.g. to the main Leisure Centre and on Sunday there is a meeting after evening service. Nevertheless there are several problems.

"We set the Youth Club up because there was nothing on the estate. At first we got over 80 coming. Hardly any of them had anything to do with the Church. We got all the hardnuts off the estate. Sometimes its very hard because everything that gets broken in the Church goers blamed on the Youth Club. I suppose most of it is done by them but it'd be nice sometimes not to be blamed for everything. There's some on the session would like to see the club closed.... We got so many toughs that a lot of the girls and softer ones got scared away. Now the UDA's started up football on a Tuesday night. They see it as a way of recruiting people - through football. We've lost a few through that. The UDA's very strong on this estate." (Presbyterian Youth Club Leader)

Football and the Flute Band are seen in the Churches in Rathcrone as ways by which the UDA and Orange Order continued their existence. On this estate, the people in the Churches see their task as providing an alternative to youth paramilitarism. Often the Youth Club is the only link the members have with a Church. Sunday night meetings are intended to be based on discussion rather than recreation. Often the intention has to be understood loosely.

"As long as people don't mind a barrage of insults it works great. They are interested like. They ask us questions about our faith and so on. At least they come." (Youth Club Leader)

Youth Clubs of this nature present the Churches with a major challenge. In one sense they upset the decorum of expected Church behaviour in Northern Ireland. On the other hand such Clubs are often the only contact such young people have with Churches at all. The leaders of the club seem to feel pressured on both fronts. Certainly the leaders took the task seriously.

"On the 11th Night we go round. We try and make sure they don't get into trouble. We also take them away sometimes - to Corrymeela, to the Mournes. But there's a lot of poverty on this estate. Last year we

organised a trip to the Giant's Causeway. All the kids had to do was bring a packed lunch. I had a couple at my door asking 'can we go if we haven't got a lunch.' There wasn't even somebody who would make them a lunch." (Youth Club Co-leader)

The Church of Ireland has a smaller Youth Club. Although they meet on a Saturday they have not been able to attract many members.

"We have a very small Youth Club. We've more leaders than members! Youth Ministry is one of my weakest area's. I've tended to try and stimulate other things." (Church of Ireland Woman)

The Churches are also centres of activities for other meetings on the estate. The Mother's Union and the Presbyterian Woman's Association both have groups in the area. Each of the Churches run groups for prayer and fellowship in the middle of the week. The Presbyterian Church is divided into 'Kinship Groups.' These are small 'Cells' of 20-30 parishioners who meet in each others home.

"I find the kinship groups the most important part of my Church life. They're much closer and people share more deeply." (Kinship Group Member, woman)

The Church of Ireland have a coffee morning every week as well as Wednesday Night meetings. These are known as 'Saints Alive'.

"We meet every Wednesday for praise and teaching. It's a great door in. Its been a great encouragement over the years." (Church of Ireland man)

The introduction of an ACE-scheme in the Presbyterian Church has led to a number of innovations. The most significant has been the introduction of a lunch-time cafe on two days a week. Despite the fact that it is new, it is well-attended at present. In addition the Mother and Toddler Group has been able to establish a more regular routine. The Group itself, the only one of its kind to operate on the estate was the brainchild of one woman with her own young children.

"I don't have a committee. I'm not really into committees. I see this as part of the Church. I had a baby and just began the group. Its a break for the mums. We don't get grants because we don't have a committee. We

don't have speakers because for us the main thing is a break. We have the VSB Toy Library and the Dental Health Officer. Its the only Mother and Toddler Group on the estate. There's a couple of playgroups for over 3s but nothing else, not even swings.

Our minister was very supportive when I wanted to set it up. I'd love some more assistance. I heard of one group in Windsor Baptist where they do Arts and Crafts which would be lovely, but they've a whole group of active women. Our mothers come from all over the estate. Most don't go to the Church. I think its important to keep it linked to the Church. I don't want everyone taking over."

This story illustrates the degree to which the Churches extended to the sphere of providing community outside the home. For many people one of the most crippling features of life in Rathcrone is loneliness. This is one area in which Churches continue to be sources of support.

The Presbyterian Church has a Pensioner's Club. This is a meeting for older people every Wednesday afternoon. This too is an important feature of Church support. In each case, the support may be as important for those who instigate and organise such clubs and groups as for those who attend the events. Bowling Clubs flourish in all three Churches. These too are important social occasions. As one clergyman remarked.

"I often get the feeling that there's a Church attached to the bowling clubs rather than the other way around."

Rathcrone Churches were an important element in the community, part of a wider picture whose other elements were dominated by the UDA and the Orange Order. The Drinking Club, the Tenants Association, the Boys Football and the Flute Bands were regarded as recruitment centres for these. Of course, the two (UDA and Orange Order) are not synonymous. Nevertheless, the people in all three Churches who I spoke to tended to regard the UDA with horror and the Orange Order as declining. It remains true however that the Churches, the UDA and the Orange Order were the three main structures within which social life was lived.

Walkerstown is dominated by commuters who work outside the area. Houses are privately owned and there is no sense of uniformity in the area. Among young people, there are a considerable number at different schools on offer. Children in the area attended local schools or travelled to leading Grammar schools nearby. This has the effect of scattering the community in various directions. People may be prepared to travel further for their social life together. Walkerstown does not give the impression of being a tight-knit community. The Protestant Churches seem to be concerned most deeply with the decline in numbers:

"Parish Organisations are very difficult. You get the children until about 11 or 12 and then they drop out. This does cause me a lot of worry. I find a problem of leadership in the area..... There is a reason for this in that the child population is decreasing. I've about 500 homes of which 200 are aged 65 or over. We have about 100 in the Sunday School. When I reckon that there's only 200 in the school I think its going quite well. Quite a number of them are dropped off in the car, and that worries me. Also I am saddled with the less attractive organisations. I only have the Church Lads Brigade while the Presbyterians have the B.B." (Church of Ireland Rector)

"The Girl's Brigade still holds on but the Boy's Brigade has declined. It used to be packed but it's nothing to what it was. It's outside our control. It's a discouragement to me. You nearly think it's a failure on your part. If it wasn't for people coming back we'd have nothing. My biggest elders districts are all in Dunroe and beyond." (Presbyterian Minister)

The biggest fall in numbers is felt in the youth area. Both Presbyterian and Church of Ireland have youth clubs and Sunday Schools. The opposite is true for the Catholics.

"At one time this area would have been predominantly Protestant. Now there's very few Non-Catholics in Lower Glenfoot Road. This has been evolving over the last 15 years." (Catholic Teacher)

St. John's has a very large Youth Club which competes with other Youth Clubs in the Belfast and South Eastern Education Board areas. Walkerstown also has a State Youth Club in the centre of the Walkerstown. It too is suffering from the general decline in numbers in the Young Protestant Population. For St. John's, it appears to be very important that the club participates in cross-community events.

"We'd encourage our Youth Clubs to engage in inter-club activity with State Sector clubs. The Anglo-Irish Agreement seemed to block things from the Protestant side... one of our Youth Clubs was attacked." (Catholic Priest.)

The Parish also has Scout and Guide troops with all their attendant junior sections. Both are affiliated to their respective Catholic and Irish national organisations. Despite mixing at sporting level the reality is that each Church in Walkerstown runs its own events.

"We don't have very close relations with the Roman Church... All our youth organisations are parallel (Church of Ireland Rector)

The same is true of other organisations in the area - PWA., Mothers Union, Legion of Mary and so on. Social life is lived in a particular Church not across denominational divides.

The Orange Hall in Walkerstown stands close to the main cross-roads on what has become the "Catholic side" of the street. Nevertheless the Orange Hall has as yet escaped serious damage. Unlike in Rathcrone, both Presbyterian and Church of Ireland Churches have strong Orange elements.

"I've got a good few Orangemen in my congregation. Nobody'd stop them using the Church, but we're no good because we're off the main road in the backstreets. You have to be seen." (Presbyterian Minister)

The Order is an important element in Protestant culture. It must be stressed, however, that the influence of any one group is limited in an area which has seen the erosion of a collective sense of belonging. Both established Protestant Churches were primarily worried about decline.

"The Roman Catholic school and chapel have been a great attraction. The Presbyterian cause doesn't flourish. There's no hope here. Sunday School going down and the Organisations going down. The age-group which is loosing most is the children." (Presbyterian Elder)

"In previous times Walkerstown was a very Protestant area. In the last few years changes are taking place, Walkerstown has become more Catholic. I don't want to use the word fear but people talk about it. Every house in Beechlawn changes. I know the same things happened in Ballyray." (Church of Ireland Rector)

The growth of 'suburban individualism' is particularly strong in areas like Walkerstown which have become dormitory areas for people who work elsewhere. However the problems of decline on one side are mirrored to some extent by the strong growth in the Catholic Parish.

All Churches have bowling clubs, there is a badminton club in the Presbyterian Church and a table-tennis club in the Church of Ireland. Although the Churches emphasise their own changes, there are no other meeting places of similar scope in Walkerstown. When Churches disappear they do not appear to be replaced with other vibrant social centres. Perhaps the search for closer community is part of the explanation for the growth of house-groups. In Walkerstown there is a strong Christian Fellowship.

"We meet every Sunday in the Bible College. You'd get 140-150 people. 95% are committed Christians. We'd see ourselves as a community. Our particular burden is with the poor and needy. We'd have male and female leaders. I'd be very keen to get women involved" (Fellowship Member, Male)

The Fellowship have rented out an old house in Clonderg. This they use as an important focus of their work (including ACE). Much of their work is with ex-prisoners and also with the elderly. They have a pensioners club one afternoon every week drawing pensioners from all over the area. The fellowship has become, for many of its members, the focus of their social lives as well as a personal commitment.

Drumglass is separated from Clonderg by a ramp and a small open space. There are plans to build a major road on the open space so cementing the psychological divide. The lives of people in Drumglass and Clonderg, though geographically close, are lived in virtually total separation. It is a vivid example of Northern Ireland's voluntary apartheid. Drumglass has one central Church. More than elsewhere, the Church leadership is actively involved in 'political' divisions on the estate. The position is complicated by the fact that some 'religious' adherents of the Church are 'political' opponents.

The main social centres on the estate outside the Church are the two drinking clubs, the nearest pub and the Activity Centre. The drinking clubs are at each end of the estate. One is controlled by Sinn Fein the other by the Workers Party. This means that large numbers on the estate do not go to one or both. The Church is probably the one building on the estate where every resident has been. To this extent what one observer said is true.

"The Church is the hub of everything on this estate and the priest is the centre of the hub." (Youth Club Leader)

Nevertheless this place at the hub is not unchallenged. In terms of social life the Church is responsible for the large Youth Club on the estate. At present the club has 400+ members registered although perhaps as few as 80 will turn up on any one night.

"We had 330 members last year and that was a terrible year for us." (Youth Club Leader)

The Club is regularly vandalised. There are now only three windows left in the club building. Two of these are covered over with iron bars and one with a metal grill. Church involvement in the club is through the management committee chaired by the local curate and with representatives of the schools. The alternative to organised youth clubs on the estate seems to be hanging around on street corners. There is a high level of vandalism in Drumglass and this too is attributed to different causes.

"I'd say unemployment is the biggest problem. For men on this estate they don't have any dignity. The need for a macho image means that the paramilitaries are the next best option." (local Man)

"The majority of kids I work with on the joyriders project come from that local school. The youngest is 17, and the oldest is 24. Their problem is often literacy and numeracy. The school's not doing its job." (local man)

Social Services and Healthcare are located on the nearby and newer Ardbann estate. The result is that nearly all the facilities for Drumglass itself are centred on Church premises. The Church circulates a newsletter to every household in the parish. There is also a family centre which has an organised programme. From Monday to Thursday every week there is a 'cultural programme'. This involves the teaching of Irish language and culture to a number of Groups.

"We teach Irish language, Music and traditional dancing. We get the mothers and the 5-10 year olds. It's an interest of mine. We get 10-14 year olds but what with homework we get them less. We have a couple of weeks in the summer as well. I see it as a way to work between Sinn Fein and the

Church." (Family Centre Co-ordinator)

The Irish language is the subject of revived interest in Drumglass. The Irish playgroups and schools movement have a number of supporters in Drumglass. The interest remains confined to a minority. It is significant nonetheless. The Irish cultural activity in the Family Centre is partly seen as a means by which Sinn Fein can be hindered in claiming a cultural monopoly.

The Family Centre has a creche, a playgroup and a Mothers Group on Tuesday and Thursday morning.

"The Council ignores this area. Everything is from the parish. They see Drumglass as a Provo estate. Does the Council know that Drumglass exists? We have a programme of speakers and outings. We also go on weekends away to Corrymeela." (Family Centre Worker)

The mothers club is well-attended. Nevertheless as the co-ordinator pointed out.

"Because of the position of the Centre we maybe only reach a half of the people we might reach."

The importance of social events can be illustrated by local reaction to the ending of a women's night in the family centre. Recently this was stopped as part of the Church's drive against alcohol. In some circles this has given rise to annoyance.

"This priest has stopped the Mothers Night at the Family Centre. The women would go down and take their own drink with them. They'd have a laugh, good crack and stagger home. But this priest is very anti-drink. He said that they could all go down to the Hitching Post (local pub). But it was different. A lot of men let their women go because they knew there was no other men. Now they won't let them go. As well as that the women got less hassle." (Local Woman)

The lack of alternative facilities means that a Church decision on, for example, alcohol automatically becomes a general policy for the area. This monopoly of decision-making, facilities and funding means that Church-critics are left with an easy target. Suggestions that the Church acts as the surrogate State in West Belfast take root easily.

The Family Centre remains the venue for bingo on Wednesday and Sunday nights. This is well-attended on both nights. Outside drinking, alternatives to Church venues are difficult to come by. The Tenants and Community Association had Government funding cut, due to suspicion that it was dominated by IRA-linked groups. At the same time funding to all Community Groups was now seen to be subject to political vetting. The cutting of ACE money from such groups has become something of a cause celebre in West Belfast.

"I'll say this for the government - they got their facts right.... The Probation Board and Social Services give money to the Provos by other means." (Catholic Worker)

"All the Community Groups have had their grants cut. We got £90. But there's not much of that goes for guns." (Woman's Worker)

Some of the groups which had their funding withdrawn were based at the Drumglass Activity Centre at the centre of the estate. The Centre is widely regarded as a white-elephant which is likely to close.

"There were no facilities in Drumglass until 1981. This changed in 1981 under pressure as the Government threatened the Council through the Department of Education that they would build a community centre. To stop this the Council did build a centre but not a community centre, rather an activity centre. It's run directly from Council headquarters, and is shortly to be closed under privatisation... The Council's responsibility is to provide recreation facilities. It (the Centre) is used but it's being priced out of people's pockets. There's 80% unemployment among heads of households on this estate." (local S.F. Councillor)

The Church also provides groups for handicapped, mostly related to faith issues. These are known as SPREAD Groups. This supplements a community group for handicapped people which meets in the activity centre every Saturday morning. As we shall see, there is also provision through ACE for work with old people.

Perhaps the position of the Church in Drumglass was best summed up in two statements.

"We'd be seen as the opposition to the IRA. They'd see us as fairly stiff opposition I think." (Catholic Church Worker)

"My attitude is that the Church is solely there for religious activity. It's there to look after the soul. The Church is highly involved where it shouldn't be. It owns all the land that's available. They've three schools and ACE schemes. Its now trying to purchase the old heating plant and it'll probably succeed. All the buildings are owned by the Church." (local man, Sinn Fein Councillor)

The official Church is the biggest institution in Drumglass. It retains its function as part of the umbrella under which social relationships are made. Increasingly it finds itself driven to adopt a stance as a 'party' in local disputes which make it difficult to retain the universal position of the past. Unlike Walkerstown "the Church" is a singular, it is not 'fighting' or 'struggling with' preserving denominational purity. Instead there are intimations of a power-struggle between various groups on the estate. The boundaries are not absolute but the issues at stake are very visible.

The grip of the Church leadership as an ultimate authority seems to be weakest among the young on the estate. School teachers and youth leaders noted the seemingly permanent problem of vandalism and indiscipline in the area. It was clear that the permanent economic depression, de facto a reality since the building of the estate, has had a deep effect on the area.

"Discipline is our biggest problem. A lot of the children in this school come from one-parent families or broken homes. About fifteen years ago that was unheard of. Its significant now. We're talking 20, 30, 40 families in this school. That unsettles the kids". (Primary School Headmaster)

The Churches and Public Life

(a) The Churches and Social Services (including ACE)

Walkerstown shows no signs of severe economic depression. Most of the households in the area do not suffer from unemployment. This contrasts sharply with Rathcrone, where the Churches survey recorded "Unemployment among the heads of households who are available for work at 57%." These were virtually all long term unemployed people with a wide range of skills and work experience. It contrasts even more sharply with Drumglass where unemployment among the same group was estimated by Social Services as over 70%. This was offset slightly by the numbers of young people in training programmes and by the fact that larger numbers of women work than men.

In Drumglass the economic deprivation of the area is immediately apparent. Housing conditions, vandalism and a certain gaunt look on many faces confirm the strains of life. Many who gain employment seek to leave the estate, meaning that the community on the estate itself is always dominated by unemployment. This is noticed even in the schools.

"The parents are very keen that their kids do well. They want their children to go on and they see education as their way out. All our school functions are well-supported... The biggest problem is very high unemployment. We're even worse hit by it on this side of the estate than the other primary school on the estate. It causes an awful lot of stress. We're made very aware of it.. We've had a lot of parents who're upwardly mobile. If they can they move to Walkerstown. Some move the children to St. John's. Its seen as more prestigious, middle class." (Primary School Headteacher)

The Church in the midst of this situation has become involved in searches to find ways out of unemployment. In this they have been heavily reliant on the governments's ACE schemes. Initially the Tenants Association on the estate also had an ACE scheme. They ran a benefits advice centre and a campaign to encourage people in Drumglass to apply for benefits. There were allegations that many Tenants Associations were fronts for the IRA and that government money was being channelled through West Belfast Groups to the Provisionals.

"We had a very good Tenants Association with six ACE workers who were running a Dole take-up campaign. In my opinion it was the best Community Groups Association in the area. It was very, active. Two years ago third Hurd (Secretary of State for Northern Ireland) made a sweeping statement and ACE-funding to the Tenants Association was cut. At the present time its trying to revamp itself. Its a bit crazy. The Tenants Association gets a flat from the Housing Executive. The only government body that stopped was the DED (Department of Economic Development, sponsors of ACE). You have the scenario where the Tenants Association were punished because Drumglass returned a Sinn Fein Councillor to represent the majority view. Douglas Hurd has politically vetted Drumglass." (Tenants Association ex-chairman)

But as we have already seen there are different views on the estate of this phenomenon. The result is that the Church is now the main means of bringing funds into the community. This has led to allegations that in West Belfast the Catholic Church has become an arm of the State. While this is a very shallow analysis it has political effect. Church projects are not lay projects. There are clergy on every committee, more often than not in the chair. This applies to ACE Schemes, Youth Clubs, Schools and Parish Groups in Drumglass. This leads to other biases in non-State agencies.

"I'd like to apply to N.I.V.T. for more funds to employ Mary to work permanently with old people. But they're very anti-Church. They're all for democracy that works. Where is the community group that doesn't get dominated by cliques? They end up dominated by three or four strong men." (ACE-scheme co-ordinator)

"The way I look at it is that there's gangsters everywhere today and you might as well have holy gangsters." (Local woman)

"The thing about the Parish is that its a more permanent thing. They're here for longer. Other things set up and close down or somebody might run off with the money. Its less likely to happen with the Parish." (Local man)

"One of the problems with some Sinn Fein thinking is that they see it as take the money and do as little as possible. The problem is that if you want some community work done you're sunk with this attitude." (Local man)

The Church leadership finds itself in a dilemma.. The clergy are open to widespread suspicion of enjoying the concentration of power to themselves.

"All the ACE-workers are going to run through the Church. They're going to say yes or no to everything." (Local community activist, woman)

"It's like Hitler. They've (the Church) got their fingers in every pie. Its empire-building and I don't like it. I'm a Protestant. I only came here cause I married. The kids go to Church with their dad. Not that anybody is any better. They make you do a course before you get your child christened, its ridiculous. They came to my house with a video. If I'd seen them coming I would have been away up the road." (Local woman)

"Everything is run by the Church and the Council. The people control none. The people know better how to use facilities better than the Church." (Sinn Fein Councillor)

There are widespread accusations that the clergy are patronising in their approach to social issues. This now extends to the Church's monopoly on the provision of local work through A.C.E.

The fact that ACE schemes have a professional structure means that while they are attached to the Churches in name, they do not require any commitment on behalf of members of the parish or congregation, except those directly involved. In Church schemes this involvement is clerically led. Drumglass A.C.E. Centre stands adjacent to the Family Centre. It acts as a centre for 46 ACE workers under a full-time manager. A second core-worker is responsible for the Family Centre. There were and are immense problems on the estate.

"One of the difficulties in deprived working-class areas is that people are used to scratching a living. They take what benefits they can get. A lot of people taking these jobs were broken people. I had a lot of people nipping off, not doing their hours. When I came the ACE scheme was a local joke, because people didn't do any work. The scheme started off with Church members and the workers weren't supervised. They relied on the choir and a few people. Some of them were very unreliable. Then there are other problems. Because we look after play areas and walkways the people have become very dependent on them. The first year I had to physically go out and supervise the work. Round the flats, 500 of them, you'd have been lucky if 100 had bins. They were rat-infested. The young ones who lived there had rip-roaring parties. Its improved now. The men go round and some people keep it a bit cleaner. The main problem is lack of heart. We're just nibbling away hoping there'll be a ripple." (ACE Co-ordinator)

ACE workers do Environmental Improvement, work visiting the elderly, run the cultural programme (Irish), help in the family centre, creche and playgroup. There was a widespread sense that the men on the estate could not be interested in programmes except employment.

"I feel sorry for the men. A man round here is nothing if he hasn't a job." (Local woman)

"The only thing which will interest the men and get them out is work." (ACE Worker, man)

The ACE scheme management see this as an important part of their function.

"The other thing we do is build up the people's confidence. We help keep up hope. There was a guy who phoned today who I had to sack before. He was a real mixer, very clever but in the wrong sort of way. Now he wants a job again. I was very surprised he rang." (ACE co-ordinator)

Drumglass people seem to have been encouraged by apparent successes on the neighbouring estate. The Church is involved in negotiations to take over the heating plant to use as a workshop and training centre. The only local group who could hope for funded backing from Government sources is the Church. While this is seen as the only way to avoid public money going into IRA coffers it leaves the Church with local monopolies making it an easy target, and upsetting local political balances. The Church can argue, of course, that it is 'the community group' par excellence. Nevertheless it concentrates power-rivalries at local level against the Church and increases the sense of the priest as the centre of the hub of the estate. This has serious implications for the relationship of Church institution and parish.

ACE has resulted in paid work with old people. It has increased the amount of Social Services being undertaken under Church auspices which may not be the same as work done by the Church. ACE has confirmed that isolation, fear and loneliness are the biggest problems facing the elderly. Care which ends abruptly after a year creates its own difficulties. St. Brigid's are extremely alert to the possibility that they might be being used.

"I don't think Social Services care. They come and then they leave again. People just think they've come to lock up their children. We don't want Social Services or Housing Executive to get us to do their work." (ACE Worker (with elderly))

"I think all care and caring for the person has gone. They (Social Services) are just doing their jobs for the money. Some of the people on the ACE scheme too, they just do their jobs. But see the crowd of girls I have now, I'd love to get them kept on." (ACE Worker - Co-ordinator with

Elderly)

"We don't have a direct link with Social Services. They want our help but not our knowledge." (ACE Care Worker)

The sheltered dwellings for elderly people at the back of the estate are used for a weekly get together for old-people. The dwellings are meant to be looked after by a married couple who live in and act as wardens. In Drumglass nobody applied for the job. ACE schemes of local people have filled a yawning gap in this area. Most of the workers with the elderly are part-time and women. The question remains as to what happens to worker and old person after ACE?

The other group involved in intensive pastoral work on the estate are the nuns, members of the order of the Sisters of Mercy. The convent is on the estate beside the Parochial House. These are six sisters working in Drumglass.

"There's quite a number of single-parent families. It reinforces the view that families are breaking down all over and society's becoming more unstable. It's not confined to Drumglass. We work in areas. I have one block and everyone else has an area. We'd kind of be 'responsible' for an area.... I've found out about the emergency services. We don't seem to be dealing with housing. We'd be quite involved with the sacramental work of the Church. We have a pre-baptismal course... We do a home visit. Then the mother comes up here after the baby's been born. For me its a great way to meet people and make contact. As well a that there's confirmation. I'm on the board of St. Brigid's Primary School and I'm the minutes secretary. The Principal asked me if I'd come down to confirmation. St. Brigid's is one of the Primary Schools. I'm on the committee for St. Brigid's and another sister's on the board of St. Anthony's.... It seems to me that the sister's have grown up with the parish. One teaches music in the schools and she has the choir's. She develops them after school hours and gives them private tuition. Her mission is music. The Sisters work with the people. The people don't need much support... We work like a family." (Sister)

The Sisters are well-known throughout the estate. Of course they are not free of their critics. In some quarters, the division of the Parish into area's has been criticised as contributing to the division of the area.

"The other problem in this area is that the Church divided the community. In 1978 the Church set up committees in each area to see who could raise the most money for a chapel and compete against each other. It's a big problem. The Church in their wisdom did this just to raise money. Most people here don't say they come from Drumglass. They come from their original place. That's been a problem - no Drumglass identity." (Tenants' Association member)

This illustrates how easily the Church can be blamed for all the problems of the area in part because of their powerful position and their claim to extend over the whole estate, something no other group in Drumglass can claim.

The role of the Sisters is an important one. They are often the direct face of the Church. To some extent they are an intermediary level between clergy and people, although their base in Drumglass is deep.

"The sisters came here before there was a parish. There is no parish Council. The result is that the sisters carry a lot of the parish work." (Sister)

Nevertheless the approach of Sisters has its own critics.

"When we started the nun came over and after the meeting she said she'd like to give a talk on the Billings method of contraception. We said no, 'cause they have classes in it every Tuesday in the family centre." (Local woman)

"Another sister came over and asked us to join 'Life'. I said to her 'we're all against abortion here but what do they say about contraception?' Sister said you weren't allowed to use artificial methods. I said "Well we'd be hypocrites if we joined because there's women in our group on every sort of contraception. Mind you we're all against abortion. We did have the women doctor in who showed us all the things, like a coil. Some people had them in but they'd never seen them". (Group organiser)

"There was a nun who wanted to teach our women how to be 'economical', she wanted to show people how to 'economise', how to bake and all. But she wanted to go into their houses. So we said no, we let her run classes. People know how to bake." (Local woman)

The Church in Drumglass is the major local agency for social services, A.C.E. work and community facilities. As a result it has all the benefits of power and has set up all the accompanying power struggles. As such it is in danger of becoming seen as external to the people, amidst the people but not the people. This is not the case at present but some of the elements of this shift have emerged. While few in Drumglass regard the Church as 'British' or 'enemy' it is widely regarded as an 'authority' with all the accompanying problems.

Rathcrone too has a problem of unemployment. As in Drumglass the strains of modern living are immediately apparent on the estate. The Primary School is the first place where the problems emerge.

"The estate itself has a hell of a percentage not working. About 40% of kids come from single parent families, mostly the result of marriage break-ups. There's only a mother at home. Not many of those mothers have job... Until they changed it, about half the school were entitled to Free Meals. Even since the change we have about one third still eligible... I'd see parents here with social problems. The worries are about not paying rates and electricity bills and the effect on the kids." (Primary School Head Teacher)

There is also a high proportion of elderly people on the estate. This too contributes to the numbers of people seeking assistance whether material or personal. The Churches in this situation are the most organised groups on the estate. They too have used the A.C.E. schemes to provide employment and meet some of the perceived needs of the estate's people. Unlike Drumglass, the Churches do not have a monopoly on ACE work. Local Social Services combine with a local group set up to promote employment on the estate. They are responsible for environmental improvements on the estate and run a number of activities for the elderly in the Activity Centre. This imbalance between funding in Drumglass and Rathcrone does not appear to be a matter of money. Rather in Rathcrone the State agencies can monitor their finances more directly. While it is true that suspicions of fraud led one group to lose their backing there are still projects outside the Churches. The atmosphere between the community groups and the Churches is not fraught with the same bitterness identified in Drumglass.

Three of the Churches in Rathcrone work together on the Rathcrone Council of Churches. Together they manage the Rathcrone Caring Office. The Office is a small cottage shared with the N.I.H.E. office for the estate.

The fact that it is a Church-run organisation is seen by the Churches as a positive matter. The idea grew from the experience of the Methodist Minister with an ACE scheme set up in another area of Belfast.

"I suppose the Ministers of the three Churches saw the need at the start. All the Churches have latched on to the ACE-scheme. Its a good way for seeing to the needs in the area. The Methodist Minister is Minister of Dunlure where there was an ACE scheme. He was the most interested. We're officially a branch of Dunlure Community Services. Now the Presbyterian Minister is interested. We get on very well. The Housing Executive gave us these houses, and there's not many houses free on this estate.... We started in 1986. The Methodist Minister saw this as an opportunity. We have seventeen ACE workers. We're under the umbrella of Dunlure Community Services. They do some of our administration. There's another scheme in Ballyray. We're three together. The DED encourage this trend of groups coming together because ACE workers now have to have a proper training." (ACE Work Co-ordinator)

"I saw the estate and it's needs. I thought the Church, if its to be the Church should do something. I saw it as a way to get people off the dole. I think the Church should take a leading role in the community. If that boils down to one Church then so be it, but if we can do it together so much the better. Together we are 1400-1500 people... If you look at the teaching of Jesus, he looked at the whole person. I feel we have to be with people where they are. We can no longer wait for people to come to us. It makes folk see that we care wherever we are. If we achieve that we've achieved a lot. Its in a quiet way. If people want it, that's it. I know now that people who wouldn't go near a Church would come here (Caring Office) because the Churches are involved and you can trust it." (Methodist Minister)

The work of the Caring Office covers a number of areas. There as a scheme for visiting the elderly, ensuring that they have company and their material needs met e.g. paying bills, shopping done and so on.

"We have an environmental project which employs eight men. They do work for pensioners, one parent families and people on low income. We do grass-cutting, windows, decoration and odd jobs. Then we have home-visiting for pensioners or people in need of a chat. The home-visitors are all part-time but they're very important because they keep up contact. Some people need a lot of attention. Others don't need any. There was

one wee woman who didn't let our worker in. Our other thing is our job-search. We've one worker. She does benefits advice and job search. We'd like it to be more used. When all the benefits changed we did a benefits uptake scheme from January to March and that was very busy. The DHSS encouraged us to do that, it took some of the heat off them. People came to see our workers not them.

Then we've a self-help group for depressed people. There's only three in Northern Ireland. They do all seem to get help from it. We've eight or nine regulars. They drop away and then they come back. They're all characters. We put up posters round about. We put leaflets round the doors when we started. We do our best round the doors." (ACE Co-ordinator)

The ACE scheme has led a number of people to get involved in community work. In Rathcrone, the Churches appear to be in this work. In Rathcrone the A.C.E. Project had an open relationship to Social Services and the Housing Executive.

"They let us use their premises. Even if we do criticise them we do it privately. They see us as a group who want to work with them for a better community. If you're not out to knock them, they're happy to help you. There's a woman from Social Services who gives guidance." (Methodist Minister)

The Churches have been paid to do large amounts of community work, recruiting locally. The fact of local recruitment does mitigate the implications of Social Work as a 'profession'. It nevertheless involves 'the Churches' as 'agencies' with 'employees' rather than 'communities' with 'members'. The relationship of agencies to clients is not the same as that of Churches to their members. In ACE this distinction is seriously blurred.

It remains to be seen whether ACE work eats into the Church as 'the community of the people'. In the meantime it provides temporary employment and a number of services.

Some of the problems of services which become seen as 'charity' are illustrated in the case of the nearly-new shop. This is open for two afternoons each week in the hall of the Methodist Church. Half of the profits go to the Methodist Church and half of the profits go the Caring Office.

"We'd heard before that 'thrift shops' hadn't worked just from people chatting. Then we thought with the ending of single payments maybe it would be needed." (ACE Co-ordinator)

"I want to advertise our shop in Walkerstown and Milltown. People might prefer to travel a wee bit for their clothes. A lot of people don't like the idea that the original owner might see them wearing their clothes. Everybody would know you've been to a thrift shop. They don't like to be seen in second-hand clothes shops either. If it was a wee bit out of their area they might come." (Local woman (thrift-shop volunteer))

The Presbyterian Church also has three ACE workers employed under a different management. The Presbyterian Church in Ireland Board of Social Witness has a scheme whereby a central management based at Clifton Street in Belfast allocates ACE money to congregations throughout Northern Ireland. The first full-time worker, only became an ACE-worker after a year's voluntary work.

"I gave up my work. I felt called to do something for the youth of my own area. I live on the estate and grew up here. I was very much supported by the congregation. I just decided to live on faith. Somehow, whenever I needed money the money turned up. I had a bit saved but not much. Then Clifton Street offered us the ACE posts." (Youth Leader, woman)

The ACE scheme also provided two part-time posts. The ACE workers have supplemented the congregation more by enabling them to be paid for work which was previously done voluntarily. This includes Youth Work, Counselling and Visiting. The groups which meet in the Church, elderly, mother and toddler etc. can be provided with tea and coffee. The biggest development was of a lunch-time cafe on Mondays and Thursdays. All the cooking, preparation, serving and clearing was done by the ACE team. The Service was advertised by a door-to-door leafleting campaign. Prices were kept to the cost of the food.

"Since we started in September things have picked up really well. We'd get from 30 to 70 people in each lunch-time." (Part-time ACE worker)

Nevertheless the drawbacks of reliance on ACE were also clear. ACE funding for two of the posts ended at the end of January. The next review of ACE-funding was not due until March. This left the Church with a dilemma. Having built up a service based on regularity the cafe was faced with closure for at least two months.

"We made an appeal to the congregation for money to keep on the two workers for another two months. I think we've got enough. The problem is that this is a congregation in a poor housing estate. We can only ask for so much. We always get when we need." (Presbyterian Elder)

In the case of visiting schemes such a gap could be very serious. Here, the workers also felt disappointed by the ending of funding by ACE given that they were ineligible for employment by ACE for a future twelve months.

"I don't know what I'll do with myself now once I'm back at home. You get very used to the company, and the money." (ACE Worker)

The ACE scheme has certainly enabled the Churches to expand into areas they had previously not touched. It appears to have given hope and restored some dignity for many of the workers, at least in the short-term. As in Drumglass, many people regarded it as a question of nibbling away at a large problem.

"Unemployment and loneliness are the biggest problems. Isolation is awful. I was encouraged yesterday when some old people got together at their own initiative. A lot of people bring it on themselves. There's a lot of things on. The estate is full of depressed people yet we only get eight or nine people to our group." (ACE work Co-ordinator)

The biggest advantage the Churches have in both Drumglass and Rathcrone is that they are permanent presences. The people who work for ACE live on the estates. The congregations and parishes which support them are people on the estates. There is certainly distance between the clergy and the laity. None of the Rathcrone Ministers live directly on the estate. In Drumglass the Parochial House and Convent stand set apart, as the largest houses on the estate. In both cases this may be a self-preservative distance or the desire of the congregations. Nevertheless, the permanence of minister and priest is considerably greater than that of Social Services or the officers of the Housing Executive. The "Social Service" they provide can be qualitatively different to that of statutory bodies. Nevertheless they are faced with different pressures - on the estates from Church structures and hierarchies and now from statutory agencies.

Middle-class Walkerstown has an entirely different atmosphere to both Drumglass and Rathcrone. None of the Churches employ under the A.C.E. scheme. The one exception is the Walkerstown Christian Fellowship which has a centre in Walkerstown House on the Clonderg estate.

"This would be a middle class parish with well over 90% employed, quite a lot with two incomes. The Protestants are poorer. Most of the Housing Executive houses in this area are occupied by Protestants." (Catholic Priest)

Because Old Walkerstown Parish takes in Rathcrone this gives a local exception to the stereotypical norm of Protestant rich, Catholic poor. The Church of Ireland Minister made a further distinction.

"Here the Presbyterians are the professional classes. We have more working People. The Presbyterian parish is much wealthier. Walkerstown parish has little unemployment. There are people on minimum retirement benefit but there's not much unemployment." (Church of Ireland Rector)

Walkerstown has a high percentage of older people especially among the Protestants. There are a number of special meetings for older people run in the Churches. None of this work is State-funded. The exception to the rule is the work of the Christian Fellowship.

"We started up an ACE-scheme, and we employ 24 from it. We do home-care work. That's alleviated a lot of the loneliness. I remember at the time of EEC Butter distribution I met Senior Citizens in Clonderg who turned their lights out because of fear of electricity bills." (Trust Co-ordinator)

The group do work in a number of areas based in a house in Clonderg estate which they use for a number of purposes. The work grew out of personal commitment.

"I'd always been involved in prison work gathering money. After I became a Christian. I had a real heart for the needy, and I continued visiting the prison in a Christian context. So there were a few conversions. We got a couple of houses for prisoners coming out of prison. Then we got this house, Walkerstown House. The Housing Executive were about to knock it down. Prisoners aren't homeless until they leave prison. There's nothing worse for people coming out of prison... This house belongs to the

Housing Executive. At the moment open Door might buy it and invest £250,000 in it. We were called Walkerstown Christian Trust. Now we're called LAOS. A lot of Churches would be very suspicious of us because they fear we go in for 'shepherding'. We never had it here. There was a lot of pressure but we were always very much against it.... This building would be multi-purpose. Once the Housing Association (Open Door) invest their money we'll have ten flats for homeless people. Its not necessarily young people. Within the next few years I see a big problem of homelessness. You'll have more and more of this. We already get enquiries from Social Services and Probation. We also have two community flats for people who need a lot of support in Rathcrone. We run a playgroup in Walkerstown Primary School. We'd enough enquiries to run two. We have about £100,000 per year. Its an arm of the fellowship. For me this work has shown the loneliness and the problems there are in Walkerstown. I realised that is so easy just to got to Church and not to take notice. At a certain point I made a decision. Its about trying to get the balance of having fellowship with other Christians which knits people together and being involved with the community, getting alongside people. I feel in evangelism you have to have some credibility. I was reading a report recently which said that 80-90% of people who become Christians do so through friends who've become Christians." (Trust Co-ordinator)

"In the end of the day it's about helping people to know Christ. At the heart of our work would be the message of reconciliation a two fold reconciliation between God and man and within the community. The last thing I'd want it to be is just a Social Gospel. We'd see the object as being reaching people. We would pray for people. We have Bar-B-Q's and at that we share the faith with them. At times we'd have gospel meetings and healing meetings." (Trust Member, man)

ACE-schemes in this area have an ambiguous impact. The money and the employment are clearly welcome. The fact that most of the workers live in the areas and are not employed because of professional qualifications means that the services do not duplicate social services. However the attachment of ACE schemes to Churches may have more to do with Government and Church institutional politics than with many members of congregations and parishes. The schemes are Church based for political reasons and the Church 'ethos' is a political guarantee rather than a Christian context. In Drumglass it results in a sense that the Church is the local establishment. The introduction of local management has clear advantages for the government and some advantages for the locals. For the Churches, however ACE raises a number of thorny problems. The Church runs the risk of becoming a passive part of government policy and more importantly the Churches may come to believe that their ACE work is the congregational contribution to local life. This it clearly is not.

(b) The Churches and Schools

Church involvement in schools is controversial in Northern Ireland. Walkerstown is no exception to this. The schools in the area are part of the fabric of the community. In Walkerstown there is a State Primary School. The Catholic schools, one Primary and a large co-educational Grammar School, are clustered around the Parish Centre. Drumglass estate has two Primary Schools and a Secondary School for boys and girls. Rathcrone has a Primary School and the Secondary School for the Walkerstown Area.

Walkerstown Primary has suffered a steep decline in numbers. This reflects both the ongoing population and the process of Protestant flight from Walkerstown.

"We declined very fast in the 70s Now the numbers are going down slowly. Its partly a population trend. We have very few Roman Catholic children. On the far side of the Walkerstown High Street there'd be mostly Roman Catholics taking up the housing. I doubt if Protestants would invest in a long-term house over there. I notice there's quite a lot of houses in Clonderg and that part of Glenfoot Road empty. We lost quite a lot of children when Prison Officers moved out to Maghaberry. I don't know if that accounts for it entirely. Its certainly a feeling that's around whether its true or not. Drumglass has had a baleful impact on that side of town. You don't get much integration. The Minister would express himself about it, parents not. There's new housing going up by the by-pass and I rang up the company advertising. They said that most of the people are from West Belfast." (Primary School Headmaster)

The school reflects the deeply pessimistic outlook of most of the Protestants in Walkerstown. The sense of slow take over, of imperial encroachment by an alien group, is very strong. The encroachment is not friendly, but it is inevitable. The Presbyterian Minister is chairman of the school boards of the Primary School and of Walkerstown High. He too reflected the sense of Protestant decline.

"Every house that changes hands here goes Roman Catholic... The main cause for this is the building of the big St. Joseph's complex. I'm Chairman of the Primary School and Secondary School boards. At one time in the High School we had almost 1000. Now were down to 600, in 10 years. We've made teachers redundant every year in the last 10 years. The Roman Catholic school have been adding to their staff. We are the extension of the Falls Road. All the streets are changing. Its one-way traffic. Their better people are all trying to escape from their own and buy in Malone."

Church involvement with schools seems to be through the school boards rather than direct contact with children.

"The Presbyterian Minister is chairman of our Board. The Church of Ireland Rector is on it. He takes the Church of Ireland children every Tuesday. He's the only visiting clergyman we have. The Presbyterian Minister's attitude is that the school does the RE very well. When I taught elsewhere the ministers all came in and took all the kids. They saw it as an infallible way to meet people. There isn't that here. A higher percentage than I expected are Church of Ireland. We have quite placid relations with the Church. What would raise a problem is that the Presbyterian Minister doesn't like the Non-subscribing Presbyterians. He's a wee bit jealous of other ministers as well, he likes things just to go on." (Teacher)

The attitude in the school towards R.E. is much more indirect than elsewhere. It indicates one end of a wide ranging spectrum.

"I'd be very delighted if the Government would cease backing R.E. and leave it to the Churches. I see R.E. as very important. To me the effective R.E. here takes place through the Scripture Union not the formal setting. I don't think the Church-School connection has done either any good in here. I don't really like denominational schools. I'm not anti-religious. I'm an elder and I play the organ in my own Churches." (Headmaster)

The sense of decline is added to by the obvious buoyancy of the local Roman Catholic school. The Protestant Primary School has declined to 200 pupils. There is a sense that integration is impossible and the blame for this is placed on Catholic policy.

"The priest and headmaster of their school are hardline on Catholic children going to Catholic schools. It appears that the Church doesn't like it. Under E.M.U. (Education for Mutual Understanding) we've very good relations with St. Peter's in Dunroe. Our P7s go to games together every Friday at Olympia on the Boucher Road. We've had no problems there. I thought there might be more problems because the local Free Presbyterian Minister sends his children here. Nothings been said." (Headmaster)

The Catholic Primary School is bursting at the seams. There are now 35 classes, five groups each of P1 to P7s. The total number of children now exceeds 1100. This figure is very seriously distorted by the difference in the catchment areas of the two schools. Nevertheless the growth and decline which the figures would suggest remain true. The contrast in atmosphere could not be more stark.

"We do a lot of our teaching in mobiles because the school has grown so fast. At one time this would have been predominantly Protestant. Now there's few non-Catholics now. They used to be very well intermixed. Its not so true now in Walkerstown." (Teacher)

The attitude to the place of the Church in the school reflects Catholic tradition throughout Northern Ireland:

"We depend on the parish. If you like its like the three musketeers, the school, the parents and the parish. That's what we try to get. I'm very happy with it. The only things I'd like is that the parents did more. The parish is very involved. We've a parents association and its second to none. The parish priest is president and I'm vice-president and they have a chairman and a committee..... The fact of being a Roman Catholic school is essential. There's no justification for Roman Catholic schools except to further the Catholic faith. At the primary level its very important that the teachers have an active faith. The preparation for the sacraments has to be done with conviction. I'd go 100% for that. The main function of the Catholic school is to prepare the children for the sacraments." (Headmaster)

The centrality of the school-parish link and the place of the sacraments underlines the differences in approach between the State (Protestant) and Catholic schools. The importance of committed teachers indicates the degree to which Catholic schools are conceived as an integrated part of a whole community. This internal integration no doubt eases many problems within the school system. The difficulty arises because this internal integration contrasts so sharply with external disintegration and the almost explicit sense that the separateness of Catholic education is necessary because it is 'closer to the truth' than the Protestant alternative. The intimate relationship between integration and disintegration is what makes this question so vexed. Within the fold, there is a generous openness at times, represented in the comments of one teacher.

"Our education is based on two precepts; Love God and Love Your Neighbour. I've a very simple view of religion. I try and do my best. I curse like a trooper when the time comes. We've room for the sinner." (Catholic teacher).

At the same time there is a suspicion that the education on offer elsewhere is wanting. There is a necessity for Catholic children to be educated separately which lies even deeper than the failings of the State system. This can be read as an implicit claim that the Catholic Church has more of "the truth" than any other group including other Protestant Churches. The line drawn by St. John's Parish is in terms of day to day schooling. They are enthusiastic supporters of E.M.U. and of contact to reduce threat.

"We support E.M.U. completely. St. John's is linked with Ballyray Primary School and St. Peter's is linked to Walkerstown." (Parish Priest)

"We're combined with Ballyray Primary under the E.M.U. scheme. Beforehand we were part of a NICED pilot project which included a whole group of local schools but our nearest neighbours are Ballyray. We've a combined trip to the baths for P6 and P7 on Wednesday. We get the odd talk about Linfield and Celtic. Last year we went with the P7's to the Share Centre near Enniskillen. Then the P3's put on a joint play before Christmas. We've just started to share resources for computers. We have a computer and the teachers from Ballyray come up here and use it." (Headmaster)

The commitment to EMU is complete provided it is within a parallel system rather than complete integration.

In Walkerstown both Catholics and Protestants share the same territory. The State School seemed more concerned about Catholics 'not allowing' their children to attend State Schools, while the Catholic school was keen to encourage cross-community meetings within the context of separate schools. The objection of Catholic schools to mixing was the loss of a Catholic 'ethos' while the Protestant school preferred to consider removing Religious Education from the school curriculum. Within such circumstances dialogue on fundamental issues is clearly very difficult.

The situation on the estates is different primarily because the schools serve areas which are exclusively Protestant or Catholic. As such there is no local dispute about schools, no local divide, primarily because the divide is already in place through the fact that the estates are residential ghettos.

Drumglass was initially planned as a mixed estate. The onset of the troubles led to a Protestant withdrawal and an influx of Catholic families fleeing intimidation in other parts of Belfast. Initially there were two primary schools on the estate, on Catholic, the other part of the State (Protestant) sector. In 1973 the State primary was handed over to the Catholic Church to become St. Anthony's Primary School, a second maintained Catholic school. This took place after the massive influx of young Catholic families into Drumglass in the early 1970s and the flight of Protestants. Both school boards have a priest in the chair. Nuns from the local convent of the Sisters of Mercy serve as secretary of the Governors.

"I'm on the board of St. Brigid's School and I'm the minutes secretary. St. Brigid's is one of the primary schools. Another sister is on St. Anthony's board." (Superior, Convent)

At present St. Anthony's has 300 pupils and St. Brigid's has 495.

"We're at the pit in terms of numbers. At one stage our numbers were up to 700. Our purely local intake would be around 400 now. For teachers a new area is great, a lot of promotion. We'd three redundancies this year! We'd have a lot of upwardly mobile parents who'd move to Walkerstown. They'd move the children to St. John's; its seen as more prestigious, more middle class." (St. Brigid's Headmaster)

The involvement of the Church in the school is regarded as not enough rather than too much.

"Catholicism is the major factor in the school for the children to be brought up in and practice the faith. Its a Catholic school. That's why the

parents send them there. There's two main sacraments in the schools. Its a way of bringing the whole community together in the preparation for the sacraments. The majority of the children would try and behave in the Church's way while they're here. The ones that run with the gang tend to adopt the values of the gang and forget the school. Joyriding is due to lack of parental supervision. its nothing to do with deprivation. If you get a clique, they cause all the trouble.

The Board of Governors is the Parish Priest, the Curate, a nun, parents representatives and nominees from the S.E.E.L.B. The Parish Priest is the chairman, we see him quite often. You find that the Church take care of schools.

I think the Church should be even more involved in schools. I said to the Parish Priest that he can walk into any class at any time he wants. Priests are few and far between on the ground. He's on that many committees. He's got an awful lot of work." (Headmaster, St. Brigid's)

The integrating factor of the school in community life, and of Catholicism in public and private life are here brought into relief. School is part of the training for values in an integrated society. The problem is that it is only integrated in a ghetto. Outside the ghetto, schools are clearly divided. Nevertheless the schools may reflect the reality of division as much as they cause it.

"I use the analogy of the three-legged stool; Parents-Church-School. If one leg is missing or falls...... The prime educators are the parents. If they fall there's not a lot the school or the Church can do. I can't see the faith being passed on in an integrated school, especially in the primary school. Even in the early years of secondary its important that its Catholic. I still say you need the Catholic schools. After fifteen its important that they see other faiths. It's important that the Church schools educate the children in our faith. You can educate the children for tolerance." (St. Anthony's, teacher)

This highlights a problem of perception which appears to pervade public discussions on the Churches and education. Catholic schools have no sense that the state schools will adequately reflect their values and teaching. This is expressed positively in the sense that Catholic schools add a dimension seriously lacking in state schools. It is also expressed negatively in the sense that Protestantism is characterised as 'inadequate' or 'lesser' in terms of the teaching of children. In the context of Northern Ireland, the 'other faith' referred to above is Protestantism. The implication is that Protestantism is a separate faith, not that both are varieties of the same faith. It assumes that there are clear lines between two monoliths Protestantism and Catholicism. The much messier reality is forgotten, and the divide appears as a wide gulf rather than as a historical fact in a context of diverse beliefs.

Drumglass does not have a partner school in the EMU structure. The difficulties of bringing Protestants onto the estate may be part of this. This was certainly part of the reason why Police Community Relations no longer work in Drumglass.

"We will take part in EMU, but we have to find a Protestant school. We're into football and netball leagues so the children do meet up. In the early days we were involved with Police Community Relations. The way things were, parents objected to the buses because they feared that they might be targets." (St. Brigid's, teacher)

If decline is the problem at Walkerstown Primary, and excessive growth the problem in St. John's then discipline and vandalism are teachers greatest worries in Drumglass. This is related by many people in all Catholic areas to the erosion of the family as the central unit of the integrated Catholic community. There appears to be considerable anxiety in both working-class and middle-class areas about this development.

"Discipline is our biggest problem. A lot of the children come from one-parent families or broken homes. About 15 years ago that was unheard of. Its significant now. We're talking 20, 30, 40 families. That unsettles the kids. The people are very kind but there's areas of hoods. We're heavily vandalised. There's never a week goes by when we're not vandalised. They just create a mess. I think we're one of the worst. We're going through a bad phase. Once it causes so much damage we had to send the kids home. Once school records go, you never get them back." (St. Brigid's, headmaster)

"We're now getting a lot of kids from broken marriages. This year we've been involved with half a dozen cases at least. I never remember it like that. It seems to be on the increase. I do think that there's a general falling in the religious commitment. Maybe its a good thing. The old dogmatic

people did what they were told." (St. John's P.S. Headmaster)

This would appear to indicate that there is a growing problem for the Church within the traditional Catholic community, in the sphere of Church influence on social teaching. We saw this in the area of family planning above. We can now begin to see it in the sphere of family break-up.

The Primary Schools in Drumglass are integrated into the community. The same cannot be said of the Secondary School, St. Patrick's. Even within Drumglass the school has a poor reputation.

"There's only 220 pupils instead of 900 in St. Patrick's because its reputation is so bad. The majority of the kids I work with [on the anti-joyriding project] come from that school. There's problems of literacy and numeracy. The school's not doing its job." (Community Worker)

"I wouldn't let my kids go round with the ones from that school." (Local Parent)

"I'd be surprised if more that 10 or 11 out of a possible 55 would send their children to St. Patrick's. Part of the problem is that a lot of the girls don't go. Their mammies went to St. Louise's so that's where the kids go. A lot would be sent to St. Genevieve's. St. Patrick's has a very bad reputation, but whether its deserved or not is another matter. The boys that they're getting are the weaker boys from this school." (St. Brigid's, Headmaster)

In a setting of bad reputation, community violence, endemic unemployment and disintegrating family life, St. Patrick's operates in a difficult context. All of the features reinforce each other - unemployment, violence, family breakdown, school reputation.

"This school was built because of the growth of the estate. We spent eight years in mobiles before we got our building. Our situation is made worse because the people are from West Belfast and are ignored by the Council." (St. Patrick's Headmaster)

This means that the school has faced additional opposition from the local Council;

"We have a situation here where we're the only school in Northern Ireland ever to take the local authority to the Ombudsman. We originally went for political and religious discrimination but the Ombudsman can't deal with that. We used the Council Community minibus and it went Dublin to an All-Ireland GAA final. It was alleged that on the return people waved tricolours. Somebody told the paper and the Council banned us from the Minibus for three months without a hearing." (St. Patrick's Headmaster)

For the moment, it is important to note that the school is not a community focus. The continuing attachment of Drumglass people to other institutions in West Belfast, including both Secondary and Grammar schools emphasises the lack of identity with the estate and the feeling of belonging to a wider West Belfast community.

"Facilities are very limited. There's isolation here.. It's a reluctant community in a hostile area with hostile government from the Council... The neighbouring areas are regarded as places of discrimination. Our youngsters wouldn't sign on in Dunroe or go to Dunroe Tech."

Rathcrone does not suffer from the same sense of discrimination by the local Council. The schools, one Primary and one Secondary, are generally well respected in the area.

"We're (clergy) all on the board of the Primary School. The school runs quietly, and the headmaster is a vociferous man." (Presbyterian Minister)

The main problems faced by the school are the effects of chronic social deprivation on the children. Unlike in Drumglass there is or has been virtually no problem of vandalism.

"This is a working class area. All children live on the estate bar 5% who live in private houses or have grannies who live on the estate. The estate itself has a hell of a percentage not working. About 40% of the kids are from single parent families, mostly as a result of marriage break ups. Often they have only a mother at home." (Headmaster, Primary School)

"There's very little damage or vandalism. Even teenage boys. I never chase anybody out after school, even teenagers. There's fellows drink in the sheds sometimes and by and large they take away their empties.

There's a couple of football pitches. This seems to have worked in terms of vandalism. Grafitti hasn't happened on any large scale. We've had a couple of break-ins, none in 1988 though." (Primary School Teacher)

This sense of a calm relationship with the local community is largely reflected by the secondary school.

"There has been a lot of graffiti and some vandalism on the estate, but we've not had too much of it in the school... We run an interview system whereby the parents come in to talk about their children. 95% of parents turn up. We've a lot of support in the sense that they'll come in and talk to us." (Secondary School Headmaster)

The S.E.E.L.B. has developed the facilities of both the Rathcrone schools.

"We have an Adult Education centre open day and evening. We also have an ACE scheme with three workers run by the Council, the school and the Education & Library Board doing environmental work. I look after the day to day running of both." (Secondary School Headmaster)

This contrasts sharply with perceptions of the Council in Drumglass. The Council is perceived as friendly and co-operative. This in part accounts for the absence of any siege mentality in Rathcrone. The Churches relationship to the schools is fairly standard for Northern Ireland.

"The Churches are fairly active. They have direct contact with the school. The Free Presbyterian, Presbyterian, Methodist and Church of Ireland clergy came into the school once a week on a rota basis. The Free Presbyterian is not on the school board. All the others have representatives on the board through the clergy. That's three out of nine. There's no hassle. The Churches have never fought over the board.. We don't actually go to the Churches. Our carol service used to be in the Churches but we can use more children in the school." (Primary School Principal)

"Four clerics are on my Board of Governors, four of nine. We would have contact on issues of common interest-assemblies, times of heightened tension, families in need and so on. They come into the school but not on a planned timetable." (Secondary School Principal)

The institutional Church-School links are considerably weaker, highlighting

Catholic fears that non-Catholic education does not further religious belief. The teachers in State schools in Walkerstown and Rathcrone either regarded religion as a matter of private concern or as a matter of secondary importance in the school curriculum. The Catholic schools regarded the passing on of the faith as the primary task of the schools. This is a fundamental division of attitude. In State schools religion is taught as one subject under a transcendence of "scientific" truth, whereas Catholic schools teach all subjects under a transcendence of "Catholic" truth. Perhaps the schools problem rests not so much on the Catholic/Protestant divide as on the difference between Catholic and liberal state conceptions of 'truth'. It may also lie behind the different emphases on the Natural sciences and the Humanities perceived in different reports, especially as they effect Catholic girls.

The Rathcrone schools have not taken part in E.M.U. although both professed a commitment to cross-community work. Nevertheless the headmaster of the Secondary School made qualifications which are as important as the commitment:

"We have had one or two visits combined with Catholic schools in Ballynahinch, such as the Ski trip. We don't go with local schools because it would cause trouble. There's the possibility of discrete informal contact and I'd support that. But I wouldn't want to see the thing being forced formally from outside. Its not forced by my governors but the government might do it mandatory. I wouldn't recommend it. I can see it creating a reaction from the paramilitaries. I don't come under any pressure from paramilitaries, though somebody asked for a change in our history course. They never came back.... I have some personal contact with the principals of the Catholic schools. We have things in common. There's not a lot on pupil level." (Secondary School Headmaster)

"I would know the heads of local schools - Roman Catholic too; St. Peter's, St. John's, Drumglass. We meet at head-teachers meetings, at in-service causes. The Board has a system of local teachers meetings. We have a special learning unit and it serves all schools in the area. We were a bit slow off the mark with EMU. All the local Roman Catholic schools were snapped up by other schools. We're not really near any others. St. Peter's twinned with Dunroe and St. John's with Ballyray. Its not a matter of principle. Apart from that there's Netball and Football matches with St. John's and Drumglass. The children are friendlier with St. John's kids than with any other." (Primary School Headmaster)

The implication is that we can trust our professionals to meet on 'business' issues but outside sport we cannot trust our children. The obvious EMU partners for Rathcrone Primary are in Drumglass where social conditions are much more similar than St. John's. Nevertheless this might arouse considerable local opposition and be considered too risky. This consideration was also noticeable in Drumglass.

One further feature can be noted about schools. The qualifying examination for Grammar Schools is a notoriously bad measure for school performance. Nevertheless there was wide variation between the area's in this study in the results obtained, and the degree to which it was considered a problem. In Rathcrone, performance was a major preoccupation.

"Academic performance is very poor, though its a bit better than inner Belfast. Education is not a priority for most parents. School is accepted, I have to say, because they don't think about it... Only 10% would get to Grammar Schools. The kids go to the local secondary schools. Our biggest problem is that we can't improve the academic standard. There's very little aspiration. We've changed the curriculum but it hasn't really altered performance." (Principal, Rathcrone Primary School)

This contrasts sharply with experience in Drumglass where academic performance is not a major worry. The motivation of parents for their children is also much greater.

"The parents are very keen that their kids do well. They want their children to go on and they see education as their way out. Last year we'd a 25% pass rate at eleven plus. It's not the way to judge a school, but it gives the parents choice." (Principal, St. Brigid's Primary School)

The contrast is notable in the light it casts on the make-up of the two estates. Rathcrone is a settled estate, largely popular with the residents. A number of people commented on the recent growth of cross-generational extended families on the estate. Public discipline is not a problem. Academic aspirations are low. There is little sense of people trying to 'escape' the estate. Drumglass is to some extent the reverse. Problems of vandalism and violence are serious, but the people of the area seem to view education as an escape route. Drumglass is not popular with Housing Executive tenants and there is a sense in which the community has not recovered from the trauma of the intimidations of the early 1970s.

The contrast with middle class areas is even starker, explicable by more 'traditional' explanations. The remarks are recorded here for comparison:

"Between 40 and 50% of our children qualify for Grammar Schools. Last year it was over 50%. The lowest we ever had was 43%. Last year we were bumped up because of the court ruling on girls." (St. John's Primary School Principal)

"We do reasonably well in the 11+ here. About a third qualify. We've university lecturers children at one end and we've families who're more backward. Its quite comprehensive, very healthy except that its largely Protestant." (Principal, Walkerstown Primary School)

(c) The Churches, Communities and Violence.

The Churches in the Walkerstown area have all experienced violence to their members. The nature of this violence varies considerably, from damage to property , joyriding and theft to shootings, bombing and times of effective "community siege". In general, the four largest denominations have all consistently and openly opposed illegal violence by paramilitary and terrorist groups. This has been concentrated in a different way on the ghettoised housing estates and in less obviously divided areas.

In the housing estates the Churches are involved in the politics of violence on and from the estates. The Churches are parties to a community dispute as to whether violence is a legitimate method of political action. In Rathcrone the three larger Churches are clearly separate from the Free Presbyterians on this matter. The three larger Churches are uniformly seen, and see themselves, as the main opposition to UDA or illegal violence on or from the estate. This has meant that they have supported the security forces in different periods. e.g. the aftermath of the signing of the Anglo-Irish Agreement, and have seen their social position as providing alternatives to paramilitary activities and clubs. In Drumglass, the Church is often identified as the main local opponent of IRA and Sinn Fein activities, the internal opposition. In this sense the Church's organisations are staunchly opposed to IRA-activities. In both cases, the Church ministers to people who are involved in both sides of this political divide.

In Walkerstown paramilitaries have a less pervasive presence. Among Roman Catholics there is no IRA club. The Catholic population experience paramilitary violence 'at a distance' in that it is not integral to the structure of their community. Among Protestants, the UDA is not as organised as in Rathcrone. The Churches are actively concerned about the effects of violence on their people rather than on the response. The community's response is reflected in strong support for the security forces. The effects include fear, effect on property values increased car and house theft and an awareness of encroachment. The Churches are part of the established group who represent broad consensuses in their own communities. As such they do not see themselves as 'parties', nor or they seen as such.

Rathcrone is marked by a strong 'loyalist' presence. UDA recruitment posters hung from every lamppost while I was on the estate. The very permanence of the "Rathcrone says No" at the main entrance to the estate is a sign of some importance. Nevertheless the stability of Rathcrone is also striking. In the Churches survey of 1987 'only' 18% of houses had ever suffered vandalism. Of the 530 households surveyed 71% said that a police presence was required and only a very small percentage objected. This may have something to do with the very long stability of occupancy on the estate. Of 719 households 522 had been in tenancy for more than 10 years. Of these 639 (82%) declared themselves 'totally happy' with the estate. There has been very little direct political violence on the estate. The UDA is closely linked to the area.

"The UDA are strong in social things. The community centre had to be closed down because of embezzlement by the committee. It reopened again but its under the Council. A couple of streets are named after UDA men. They've put up new signs in memory of their heroes but we all still call them by their old names." (Woman, local resident)

"There's the UDA ones on this estate. Very strong. Its in certain families. Every now and then they get active. Everybody knows who the big boys are." (Man, local resident)

In Rathcrone there are two issues of note. First, the development of intimidation on the estate and second the shifting relationships with the police. The Churches in both cases have been the public bodies most able to counter intimidation.

Intimidation against families seems to happen in waves. There are still a number of Catholic families on the estate. Mostly they are quiet but they have faced considerable pressure at times. In the event, the Protestant Churches become their strongest advocates.

"In the last seven years we've had a number of Roman Catholic families put out. We clergy have then gone to the victims and said to them that we really want them to stay. We told them we needed them to stay. At the same time we can't ask people to put their lives on the line. Any Catholic families I know and there's maybe 35 on the estate, want to stay out of trouble. But one family I know whose lad's in the CLB has been petrol-bombed twice." (Church of Ireland Rector)

The Community Association has a reputation of being close to the UDA. Nevertheless some members of the Walkerstown Fellowship participate also.

"I'm on the Rathcrone Community Association. It was set up by the UDA but they're not all UDA. I see my role as very much bringing hope." (Fellowship Member, man)

The 'second wave' of intimidation has taken place since the signing of the Anglo-Irish Agreement. This has mainly affected relations with the police.

"We've had a parishioner who had to leave. He was in the police. We had another one who had a bomb attached to his car. We've a number of police families. Two that I know of moved under paramilitary pressure. One I know of considered it and stayed. I'm glad he did." (Church of Ireland Rector)

"The Police have come under terrible pressure since the Anglo-Irish Agreement. We've had a number of cases of people leaving, direct intimidation." (Presbyterian Minister)

"I don't feel isolated. One reason is that we work together. After the Agreement there was a lot of pressure on police families. We decided that we'd speak out against intimidation in all three Churches. We spoke on the same Sunday and put articles in our magazines. It was interesting how much support we got." (Methodist Minister)

"At the time of the signing of the Anglo-Irish Agreement the whole estate was closed off. There was barricades at the front. Notes went through the doors telling people to put their flags up. My dad did. I was disgusted. Loads of people hung out their flags who might not have bothered because

of intimidation." (Presbyterian Woman)

"The vast majority of people still look to the clergy to give a lead in a time of crisis. For example at the time of the Anglo-Irish Agreement the extreme Prods were turning against the police. People still looked to the clergy. We've something unique here, at least unique to me. There's a strong bond between the Churches. In anything important we'd make sure that we're together." (Methodist Minister)

The three main Churches are united against local intimidation. Certainly compared to other agencies, e.g. State Social Work, Police or Army they have a far greater chance of being part of a successful outcome because they are in and of the community. The fact of their unity is at this point very important.

"We know each other fairly well. We do lots of things together, especially with the Methodists. I suppose we're on our way to remembering that we're Christians first and Presbyterians second. The Orange Order don't march to the Church. They're not strong in this congregation. I think they think they're not allowed. But you know, nobody has ever asked me. If they did maybe we'd have to be open to that too." (Presbyterian Minister)

"One of my members said to me "You know there's no point in talking to any of the clergy on this estate cause they can't be divided. The Orange Order don't get any marching to any Church. We'd see that as divisive." (Methodist Minister)

"I think the contacts good on this estate. We have a good relationship together. Its my best experience of inter-Church relations. This is far healthier than a formal Council of Churches.... There've been a few hiccups but we've always talked them out." (Church of Ireland Rector)

Nevertheless there is a more sinister aspect of intimidation:

"My father actually walked out of the UDA. They say there's only one way out. So we were all in fear. Not so much now cause we've God with us. All through my dad's life we used to talk about fear gripping your stomach and he said he'd had it all his life about the gunman standing at his door. My dad doesn't sleep now. I don't know if he still fears. He made a stand against them at the time of the agreement and he was condemned for it.

He's still there though." (Woman, resident)

"The attitude to the RUC has totally changed. On the 11th Night they burned a sign saying burn the RUC instead of burn the Pope. The Free Ps say they won't obey the authorities because they're not doing the Lord's Work." (Presbyterian Woman)

While I was on the estate one incident illustrated this change. The RUC were able to walk into the Presbyterian Church youth club during the evening. Six patrol men came in and sat chatting with the members while drinking a cup of tea. The atmosphere was relaxed, with jokes flying between the police and the club members. During the unplanned visit, they arranged a five a side football match between the club and the police and the club members asked whether they could visit and go round an army assault course. The following weekend an incident occurred in Walkerstown. Two youths from Rathcrone robbed the Social Club in Walkerstown. While they were escaping, the police shot at them, injuring one in the head. Reaction in the Church groups was mostly in support of the police.

"Those two lads are always causing trouble. They're a pair of bad nuts." (Presbyterian Elder)

"Your man was shot last week robbing the social club. My own reaction was if he hadn't been there ,he wouldn't have been shot." (Church of Ireland Rector)

Other reaction on the estate was much more hostile to the police. A leaflet was passed through every door in the estate condemning the RUC action and calling a protest meeting.

"We have had to cancel our football match with the RUC. We had arranged it but the boys won't come now." (Presbyterian Youth Club Leader)

This illustrates the ambivalence in Protestant Working Class areas towards the police. While it is in no way comparable to the antagonism to all Crown forces in Drumglass it represents a considerable shift. The Churches in Rathcrone are confronted with violence as a fact of life in their own area. Their primary concern is the reaction to this violence rather than general political statements. The same has become true in Drumglass. Peace and violence are not abstract concepts to be striven for but realities of everyday experience. "The Church's response" in such a situation is clearly of many types. At one level it is providing a focus for those opposed to violence as a means of politics. At another level it is an institutional response where professional Church representatives, the clergy, speak out. Their view is somehow "more official" or is held to be "more Christian" than the laity. When people demand that the Churches "do more" it is often at this level that "response" is measured. More profoundly, Churches claim to witness to a deeper fact of peace.

"About five months after I'd been attending the Free Presbyterian Church I was laughing when all of a sudden a cloud of doubt attacked me and all these things happened. My husband asked me what was wrong. Everybody noticed. By this time I was totally gripped with fear. My mind went berserk. My friend came to the door and I thought it was Satan to take me away. She took me to all these Churches. The only person I wouldn't go to was the Presbyterian Minister. Nothing worked. Then this day I was watching the TV and it ended up it was a Catholic on it. I thought "He loves the lord." What they (the Free Presbyterian's) said wasn't true. I saw the Presbyterian Minister just walking around the estate and I just ran over to her, and the love started coming, the deep love. From then on its just been each day." (Woman, Rathcrone resident)

"I became a Christian about eight years ago. I was from a traditional loyalist background, paramilitary, UDA, as were most of my family. I've a brother in prison. I got married, had a baby. I was in some mess; UDA, drink, marriage on the rocks, drugs. I met these Christians. I went to this meeting and got invited to a house group. I was affected by people not sermons. At last I saw people with real hope... I read this thing recently which said that 80-90% of people who become Christians do so through friends who've become Christians less than 12-18 months." (Man, Rathcrone resident)

Drumglass has experienced violence at even closer hand than Rathcrone. Indeed starting with the intimidations and the influx of people intimidated elsewhere in Belfast, there does not seem to have been a time when the estate was not associated with violence. As we have already seen, everybody was concerned to show that "things" in Walkerstown and Rathcrone were not as bad as in Drumglass. The building of Drumglass is regarded as the root of most of the social evil in Protestant Walkerstown. Nevertheless the violence experienced on the estate itself is beyond doubt more widespread than that experienced in Walkerstown.

Drumglass was also the home of two of the ten men who died on Hunger Strike in the Maze Prison in 1981 to whom a plaque is erected on the side of the estate. As we have already noted the Church has been actively campaigning against the paramilitaries on the estate.

"I've seen the Parish Priest say before the mass started: Anyone whose here to make a protest may go now for I know you're only here to disrupt things." (Man, Drumglass resident)

The incidence of violence is too widespread to recount. Our task here will be to look at responses to violence and the Churches place in the discussion on violence. We will also look at specific areas; in particular the hunger strike, intimidation, the problem of joyriding and the relationship of the estate to the security forces.

The Hunger Strike was undoubtedly the time of highest tension in Drumglass.

"During the first hunger strike (Autumn 1980) there were calls to down tools and walk out. We just decided we'd tell the kids no. We sent a letter to every parent telling them that no pupil could leave school without written permission from their parents. Without permission they would be suspended. In the event two girls walked out. We called them back and they apologised.

There were some posters put up; "support the H-Block Strikes." Teachers were worried about taking them down. So I went and took them down. I sent a note to all teachers telling them 'No Political Posters'.

The day Bobby Sands died I got phonecalls from teachers asking what was happening. I said "The school is open". The teachers weren't too pleased. So we drove in through the barricades. The signs of rioting were everywhere. At one time we'd about 100 youths at the gate chanting 'close the school'. So I went down and told them we'd close at normal time. They went away. There were workmen who were told they'd be shot and they ran off. The atmosphere was very tense. We had phone calls from parents asking was the school open. There were people stopping kids and telling them school was off.

For a whole month this estate was closed off. We were driving in through barricades and hi-jacked cars. No teachers were touched. We had youngsters who normally went to other schools off the estate who came in here. For a whole month the Army and Police were camped at the edge of the estate in Clonderg and at Walkerstown Industrial Estate. There were two roadblocks, one run by locals, the other by the army, to get into the estate.

On the first day we had the highest percentage attendance of any school in West Belfast. We had a meeting with the Priests and Primary School heads and decided we'd remain open on the day of the funeral. Then we discovered that no other schools in West Belfast were opening. Then it fell apart because the caretaker was worried about being shot, office staff were physically sick, teachers told me they were petrified. I thought 'I have a responsibility to these people' I thought I could not subject people to that. So I called an emergency meeting and we decided to close. There were some parents who slammed us for that. Some people took their kids away. Its very difficult in such a situation. We don't have a united community. We have to tread a very narrow path." (Secondary School Headmaster)

The fact that hunger strikers came from Drumglass heightened the tension on the estate. The day of the funeral and the position of the Church are remembered also.

"I'll never forget the funerals. There was so many people. People from all over, the press, people off the estate who never set foot in the Church. I felt sorry for the Parish Priest. I was in the choir. I sang at that man's funeral mass. I went because I felt I wanted to be with the Priest. When I saw all the young ones there I saw how they were. For them God was not where he is but in that box. I wanted to be with the Priest who was doing his duty." (Woman, local resident)

"The time of the hunger strike was the worst. There was black flags up for months and every time somebody died they tried to get us all out to rattle our bin-lids. There was barricades up everywhere. It was like a siege, very frightening." (Woman, local resident)

If the hunger strike represented the time of the most extreme tension, the fear on the estate of renewed violence remains. In Drumglass, the reality of army harassment and of the enemy status of the police is not a public discussion it is accepted fact. Much more present is the violence which results because of lack of any policing presence. The two most striking features are in the areas of intimidation and vandalism and in the area of car-theft by minors, known as joy-riding and the associated punishment shootings, still known as knee-capping.

Intimidation is a subtle process. It nevertheless leaves traces in views, attitudes and statements which may point to very concrete memories. In Rathcrone we saw how flags were flown at the time of the Anglo-Irish Agreement. In Drumglass the Hunger strikes were associated with intimidation of institutions who remained open.

"I would be regarded as anti-provo because I'm part of the broader peace movement. At one stage the army took over the school. I was accused of being a collaborator and I had to defend myself. My position is stronger on the estate because I stood up." (Secondary School Headmaster)

"The community centre wasn't built because of political bickering. I had to tread softly with Sinn Fein because they had an ACE scheme too through the Tenants Association. They had an Advice Centre for Benefits take-up. Their funding stopped and the Centre's not opened most of the time now." (ACE scheme co-ordinator)

"Paramilitaries seems to be the main reason why men don't get involved in the community. The men are scared of getting pressure so the women get involved." (Local woman)

"By and large we escape political violence. There's no politics in the school. But the kids and the area don't escape the violence. It's a very republican area but it's very factionalised. A lot of the parents of kids in the school have been lifted. I'd say that if it came to the vote about 50-60% would vote Sinn Fein. I take very little to do with it. We're very heavily into the Catholic ethos in the school, including the attitude to violence." (Primary School Headmaster)

"Sinn Fein burned my van because we opened on the day of the Milltown funerals. I have to be very careful because we're in wooden huts and I could be burnt down. Still I have to sack boys at times and you never

know..." (Local Man, Drumglass)

The situation was summed up by one woman in the Family Centre who said:

"I don't know what I'm allowed to say. You'd be afraid to open your mouth on this estate sometimes." (Local woman)

The estate is so factionalised that people on the estate often feel under threat from one another. There is no unity on the estate beyond a general detestation of the Security Forces, the Council and Politicians. Beyond that there is deep antipathy between the workers party and Sinn Fein, between the Church and the IRA and between other residents and young delinquents. The level of violence, combined with a notable increase in family breakdown add to the sense of the estate as depressed. The sense of frustration is best caught over the issue of joy-riding. The stories are legendary and many.

"We couldn't get to sleep last night until four in the morning because they were racing around. If I could get my hands on them.... All these schemes for them, its ridiculous." (Local Woman)

"The other night this lad came to my door and he says 'We've got to take your car.' So I called to my husband up the stairs 'There's a lad here says he's got to take our car.' My husband came down with the cross-bow. They haven't been back." (Local woman)

"They take these cars and they strip them and burn them. They were at it again last night. There's a shell sitting out the back. They sell the parts. They steal certain cars, they get orders for them." (Local man)

"The biggest disturbance in this place is the joyriders. In Derry there was no joyriding only hijacking. Here the kids take cars and the paramilitaries try to stop them. In Derry nobody took cars except the paramilitaries. Funny that." (Convent Superior)

As we have seen there is some local scepticism about schemes to counter joyriding. Punishment shootings, while not supported, are often seen as a last resort. "The hoods", short for hoodlums, or unclassified vandals, are generally despised.

"Joyriding is due to lack of parental supervision. It has nothing to do with deprivation. If you get one clique... There's about two or three gangs and they cause all the trouble." (Schoolteacher)

"There's numerous ways of dealing with Joy-riding. We do social skills, discussions, leisure, education and outdoor pursuit activities. This is an alternative for the energies these young people possess. "It's just as good as being in a car." The problem is that these young people grow up in a society which doesn't give a damn about them. School, older people, no identity which is transferred from older people. Its the only way for the kids to get attention. We have a group of nine and none of them have taken a car. It takes a lot of energy. You have to get a community that cares." (Community Worker with Joyriders (LINKS))

"The underlying problem is unemployment. For boys the macho image means that if you haven't got a job, the paramilitaries are the next best option. The girls all run with that too." (Youth Worker)

"I don't agree with punishment shootings. I've said that I'm against shooting joyriders. Its just that the community wants a pound of flesh and they look to the IRA to get the pound of flesh. But its not an IRA problem its a community problem. You have a community which says they're all hoods (from hoodlum). But its not organised in that way. In West Belfast in that age group it's become endemic. Its a government problem. Facilities in Drumglass are nil. The people they should ask are the community." (Sinn Fein supporter, Community Worker)

This reflects a number of contradictions. The commitment to "the community" appears to contradict the sense that joyriders should be handled with understanding rather than violence, given the community's demands for a pound of flesh. The Church is deeply involved with all of these issues. It is the fact of intimidation which the government uses to show the need for institutional Church involvement in ACE projects. The Church's organisations, schools, youth clubs, family centre, ACE programme are aimed to provide opposition to this breakdown. This has had violent consequences for the clergy.

"The last priests were brilliant. Father O'Callaghan was like a father for the whole estate. Father Doherty used to take the petrol bombs off the lads. He also used to stop the car stealers. He had his flat burned down by a

gang. The people were behind him though. They helped him rebuild his flat." (Local woman)

The sense that the estate was behind the priest was not conveyed immediately, according to one worker in the family centre:

"The priest who challenged them doing punishment shootings got a gun put to his head. Another time they burned down his flat. Afterwards he told me he felt as if everyone in the parish was against him. In fact most people were for him but they were slow in coming forward. Gradually they did and he felt more understood."

The Churches are therefore part of the network whereby social order is maintained without police. This takes place through the consistency of Church-School-Family, but its influence may be largely unseen in that it consists of a lack of breakdown. It is not measurable, and nevertheless the Church remains the centre of moral life. On the estates Church and family 'norms' are the only present structural alternatives to the IRA and paramilitary justice.

The Security Forces have no 'normal presence' in Drumglass. When they enter the estate they do so in convoys, always in vehicles and never on foot patrol. Effectively Drumglass is a no-go area for police except in the case of specific targets. Often they are associated with house to house searches have led to further objections, although in the course of the research the army's policy was apparently vindicated when arms were found under the floor of a kitchen in Drumglass. Nevertheless it is clear that the security forces are entirely an external force without real support on the estate.

"In the early days we were involved with Police Community Relations. The way things were parents objected to the buses because they might be targets." (Primary School Headmaster)

"The police and army don't come here except to get somebody or something. If they get it wrong it just makes things worse. Apart from that its just patrols of aliens. They harass the people on the Falls. This searching hasn't helped." (Local man)

The Police mount fairly regular checkpoints on Lower Glenfoot Road, checking cars and stopping traffic. The army patrol all of Catholic West

Belfast, although their presence in Drumglass was very low-key. During the Hunger-strike the police had a more permanent roadblock at the Clonderg entrance to the estate. The evidence is that the police seek to 'contain' Drumglass because they cannot patrol there without danger to life. The impression is that Clonderg is part of an imaginary peaceline seeking to wall in the barbarian horde. There is talk that a major new road will be built between Drumglass and Clonderg which would effectively separate the two areas. This is something which the Presbyterian Minister in Walkerstown supports.

"It would maybe keep the trouble out. There were plans to build a roundabout at Clonderg but I don't think that would be advisable."

The situation in Walkerstown is very different from that in Drumglass and Rathcrone. It is not 'closed off' in the sense of either estate nor is it in the control of any paramilitary group. The police operate here in a relatively routine manner, although the netting around the police station bears witness to the fact that it was recently a target for bomb attack. When violence does happen, most of it is held to stem from 'outside the area'. There was one recent, and particularly bizarre episode.

"There's a house near here was bought by two people who arrived from the Bible College. They came from Donegal or she was from the South and she had visitors. Because they were from the south that house has been bombed twice, even though they're Protestant. They had to leave." (Primary School Teacher)

"Our manager had his house bombed because he came from Donegal, on the Protestant side!" (Fellowship Member)

In general the growth of violence is blamed on the proximity of Drumglass;

"One-way traffic. Their better people are all trying to escape from their own and buy in Malone. Before Drumglass was built this was all farmland. When Drumglass was built we'd great hopes that the housing would be allocated 50-50. The Church of Ireland even came in with us on a Church! With the troubles, they'd [?] come to the door and tell people. "You're leaving at the weekend." Once the Protestant flow started it couldn't be stopped. Its now 100% Roman Catholic. The Presbyterian cause doesn't flourish. There's no hope here.... Dunroe is still solid. But

then people are moving to Carryduff, Bangor or Comber. They all move that way. I think its true that Brian Faulkner once said that he thought that on this side of the road it would all be Catholic. Its coming true..... Its outside our control. Its a discouragement. You nearly think it's failure on your part." (Presbyterian Minister)

"In the last number of years especially with the building of Drumglass and Ardbann, Walkerstown has been becoming more and more Catholic especially in Lower Glenfoot Road. This has been augmented by the Roman Catholic set-up in Walkerstown, an excellent Church, and one of their best Grammar schools. Consequently any new houses especially in Lower Glenfoot Road are Roman Catholic. The consequence could be that what has happened on the other side of the road could develop on this side. I don't mind a mixed population but I do worry when my numbers drop. I don't want to use the word 'fear' but people talk about it. Every house in Beechlawn changes. I know the same things happened in Ballyray." (Church of Ireland Rector)

"I hesitate to point the finger, but Drumglass is where all the car-theft comes from. The value of property beside the RUC station has collapsed. People can't sell their houses. We were all out again the other night because there was a bomb-scare there. There was a huge bomb six months ago which damaged a lot of the houses." (Male, local resident)

"There's a tremendous amount of car-stealing. One hesitates to point the finger at anyone but a lot of it comes from Drumglass." (Church of Ireland Rector)

The level of physical violence is much lower than in Drumglass. What is very marked is a sense of fear among the Protestants of Walkerstown about 'takeover'. The sense that territory has been lost is very deep. There has been experience of violence; recently the RUC station has been a target, the loyalist club was the site of a shooting by police of a young man from Rathcrone and there has been car-theft. Nevertheless, Walkerstown does not give the impression of a place of particular violence. What is notable is the relatively 'rosy' picture given by local Catholics.

"We once lost a Church. Petrol was thrown in and set alight. All the Protestant Churches in the area sent us money and messages of support. The Catholic people at that time were being threatened. Normally it's

quite harmonious. There was a fellow sentenced for the attack. He was from Belfast.... I suppose there's paramilitaries in Rathcrone and Drumglass but they've long since left the Churches." (Roman Catholic Priest)

"Of course the people who get it in the neck from the troubles aren't the people who cause it. Now and again you have a flair-up but mostly its great.... At one time this would have been predominantly Protestant. Now there's very few non-Catholics. Glenfoot Road has very few non-Catholics now. This has been evolving over the last 15 years. The used to be very well intermixed. Its now so true in Walkerstown. The nearer you get to Dunroe the more the pendulum swings." (Roman Catholic Teacher)

Community relations remain very tentative though violence has been contained. Instead, perhaps pre-emptive of violence and certainly in an identifiable manner, there has been a process of Protestant flight and Catholic settlement.

(d) The Churches and Inter-community Relationships.

The Churches live in an area that is united by little else other than geography. Neither Rathcrone nor Drumglass schools are linked to schools in the other community except by sport. The paramilitaries are active in both Rathcrone and Drumglass and the RUC have permanent problems in the latter and developing problems in the former. Violence is endemic in Drumglass and intimately related to serious deprivation. Rathcrone has a degree of tranquillity characterised by sinister undercurrents while Walkerstown is apparently peaceful but psychological relationships of fear dominate conversation and have led to large scale, if mostly uncoordinated, population movement.

In such a context how do the Churches operate and what is their contribution to inter-community relationships? The most developed relationships are between the Churches of Rathcrone and the Catholic parish of Old Walkerstown, both St. John's and St. Peter's. The foundations of this relationship are the unity of the Protestant Churches on the estate and the ecumenical outlook of the clergy, which has made for long-standing relationships.

"I am sure that it is more important to be Christians than to be Presbyterians. I know that his causes difficulties. On our session we have these very

discussions, and I think this view is gradually winning. We've lost some dead-wood recently. I think we suffer from feeling down at times. We need to hear that its a warm place. I feel that the spirit has taken us this far and we're ready for a new beginning." (Presbyterian Minister)

"I think the contact's good on the estate. We have a good relationship together. Its my best experience of inter-Church relations. This is far more than a formal Council of Churches. We share Holy week together and we share Easter Evening. This year we have it. People come from all the Churches to whichever it happens to be. Its a good combination of three or four clergy with a similar vision." (Church of Ireland Minister)

This strong inter-Protestant link is challenged only by the Free Presbyterians. The other three ministers, people from the Caring Office and some of the people from the congregation meet together every week with priests from Old Walkerstown. These meetings are meetings of friends, of people who know each other well from years of being together both in these meetings and at gatherings in each others Churches. They take the form of an exchange of news and a chat over a cup of tea, a discussion led by one person in the group or a particular subject and a time of prayer together. They are part of the routine. I was invited to take part in their meetings, and did so.

"It is very important for the Churches to do as much as possible. I meet weekly with the ministers in Rathcrone. We meet to pray for peace in this area, to organise services, to keep up with each other. During the week of Prayer for Christian Unity we had Protestant clergy in. We support EMU, linked in with Ballyray from St. John's and St. Peter's with Walkerstown. We'd also encourage our Youth Clubs to engage in inter-club activity with state sector clubs. The Anglo-Irish Agreement blocked things from the Protestant side. Before it we would have had 800 at an interdenominational service. Since then we haven't had the same numbers." (Roman Catholic Priest)

"We meet every week. I have a lot of friends in every Church in Ireland. We have an exchange with a Carmelite Priory in Dublin. The congregation has always been very open." (Presbyterian Minister)

"I have had a relatively low-key approach to conflict in the Protestant community. My predecessor tended to go up and curse the violent ones

up and down. I've tended not to go looking for conflict. One element is that many of that element have come to appreciate things. We've had the Parish Priest preaching in our own Church. We've been at many things in the Roman Catholic Church. He's always well received. People seem to accept it... I'm asking myself "Am I being blase?" - No, I don't think so." (Church of Ireland Rector)

"When I arrived there was a nucleus of Orangemen who saw it as very much their mission to get their minister into the order. After eight years they've probably given up. Since then some of them have mellowed tremendously. One of them, for example met the Priests at the door during the week of Prayer for Christian Unity. There were five priests and quite a number of nun's at the service. I would see the week as an exercise in encouragement of our work of reconciliation. Its a chance to learn from one another that we haven't all the truth, that there's aspects of Catholic worship and life we can learn from... I'd say I inherited what was politically the "hardest-line" congregation, more than the Presbyterians and Church of Ireland." (Methodist Minister)

The relationship at clergy level between the Churches in Rathcrone and the Roman Catholic Church in Old Walkerstown Parish is close and friendly.

"Even in public the Parish Priest will openly say in a service at St. John's that we're very good friends." (Methodist Minister)

This has spread into the congregations where the Caring Office is only one example of friendship. There are occasional joint services of worship between Catholics and Protestants even if still unusual. Between Protestant denominations joint services are now common, part of the annual calendar. Throughout July and August evening services in Rathcrone are united. Young people from Rathcrone Presbyterian and St. John's Roman Catholic meet together at times. Prayer and Healing services are attended by both and the strong influence of the charismatic renewal movement in the Church of Ireland and Presbyterian Churches has meant that the meetings between active Church members in other contexts are regular.

"Since I came I've felt a strong commitment in the Presbyterian Church. It's very difficult to keep the Church situation together. There's so many pressures. In their commitment to reconciliation they're so strong and I

don't mean the minister. The priests in this area are very good as well." (ACE scheme co-ordinator)

Within Rathcrone, the Churches are the largest groups maintaining active cross-community contacts. No other locally based groups appear to seek any cross-community relationships in what is effectively a Protestant ghetto. This has led them into some conflict with parts of the estate and means they are openly attacked by the Free Presbyterians. The Churches are one of the few open doors to cross-community contact on the estate. In a sense Church relations are the only relations not characterised by inter-community antagonism. There is further exception in the case of the Christian Fellowship which we will examine below. It is important to note that this fact does not mean that relations are easy, or that movement is free between Catholics and Protestants. However behind a Church shield provided by congregations and clergy, movement is possible. This is in itself unusual.

"I think if the Minister approaches the question of the Christianity of the Roman Catholic Church, changes take place. You can lead people into a U-turn. We've seen a change here over the last six years. I don't think ministers in Ulster realise what a powerful force they can be for good or division. I think if you're patient and caring and loving, if you're trying to be like Christ in that situation things can be done. It's a long hard slog. Two forward, one back. It would be much more difficult if there was a hardline minister in any one of the major Churches." (Methodist Minister)

The Churches, as communities of people, are able to continue some relations with each other in spite of violence. The Roman Catholic Church has been very active in this field. It is interesting is that the Churches are effectively neighbours not ministers to the same area. The Roman Catholic parish while covering Rathcrone has virtually no parishioners on the estate.

The second area of contact is maintained within the Christian Fellowship. This is interesting in that it runs outside the institutional Churches, and therefore faces different problems. Although the group is predominantly Protestant they wish to remain open to Catholics.

"A number of people in this fellowship come from Catholic areas.... Even in Rathcrone my house group is mixed. But if people knew that it would be dangerous." (Fellowship member)

A number of people within the Fellowship are aware that other Churches remain very suspicious of them, including Protestants.

"A few years ago there were meetings of all the Churches. A lot of Churches would be very suspicious of us because of "shepherding", which some house-Churches have. We never had it. There was a lot of pressure for it but we were always very much against it." (Fellowship member)

The main Churches remain disinterested in groups outside the institutions. Nevertheless, this small Fellowship has also engaged in some cross-community contact.

It is important when dealing with cross-community relationships to emphasise the context in which they take place. The ghettoised housing pattern means that there is little unplanned contact between Protestants and Catholics and what contact does take place does so outside the estate (e.g. at work). Unemployment further erodes these possibilities. The perceived bias of the local Council further limits the degree to which Council facilities are used by both communities. Beyond this "accidental" contact, inter-community relationships are a matter of deliberate effort. They do not happen "by chance". Where the problems of life on the ghetto estates are themselves great, this effort may appear of secondary importance or "too much". This is generally the situation in Drumglass. In Rathcrone the Churches, far more than any other groups, have undertaken this contact. This has become part of Church life. It remains clergy - led more than community driven, but there is no sense that the clergy act apart from or even always ahead of the laity. The limitations of this contact are immediately apparent. The fact of its real existence is nevertheless notable. If we contrast the Churches efforts with the cross-community building evident in other circles or with the caution and the fear evident in the schools, they appear remarkable. Once the ghetto structure is in place the efforts at creating relationships between communities are made very difficult. They take place only through conscious effort and planning. The possibility of friendships between people in opposed ghettos developing organically appears slight. Their scope in such a context must inevitably appear limited.

The relations between the Churches in Rathcrone and the Catholic Parish of Old Walkerstown are not repeated elsewhere in the area. In Walkerstown there are no formal contacts between the Churches, and no Council of Churches. Relations run on a pattern of each denomination working on its own. The Catholics are involved with Rathcrone rather than Walkerstown.

"We don't have very close relations with the Roman Church. We're friendly but I think that maybe I'm tired. All Youth Organisations are parallel. I am concerned with St. Peter's Church of Ireland which I must serve. I am guilty in a sense that I haven't got involved in much community work. The non-subscribers sometimes marry my divorcees without telling me which is annoying." (Church of Ireland Rector)

"I'm friendly with them (Roman Catholic's) in as far as if we do things with Monsignor.... I forget his name. I've been down at his house. Relation's couldn't be better.... I have great respect for other denominations. I'm a chaplain in Purdysburn and one of my best friends was the Catholic Chaplain. We played golf. Here we don't see each other. We do our own thing, but the relationship is very good. It used to be that the Non-subscribers were considered worse that the Catholics. Montgomery was minister in Walkerstown. They were short of ministers so they got trained as Unitarians. That's why the Presbyterians called our hall "Trinity" Hall and the badminton club is called "Trinity". They wouldn't have called the Non-subscribers Christians. The last Non-subscribing minister, in my time here, used our hymn book. 90% of their people are now Presbyterian. All the animosity has gone except some of the folk wouldn't want their minister to preach in our Church.

The G.B. and the B.B. cater for the whole of Walkerstown as the Church of Ireland's organisations do, I assume. Up until a few years ago there would have been opposition to Roman Catholic bowling clubs coming to our hall. All that animosity has gone. Probably the influence of the ministers. I've some very hardline Orangemen. I've always told them about my friendship in Purdysburn. I'd really take the line that the whole business of being ecumenical is out the window. I think we stay on our own and come together when we need to. I sort of feel that is the way. The woman's World Day of Prayer goes round all the Churches in Walkerstown and Rathcrone. There's no opposition. There's been a complete change on that score in the last fifteen years..... St. John's Roman Catholic Church gave £1,000 for the damage done to Dunlure Presbyterian Church Hall. When my hall was blown up in 1971 because the court was held there at that time, all the Protestants rang up. There wasn't one word from Father Kelly. That shows that change has come. I think things are far better done at the lower level. This business of trying to impose it from the top will never work. In our area we go along quietly." (Presbyterian Minister)

"We once lost a Church. Petrol was thrown in and set alight. All the Protestant Churches in the area sent us money and messages of support. Two of our schools were attacked and one of our Youth Clubs. In all those times we had the support of all the other Christian congregations in the area." (Roman Catholic Priest)

The local Churches exist separately at every level. Where violence to one Church building takes place, Churches of all denominations do respond. Beyond this, the troubles have not affected Church relations. In the meanwhile the Churches reflect the intense feelings involved in population change. Many Protestants seem utterly depressed by the collapse in numbers. For them the area is suffering from Catholic advance and Protestant decline. Catholics appear cheerful and optimistic and satisfied with relations in the area, aware of course of population change.

In a sense Walkerstown has suffered the biggest change in its composition of any of the area studied. The Churches have not been focuses of any alternative approaches. The fear of falling numbers dominates. The clergy reflect and share this fear. Their concern lies within their denomination. Concern is on "declining numbers" as such rather than on what might be done about fears. The result is that the Churches are mirrors of their communities - the Protestants depressed and declining the Catholics optimistic and growing.

"I don't want to use the word fear but people talk about it. Every house in Beechlawn changes. I know the same things happened in Ballyray. Its affected my work in the sense that I'm not as conscientious as I was about visiting people who move in." (Church of Ireland Minister)

"We have 1138 children in the school, five groups in each year. We keep growing." (Catholic teacher)

Drumglass as an area presents the greatest problems for inter-community relations. The problems are partly to do with the reputation of the estate. 'Drumglass' is a name usually uttered by Protestants with a mixture of fear and antipathy. Protestants in Walkerstown would not go to Drumglass in the normal course of events. There are no facilities on the estate not available elsewhere. The Industrial Estate for the Walkerstown area lies between Rathcrone and Drumglass. There are virtually no family relationships between the communities. The problems of living from waking to sleeping on Drumglass itself tend to occupy the time of people on the estate. Unemployment, vandalism, paramilitarism, joy-riding, isolation and family breakdown are the 'problems' identified by public agencies. In this context Community Relations are often seen as 'irrelevant', 'impossible', the obsession of middle class liberals and/or such a problem as to be insuperable. In the latter case, people prefer to spend their energies on more fruitful tasks. What contact between the communities does take place, does so in the workplace or in places outside Drumglass.

"Rathcrone's as bad as Drumglass. People are very narrow in their view. Rathcrone would be the complete opposite of here. There's not much contact. If they were any closer, there'd be a lot of friction." (St. Brigid's Primary School Teacher)

"Facilities are very limited here. There's isolation here. It has been a struggle to get doctors in. The Churches were mobile buildings and the schools were mobile. " (St. Colm's Secondary School Headteacher)

"There's not much cross-community work here. Any there is, we do. We have Protestants play for our badminton team. That's because we're so good. We've been Northern Ireland champions before now." (Youth Club Leader)

The Family Centre use Corrymeela Centre in Ballycastle for weekends away for mothers and their children, up to four times a year. This is a minimal contact though in the circumstances it presents an unusual opportunity to escape a ghetto society.

In this respect, Drumglass is similar to most of Catholic West Belfast. The ghettos were created in fear of violence. The violence to and from Drumglass perpetuates the fear of the area from outside and the sense of a need for protection on the estate. The deep political divides on the estate, especially as represented by the Church versus Sinn Fein, occupy any immediate attention for politics. The sheer workload on the priests, the structure of Catholic hierarchy and the immediate problems of making a life in the face of adversity are easily sufficient to absorb attention once the ghetto has been established, making Community Relations appear a secondary task, for the Churches as well as other organisations. Everything seems to be reduced to a struggle to establish control between various forces which threaten chaos (unemployment, Sinn Fein, hoodlums, joy-riders, family collapse) or offer authoritarianism (Church and also Sinn Fein).

Theology and Church in the Walkerstown Area.
The ideas of Church and of the nature of Christianity in the Walkerstown area throw some light on the thinking behind actions and arising out of experience. The Protestant clergy had no consensus on their approach to the Church and their role. As we have seen their attitudes towards one another and their attitudes to the necessity of inter-Church contact were very different.

"For me, in the end, its more important to be Christian than Presbyterian." (Presbyterian Minister)

"I really take the line that the whole business of being ecumenical is out the window. I think we stay on our own and come together when we need to.... I think things are far better done at the lower level. This business of trying to impose it from the top will never work. In our area we go along quietly. There's a PACE group. I don't go to it. In my opinion they're far better done at that level." (Presbyterian Minister)

"There's a strong bond. In anything important we'd make sure that we're together. On this ecumenical thing somebody said to me that there's no point in talking to any of the clergy cause they can't be divided." (Methodist Minister)

"We have a good relationship together... We share Holy Week together and we share Easter evening. This year we have it. People come to whichever it happens to be. Its a good combination of three or four clergy with a similar vision. There's a shared vision. One of the things I hear (on this estate) is that we all get on well. I don't find the competitive spirit." (Church of Ireland Rector)

"We don't have very close relations with the Roman Church. We're friendly but I think that maybe I'm tired. We say hallo to each other but we don't have any meetings or anything. The Non-subscribers remarry my divorcees without telling me which is annoying. Otherwise we're friendly enough. I'm concerned with this parish and the Church of Ireland

which I must serve. I am guilty in a sense that I haven't got involved in much community work." (Church of Ireland Rector)

Thus, even within each of the Churches there are major differences in approach. It is thus impossible to talk anymore of what "The Churches" do or do not do. Even in an area as small as Walkerstown within the same denomination there are significant differences. This is before we take into account the differences between laity and the clergy and between the laity. Identity with a national denomination, an institution. "The Church" does exist. The use of the term Church does not mean the same for every user. This "Church" is in itself an illusive concept. Without hierarchical or state authority, Churches have no power to impose any single direction. In an increasingly pluralist environment, the Churches exhibit two tendencies at once; ever more desperate calls back to a unique authority and an increasing inability to show unity in their own ranks. It is not clear in the Presbyterian or Methodist Churches that even a notional hierarchy truly exists. The result is that attempts to pin down "Ulster Protestantism" in a fixed ideological framework are always based on shifting sands. The only clear signal in Walkerstown is that "The Churches" in their engagement with and interest in other denominations depend on local circumstances. This carries with it the attendant risk that any attempt to categorise "the Churches" in one box, always ignores or drives out part of reality, possibly because it makes for simplicity. Categorising "the Churches" as "sectarian" ignores those whose cross-community commitment and activity often entails considerable risk and personal commitment. At the same time, to categorise the Churches as "ecumenical" is to ignore the large numbers whose ecumenical commitment is limited and others whose personal position is expressly anti-ecumenical. We can only talk of "the Church" in a particular context, since what it is, is a matter of specific relationships. Church people also have divergent views on the nature of their task.

The Free Presbyterian Church are an exception to this tendency. Here the uniformity of political and religious belief between members of all standing in the Church seems to be much stronger. It is this which gives them political and cultural significance beyond their membership.

"I see the most important part of my work as being with people, being beside them, so that I can walk into any house in this parish because I have a relationship. Whether people go to Church or not, they need their Church... My role is first a pastoral role, going out and finding the lost sheep and trying to build God's kingdom in the Church and proclaim

Christ's teaching and its implications. You're always conscious you're not doing it. You reach the problem of how far you go, how long do you make an effort for somebody. I was talking to a doctor who said, I should only go and see the sick. But my mission must be bigger than this." (Church of Ireland Rector)

"I began with a vague sense of God's calling to ministry. I saw ministry as a thing where the minister did everything. Over ten years my view began to evolve to a view where the job was to equip the saints for the work of ministry. We've around 500 families here who claim membership. There's no way one person can minister to their needs. I began pouring myself into those people who want to grow, those people who had some kind of hunger with them, a need to grow. At the same time I put a lot of time in going door to door getting to know people on paper at least. Since then I must admit I go where I see the needs. I don't go knocking on doors on a door to door basis." (Church of Ireland Rector)

"I think the main task of the Church is to be relevant to the situation and to adjust to meet those needs in the name of Christ. If the Church isn't relevant, folk will soon drift off. I think there's so much irrelevancy in the Church. In my Church there's the attitude "we've always been here and we'll be here tomorrow because we're one of the four main Churches". Down through the years there has been a loyalty to the Churches, but I think that loyalty is waning. I had a woman say to me, "When I stop finding something in your Church which helps me cope with life I won't be there". That's what its all about. I wouldn't stay myself if it wasn't relevant.

I think ministers are partly to blame in setting up barriers between themselves and ordinary people. They've put themselves on pedestals. I suppose its one reason I wear my collar so seldom. They (my congregation) know that I blow my top and that I'm human." (Methodist Minister)

"I think the clergy do have influence. More from your living and what you are rather than what you say. If the love of God was there, I'd like to think people say "that fella, ach he wasn't a bad fella." Some go away and then they get married and have children and then they look for what held their families together." (Presbyterian Minister)

"I think the presence of the spirit is the most important. I feel God is calling us on to a new challenge. What it is we don't yet know, but we are

praying for the spirit's guidance." (Presbyterian Minister)

"The task of the Priest is to preach the gospel, to look after the pastoral needs of Catholics, to educate the children and to care for the sick. In this parish we'd see the need to be a committed ecumenist. I suppose there's paramilitaries in Rathcrone and Drumglass but they've long since left the Churches. But there's a task of evangelisation of the Gospels. The Church can just talk. We can't force people." (Catholic Priest)

"Caring for the pastoral needs of Catholics." is a wide remit. Into this elastic category professional clergy can either sink or swim. As we have seen, the clergy can be swamped by huge pressures of work as well as enjoying huge power and prestige as the carers for 'needs'.

"For me the Kingdom of God is righteousness, peace and joy its within me. With all that we do, the most important thing is that in all things Christ has first place. It would be so easy to get away from that through busyness... I think we thought 'We are God's people for the time'. What I think has happened is that God humbled us." (Fellowship Member)

Theology as an academic discipline appeared much less important unless it was important as a means of explanation:

"On this estate people don't give two hoots about theology." (Methodist Minister)

The identification of communities as 'Catholic' and 'Protestant' is in relation to one another in other words 'I am Protestant rather than Catholic' more than because of a widespread theological knowledge. Difference is 'proved' by general attitudes and by more immediate outward differences in liturgy rather than in depth theological knowledge. Theology would appear to follow rather than lead community relations in Walkerstown for all but the most knowledgeable.

This is not to say that there are not deep theological assumptions in folk thinking. One example of this I found in the Parish Magazine for Drumglass. In an article, the parish priest speaks of the grave of St. Brigid now maintained by the Church of Ireland.

"By 1875 the site had long been in the possession of the Church of Ireland and it was under the aegis of their Dr. Chaplin that the restoration took

place... And a day will come too, not in my lifetime but perhaps in yours that the patrimony of Brigid will be reunited with the Church in whose service she spent her life."

What is of note here is the degree to which a fifth century saint is presumed to have taken sides at the time of the Reformation in the sixteenth century. The Church of Ireland has apparently 'usurped' St. Brigid's own Church (R.C.) until the day of the return to the real Church. Such a statement carries with it very many assumptions which Protestants could not share about the nature of the reformation and the Church. Deep within such a statement is the notion of the Roman Catholic Church as the one true Church and other Churches as lesser. In such small examples we see the degree to which culture, religion, history all intertwine to give across an unwitting message about underlying assumptions between Churches.

Conclusions

The Churches in the Walkerstown area are not monolithic. There is no consistency in the nature of each Church within each denomination let alone between denominations. In part this can be attributed to the starkly different social contexts in which the Churches operate. The reality of Walkerstown is three distinctly different areas which share very little. People live in boundaries defined by class and religion, and although the former has not resulted in violence, the residential division is not less because of it. Drumglass is, however, considerably more distant from Rathcrone and Central Walkerstown than the other two are from one another. Walkerstown remains an important service and shopping centre for Rathcrone residents, movement between the two is fluid and Walkerstown High School is on Rathcrone estate. For Walkerstown residents 'Drumglass' remains a foreign body, treated as a bacterial invasion. The Protestants of Walkerstown have preferred to leave rather than face this contamination. For the people of Drumglass, this sense that they are 'not wanted' has not passed unnoticed. The attitude of the Council has certainly exacerbated the sense of the estate as a vulnerable outpost in a hostile territory. Although no peace-line has been built, a psychological wall exists between Drumglass and Walkerstown and the groups on both sides regard one another with unsurprising hostility.

"The Churches" are part of this development. The parish-congregational system means that Church boundaries reflect social barriers. The fact that the Church is an institution with a professional paid clergy servicing, in the first instance, the immediate desires of their parish people means that there is little knowledge of these differences beyond cursory glances or occasional prejudices. There are sound bureaucratic reasons why it makes sense to concentrate resources. The result is that parishes/ congregations become ghettos. The Non-subscribing Presbyterians provide the counter-example to this. Their congregation in Walkerstown is nearly all resident elsewhere. The result is that they have little presence in Walkerstown, nor do they provide any focus for community life.

The implication is that 'The Churches' have no more idea about the reality of each other's problems, lives, goals, dreams etc. than people not in Churches. It becomes inherently unreliable to ask any one person what "The Churches" are doing, because nobody knows. There are no mechanisms for congregations or parishes to share their experiences. The problem of hierarchy (in other words. that people in senior positions have little idea of what is happening on the ground) is now exacerbated by the variety of experiences between people on the ground. If each person makes their particular experience the paradigm for the general experience then only chaos can result. There is no sense that anyone accepts that they only know part of the story.

The rural parish which transcended class divisions (see Ballytorlar) is not repeated in the urban setting. Instead Churches become places which reflect rather than transcend divisions of every sort. The extra pressure of physical violence means that people rather than being concerned with transcending division are now faced with ministering to increasing problems in their own patch. Faced with whole areas in which all parishioners share the same experiences of violence means that it becomes for each parish a universal experience. In other words: In Drumglass everybody shares the view that violence is unemployment, discrimination harassment, and vandalism. In Protestant Walkerstown violence is bombs at the RUC station, car-theft, increasing crime and the IRA. In Rathcrone violence is unemployment, the IRA and local paramilitaries. The problems of inward-looking obsession are made worse by violence between people and the estate, e.g. joyriding. In a parish, the clergy need to be very strong not to share the same view of what violence is. Confronted daily with mounting evidence of that violence, the Church professionals come to reflect the attitudes of the Church members. If they stand out against their parishes, it may be impossible for them to continue as clergy. It is easier to be a liberal Church where there is no violence.

The Church parishes and congregations also reflected the stark class divides of the area. In this regard some interesting points can be made. Working class areas were residentially segregated. There was very little interchange between Drumglass and Rathcrone and violence was endemic to some degree in both. It was very clear from our study that poverty and deprivation were major contributory factors both to the alienation of much of the population from the authorities and to the increasing difficulties in preventing crime. At the same time, the very immediacy of the crises related to poverty, such as joy-riding, unemployment and vandalism meant that community relations was sometimes regarded as a middle-class luxury which missed 'the main' point. At the same time, the continuing community divisions contributed very sharply to the isolation and deprivation of the communities. It is important to note, however, that community relations were not related in a clear causal relationship to class or poverty. In Rathcrone, Protestant Churches were much more active in this regard than in middle-class Walkerstown. At the same time, it is certain that ghettoisation makes problems of inter-community relations appear distant while problems of poverty are close. Poverty then comes to be regarded as 'more important' in an abstract sense than community relations, on the basis of its immediacy. In a sense, then, poverty reinforces the ghetto.

In theory, Walkerstown is a mixed, middle class area. In fact the mix may prove to be illusory. Already the main road through the middle acts as a dividing line of sorts. Throughout the area people of all backgrounds were aware of the progressive flight of Protestants, the previously dominant group, out of the area and an influx of Catholics. In fact the area is one in transition, in which fear among Protestants takes the form of a gradual 'moving out'. There is considerable evidence that the Protestants are very unhappy with the present situation. This was reflected in the Churches. Segregation may be less dramatic among the middle classes, but it appears that slow transitions take place along the same religious lines. All the evidence points to a continuing ghettoisation of the mind in this area. Certainly, nobody seemed to regard the change in the denominational make-up of the population as insubstantial.

In Rathcrone and Drumglass the Churches are well-attended. However it is clear that they no longer have the undivided loyalty of all residents. In Protestant Rathcrone, Church attendance is a choice, not a social obligation. In Drumglass, as we have seen, the Church is identified with a particular political approach. This appears to leave the Church in an ambiguous position. On the one hand, they are no longer the sole or final authority on moral matter and yet all appearances show that transcendent authority is presumed. Furthermore, the Church's official authority is being eroded by the political situation and by changing responses to the teaching of the Church on personal and sexual morality.

At the same time, there is some evidence in both Rathcrone and Drumglass that the Churches have become more important for those still attending. In Rathcrone this transformation to minority or at least reduced status seems to be accepted as a matter of fact. In Drumglass, the Church still operates as if it is a central moral authority for the whole area. This may account for some of the atmosphere of calm in Rathcrone in comparison to Drumglass.

In Walkerstown, the Catholic Church is packed to the brim. The Protestant Churches, meanwhile, appear to be deeply depressed by the loss of membership through population movements. The moral authority of the Catholic Church appears intact at one level, and yet there is some evidence that issues such as birth control are now no longer regarded as a clerical domain. Nevertheless, the atmosphere of the Parish is in absolute contrast to the atmosphere in Drumglass. The Protestant Churches appear remarkably unenthusiastic, reflected in a deep pessimism among many of the clergy.

In the Walkerstown area the groups most conscious of being under threat are the residents of Drumglass and the Protestants of Walkerstown. In both these cases the Churches are concentrated on the problems in the immediate area, on the despair of their congregations and on meeting their own needs. They have no cross-community outreach. The groups less conscious of being under threat are the Catholics of Walkerstown, a confident and newly prosperous group characterised by employment and growth and, more surprisingly, the Protestants of Rathcrone. In this latter case, the confidence is a relative matter. Relative to that of middle-class Protestants in Walkerstown, the confidence of Rathcrone people is based on continuing stability of population on the estate. Between these groups there is a degree of contact. The contact is nearly all through the Churches. There are no other groups on the estate engaged in inter-community relationships of any sort. The relations between clergy are characterised by personal warmth, which does seem to spread into the congregations. However while Churches can provide institutional shelters for relationship-building, they have no power to enforce any changes. It therefore depends on relationships within each parish between clergy and laity and between the laity and on the links of all people to lives and experiences other than their own. What is achieved in this regard is thus achieved in the face of considerable obstacles. Nevertheless, it appears that confidence and a relative absence of fear are more important than class divisions as an indicator of inter-community relationships.

This area also provides interesting examples of the Churches as recipients of government funding. ACE seems to have become an integral part of the Churches existence in working class areas. To some extent the cross-class acceptability of the Churches is central to the funnelling of money through ecclesiastical sources into impoverished areas. This cross-class acceptability, albeit a relative rather than an absolute acceptability once again draws attention to the integrating position of the Church institutions in Northern Ireland. Much of the controversy in working class areas over Church involvement with ACE is centred on accusations that the Church is the agent of the funder not the funded. In Northern Ireland this accusation has a class and a national appeal in Catholic areas. Indeed attacks on the Church in these areas can have numerous roots.

The controversy is particularly acute in Drumglass. The government's decision to cease ACE-funding of community groups because they come under the control of Sinn Fein means that the Church is the only feasible institutional alternative if Drumglass is to receive any part of the ACE-cake. This has led to allegations that the Church is the State in West Belfast. The picture of a Church overflowing with State bounty in the midst of a community devoid of other funding is easy propaganda for anyone with an axe to grind, however justified or unjustified. The moral authority of the clergy through tradition, made rigorous in the schools, is now directly economic. In the face of money, envy, jealously and bitterness are common among those who feel hard done by. The power it bestows on the 'winners', in this case the Church, is also a double-edged sword. A spiral of mutual recrimination begins; the Church takes and distributes the money, Sinn Fein attack the Churches role, the Church now opposes Sinn Fein more strongly by keeping a tighter rein on funds, Sinn Fein attack the Church as anti-community, people with other axes to grind join in, the Church is ever more careful etc. At the end the estate is divided into camps - Church and anti-Church represented by Sinn Fein. The Government clearly supports one side, more so now that Sinn Fein dominates the "opposition", Sinn Fein accuse the Church of being Government stooges.

This is a dangerous process unless the Church finds ways of channelling money into more broadly-based groups. Clerical domination of committees means that 'Church Authorities versus people' battlelines can be drawn. Until now the Church has failed to build alternative grass-root structures and have relied on the traditional model of ultimate clerical control. While this guarantees that no money is accidentally fed to paramilitaries, it also stores up resentment against clerical authoritarianism. Clerical leadership may no longer be appropriate in Catholic Belfast.

The Protestant Churches have a different relationship to ACE and to the State. They are not seen as the peoples allies or opponents in their relationship to State agencies. Protestants do not object to the State as such. The experience of anti-Police violence after the Anglo Irish Agreement may have changed this somewhat. In Rathcrone, the Churches are not the sole object of government funding. Church efforts are thus one strand in a larger tapestry. The continued funding of community groups, the fact that the area has four Churches not one and the relatively lower attendance in Protestant areas means that the Churches are not perceived as centres of direct political power. Distances between the Churches and paramilitaries are real, but the relative lack of authority of both in the face of the State reduces local political power rivalries. As a result, ACE funding has lost its divisive aspect of Catholic areas.

There remain further questions about ACE-funding and the Churches; to what extent should the Churches be the recipients of State employment schemes? Is the government getting its job done 'on the cheap'? Is there any attraction in funding Church schemes except that the alternatives have paramilitary involvement? Are the Churches being used as bulwarks against paramilitaries without any correspondent benefit?

There is an implicit problem in professionalism in Churches. Traditionally the strength of Churches has been as centres of community life, integral to that life. ACE, by paying certain individuals to do work in the name of the Church, may not engage more than one or two members of the parish or congregation. Thus it gives the appearance of expanding the Churches work, but only by mistaking the formal legal institution which now has long lists of extra activities for the bulk of the community of the Church which is untouched. Indeed in some cases, the existence of ACE-schemes may act as a disincentive for voluntary schemes which would be less concentrated but more voluntary. Another problem is that Churches without ACE-schemes may appear to be doing nothing. This certainly cannot be established without further investigation in each case. Rural parishes where the elderly are not abandoned may appear to be 'doing less' than urban parishes with ACE-visitation schemes.

Walkerstown/Drumglass/Rathcrone shows the Churches as institutions trying to come to terms with a changing society with a different view of Church and everywhere having difficulties adopting or knowing what their job is. Churches based in local communities have very obvious strengths. Where those localities become ghettos or places where a threat is felt by all, so the Churches become reflectors of the ghetto, unless within the Churches some wider possibilities exist. In this respect hierarchical Churches may have more choices than non-hierarchical Churches, because they have obvious links to others outside their immediate experience. Churches without local roots or strong commitments (e.g. Quakers) may wither and die. Non-subscribing Presbyterians have certainly felt this chill.

Walkerstown illustrates the diversity of Church life and at the same time each Church now faces the danger of being an ecclesiastical ghetto in which all of life is read from the ghetto, whatever that might be. Within communities under threat, theologies which offer simple explanations of why the group is under threat gather a special appeal. The Churches then become obstacles to community relations, because inter-relationship appears like a threat, a possibility of contamination or of annihilation. The Churches do not need to condone murder. When murder is carried out by individuals they can provide a framework within which that act can be 'understood' if not condoned.

In this context the Walkerstown area also provides examples of Churches who have stood against a trend. In Rathcrone this has led them to be under attack from Free Presbyterians, but the significance of this has been to seem to separate Church identity from political identity, as the Church-goers have been little affected.

SECTION FIVE: CHURCHES AND COMMUNITY IN THE WATERSIDE

"The violence is real for some children in that two fathers have been killed and others shot... Otherwise it's as normal as we can make it."

Introduction

The city of Londonderry, known as Derry, straddles the River Foyle a few miles before it enters the sea. The river divides the city into two parts, the Waterside to the east and the City or Derry side to the west. Over the last twenty years, the city has often been a flashpoint for violence, holding, as it does a central symbolic importance in the political mythology of both Unionism and nationalism. Our study took place in part of the Waterside, where a mixed Catholic-Protestant population still lives.

Most people in the city live on the opposite West Bank surrounding a historic core within the city walls. The city was a flashpoint in the violence which erupted in the late 1960s. Political conditions in Derry were held by Civil Rights campaigners to provide the worst example of Unionist gerrymandering in the province. The result of political manipulation was that a nationalist majority of votes in the city was turned into a Unionist majority of seats on the City Council. The Civil Rights slogan 'One Man, One Vote' arose in part out of these circumstances.

Violence in the city in the late 1960s and early 1970s had significant results in Derry. The most profound was the flight of the majority of Protestants from the west bank of the river (the so-called 'City' or 'Derry' side) to new homes on the Waterside, Eglinton and New Buildings or beyond. The only clearly Protestant area on the west bank is now the area known as 'the Fountain', close to the city walls, an area notable for the amount of red, white and blue graffiti and defiant sloganism.

Derry City Council now has a Nationalist majority, reflecting the religious and cultural identity of the local majority. The three wards on the west bank return one Unionist member from a total of fifteen councillors. The Waterside area returns five Unionists and one Nationalist from a single ward. This indicates the degree to which the river acts as a liquid 'Peaceline', a cultural divide which splits the City. The Waterside population is however more mixed than the electoral results suggest. Three of the area's five primary schools serve the Catholic population while many Protestants feel under threat from the growing Catholic minority in their midst. Up to 35% of the population of the Waterside are Catholic.

Within the Waterside there are smaller areas which reflect further concentrations of religious and cultural groups. Cairnhanna, Ballybrian, Campatrick, Ballymack and Clonmore are largely Protestant. Craigneill and Brian's Hill are largely Catholic while middle class areas such as Glendean and Castle Park are mixed. The result is a heady social, cultural and religious brew. The position of a Catholic resident of Craigneill is that of a Catholic on a Catholic estate in a Protestant area of a Catholic City in a Protestant State on a Catholic island. The possibilities for considerable political and denominational difficulties are already given.

Mention should be made of the controversy surrounding the name of the city. An ancient Irish settlement of Doire, anglicised to Derry became Londonderry when the land was given to the London Companies for settlement in the early 17th century. Although widely known as Derry, the official name of the city is Londonderry. This was and is regarded by many nationalists as a symbol of British colonialism. In the last twenty years many Protestants began to refer to the city as Londonderry as a matter of principle. A Nationalist majority on the City Council voted to change the name of the Council to 'Derry City Council' in 1984. The resulting uproar led to the withdrawal of all but two of the Unionist Councillors from the council. The present position is that the name of the City is the City of Londonderry and that of the Council is Derry City Council. Use of either name in certain circumstances is regarded as a highly political statement. In general, Protestants spoke of Londonderry with occasional use of Derry whereas all Catholics referred to the city as Derry. Various compromises have been adopted in Northern Ireland in an attempt to avoid this controversy. Written conventions such as L'Derry or Derry / Londonderry (leading to the nickname of 'Stroke city') have all been tried. Such compromises are not appropriate for this piece of work. Where the city was referred to, we have recorded and reproduced the usage of the speaker. Elsewhere, we have used Derry.

The Waterside is characterised by ghettos of both class and religion. The class division of housing between privately owned 'middle class' areas and publicly owned 'working class' estates is repeated here. As elsewhere in Northern Ireland the division of the Waterside into Catholic/ Nationalist and Protestant/Unionist areas is obvious. Craigneill is the largest Catholic housing estate in the Waterside. The main entrance to the estate is characterised by green white and orange graffiti on walls and pavements. During recent elections the only visible posters were those of Sinn Fein.

A large sign directed at passing cars declares 'IRA rule Craigneill.'

Nearby is a large Protestant housing estate, known as the Carnpatrick estate. The political affiliations of this area are immediate from the first glance. Kerbstones are painted red white and blue as are many lampposts and street signs. Murals of King Billy, Scottish and Northern Irish flags and Loyalist paramilitary groups are painted on gable ends on the estate. The houses in Craigneill closest to Carnpatrick lie derelict and empty, a further protective barrier, foreclosing any contact. The Ballybrian area is a large Protestant middle class area. Almost all of the housing is postwar and private. Here the graffiti is concentrated in the more rundown areas. Loyalist colours are widespread in Foyle Heights and in Clonmore. During the election the posters of the DUP and those of the ULDP were most prevalent. Glendean is quiet and characterised by an atmosphere of middle class calm. This part of the Waterside would not be out of place in any English or Scottish town. Graffiti is almost absent and there is no sign of poverty or widespread unemployment.

The Churches in the Waterside

The City Council Area has one of the highest proportions of Catholics of any council area in Northern Ireland. The 1981 Census recorded the Catholic population as 54.4%, the second highest recorded in any district. The boycott of the religious question by many Nationalists means that this figure can be increased to approximately 66%. The Protestants in the area are largely Presbyterian or Church of Ireland. In the 1981 Census 12.6% claimed to be Presbyterian while 10.6% were Church of Ireland. The Methodists accounted for only 831 people or 1% of the population while 2.5% belonged to other denominations. It appears that the Church of Ireland is stronger in the rural areas of the City Council area while the Presbyterians were strongest in the city itself.

The Waterside is regarded as one Parish by the Catholic Church. It is divided into three areas served by priests resident in each. The Parish Priest lives and ministers in the Waterside Chapel on Clonmore Avenue. Other Curates live in Craigneill and New Buildings. In general terms the Craigneill Chapel serves the Craigneill and Brian's Hill areas while Clonmore Avenue is the Church for the rest of the Catholics of the Waterside. This makes a clear class division between the parts of the parish.

The Presbyterian Church in Derry is in many ways a strange institution. The three largest congregations in the Presbytery are the Waterside congregations of Second Presbyterian, Ballybrian and Clonmore. Some 3700 people claim connection to these three Churches. Nevertheless the four congregations still remaining on the west bank claim the allegiance of 1877 people. The majority of the west bank congregations now live in the Waterside or outside the city. Many people once resident on the City side continue their connection through the Church. A glance at the register of Baptisms shows that the number of young families claiming connection to the Churches indicates a sharp decline in all of the West Bank and City Centre congregations. Interestingly all of the ministers of Derry congregations live on the Waterside including those in City side congregations.

The Church of Ireland too retains a structure which reflects older residence patterns. The two Waterside parishes are St. John's and Kilfinn. These are the two largest congregations in the city. However the Cathedral parish of St. Columb's retains its pre-eminence. The Church has two other parishes in the city; Christ Church and St. Augustine's. The clergy for these parishes continue to live on the City side.

The Methodist Church has two buildings in the city. The larger congregation meets on the Waterside. A smaller core, again mostly resident on the Waterside meets in the city centre at Carlisle Road.

There are several other Churches on the Waterside. The Free Presbyterian Church has a large Church at Cairnhanna. This serves a congregation which extends far beyond the city including members in Donegal. There is also an Apostolic Church, a Brethren Meeting Place and a Jehovah's Witness Kingdom Hall. A Mormon Church also serves the whole of the city based on the Waterside. There is also a Quaker Meeting on the City side of the river which consists of a small dedicated core.

The Protestant population of the Waterside are an unsettled population. Many moved to the Waterside as a response to the violence. Only one Church has finally closed on the west bank. It reopened as Ballybrian Presbyterian in the 1970s. Ballybrian and Second Presbyterian are the most locally based congregations with larger numbers of young families. This makes any study of the Churches on the Waterside difficult. The attendance of Protestants at Church does not necessarily reflect where they live. Any study of the Churches in the city must reflect this.

The extent of Protestant population movement has meant that the city-wide reach of the Protestant Churches is seriously truncated. Without a local tradition the influence of Protestant Churches is seriously curtailed.

This has led to suggestions that the Waterside should be reconstituted as a separate town with a Protestant majority. Population movements which are felt to be the result of fear, threat or intimidation also leave behind them memories in the people today. There is a strong sense that the drift of Protestants from Derry may be an unstoppable tide. This compounds a historical memory whose keystone is the successful Protestant defence of the walled city in 1689 against James II supported by the native, Catholic Irish. A large wall sign in the Fountain declares that 'the Protestants of Londonderry west bank are still under siege'. This sense of besiegement, of being overwhelmed by a dangerous enemy seems to have crossed the Foyle. The political representation of the Waterside reflects this unease. The five Unionist councillors consist of two members of the DUP, the sole councillor in Northern Ireland of the U.L.D.P., one Ulster Unionist and one independent Unionist. The independent left the party because he disagreed with Unionist withdrawal at the time of the renaming of the Council. He also has a colleague in the sole Unionist councillor on the City side.

The Catholics of the Waterside are aware of their growing strength. There is a strong sense of community confidence, a belief in improvement. This community confidence is the result of the changes in the city in the course of the last twenty years. Despite continuing high levels of poverty and unemployment there is a sense of advance. This is most visible in the Nationalist control of the City Council, the changing of the name of the council to Derry and in the remarkable success of the Football Club, Derry City winners of the League of Ireland and FAI Cup. The Football team play in the heart of the Catholic city in the league of the Republic of Ireland. This means that their matches are on a Sunday which further compounds the alienation of many Protestants. Attempts to portray the club as a cross-community success are somewhat misleading. After winning the FAI cup returning supporters were ambushed by stone throwers in many Protestant areas including New Buildings, just outside the city.

The Catholic Church is the most obvious unelected power in the City. Pronouncements of the Bishop are regarded as extremely important. Many regard him as the most important figure in the city. Even within Catholic Ireland, the Diocese of Derry is seen as particularly strong in terms of loyalty and attendance. This is not always regarded as positive. The power of the Church to raise money is almost legendary in a diocese which is amongst the poorest in Ireland. In Craigneill the Church and the schools are by far the most prominent buildings. A recent mission by Redemptorists in the area produced huge attendance's at mass and confession.

On the Waterside there is an uneasy balance between Catholics and

Protestants. In recent years there has been relatively little violence in the area, although there have been a number of attacks on soldiers and their families. Nevertheless there is much below the surface. Mention should be made of the Apprentice Boys of Derry and the associated Orange and Black orders. The Apprentice Boys remain an important organisation in Protestant areas. The annual parade in August is still one of the largest in Ulster, an annual occasion to recall Protestant triumphs in adversity and to reclaim the city. As we shall see they have close associations with the Churches although these links are mostly not through clergy membership.

The Churches and personal life

The Churches in the Waterside are important in the lives of many of their parishioners and members. There is considerable variation in the levels of attendance in different areas and the degree of importance attached to Church by each person. It is not within the scope of this project to attempt to quantify this attachment. What is certain is that many people continue to attach great importance to their faith and religious life.

The Catholic Churches in Derry are very well attended, for some too well;

"I'd have found Derry Diocese very traditional. The practice of the faith, attendance at Church is very high. Because this is very high, I think the clergy live out of a different model of the Church than I would envisage... A lot of people left school at 14 or 15 and their education literally stopped. Certainly their faith development stopped. They may be mature adults but their faith is not so mature" (Catholic Sister)

"The chapel is very well attended. I go myself though I'd be critical of the Church as well. It's very well supported, judging by the amount collected every week in such a deprived area, around £2,000." (Craigneill resident, male)

"People are looking for something. There' is a fierce hunger for something genuine. It's for the personal thing" (Waterside Catholic woman)

"The real needs of the people seem to be personal. Listening, giving a sense of belonging. People demand you to be what they want you to be. I m meant to be a man of God. The people hand things over to you. This man was dying and they nearly put you into the place of God. I was with

the relatives, learning myself. Yesterday I was called out to a guy who wanted to commit suicide. What do you do? God guides you. People turn to the priest. They ring if their son has been lifted by the police and so on." (Local priest)

"There is a very strong Catholic tradition on the Waterside. The Catholic population is continuing to expand. It's true in that there is a falling away of attendance at mass, though it's not very noticeable to us here." (Catholic Priest)

"The Church has a very large say in the lives of the people here. It's true in any Catholic area. Here the Church is still the strongest. The vast majority of this area despise Sinn Fein and the IRA." (Craigneill resident, born and working on the estate)

Nevertheless there is a sense that the commitment of young people is less than it was. This may mean that Derry Catholics are slightly less loyal than they were. In local terms this is perceived as an important change.

"I do believe that the Roman Catholic Church is speaking to the people. But 99.9% of the young people aren't going to mass. My son says - 'All those people just have long faces. Why don't they have the music like the coloured people do?' Every Sunday priests will read out for the dead, the sick and so on. Quite a lot don't pray for people in prison every week." (Craigneill resident, male)

The guesstimate of 99.9% contradicts the evidence of attendance at the mission and any weekly observation at the gates of the Church. Nevertheless the implication that increasing numbers of young Catholics view the Church critically is confirmed by people who work for the Church.

"There's two different things. Rejection and a sense that the obligation is not taken so seriously. In morality, young people are talking about things we never talked about; abortion, drinking, drugs, homosexuality. You have to talk about it to be fashionable. There' is a greater emphasis on the social awareness of these things and less of an emphasis on their rightness and wrongness. Sometimes it seems that all these issues are coming so thick and fast that they might lose sight of the gospels and they appear irrelevant. The gospels are as relevant now as they were 2,000 years ago. Our task is to make them relevant. If we go in and talk about

the ten commandments people drag you off into a conversation about premarital sex or relationships. We have to make the timeless teaching of Christ relevant.... I was talking to a nephew of mine who is 17 and it's a whole different lifestyle between me and him. The struggle is both ways. We have to struggle to keep au fait with their thinking. The way to talk to young people is anything but moralising. My natural way, I must admit, out of my training is to say 'you must', 'you ought', 'you should do this' 'you shouldn't do that'. You don't go up and say 'Were you at mass?'. They just seize up. It has no point." (Catholic Priest)

"We try to meet people in all the important times of their lives: birth, baptism, first communion, marriage, bereavement and death. We try to visit people too. It's a terrible discipline when there's other distractions." (Catholic Priest)

The Protestant Churches, as elsewhere, have lower attendance rates than the Catholic Church. There are markedly lower attendance's at Church in Working-class estates. Even here Churches retain close links with the cultural life of the community compared to many similar situations in other countries and for many people they remain personally central.

"My work for the WCA Centre has made me much closer to God now. Alone, I couldn' t do it. Its not as easy as just switching off at 5 o' clock. When I think things are bad, the strength comes through." (Church of Ireland, man)

"I would say that the Presbyterian Church is very evangelical. I wouldn't consider my own Church very evangelical. I don' t imagine the congregation would feel too strongly about the Billy Graham business. I would describe them as Churchy. It frustrates me a bit. I'm a strong member of the Church of Ireland. I have strong evangelical tendencies but I wouldn't call myself an evangelical. I do think, for Christ to mean anything, you need a personal relationship with Jesus Christ. Having said that, there are things about evangelical Christians which really turn me off; attitudes to Roman Catholics, some of the traditional approaches to the bible. But the evangelical Churches do have an influence on people's lives. There are a lot of people are 'habitual attenders in Churches.... Where the evangelicals are positive is that they encourage people to take Jesus seriously and to question their commitment to God." (Church of Ireland, woman)

"RE is taught by all teachers. I feel its a very important thing. We'd have, I hope, a balance between child centred and bible-centred approach. We rely on Stranmillis system heavily. Three teachers hold a Scripture Union Group. It's very well attended. They have a weekend away. R.E. is not necessarily an extension of the home. Thirty per cent of the children wouldn't go to Sunday School, mainly those from the housing estates." (Teacher, P.S., Presbyterian)

"We meet twice on Sunday. We've Sunday School in the morning. In the afternoon we have a children's meeting. The afternoon meeting has children from other Churches. We have maybe 60 or 70 children. The children range from 3 to 16. Choruses, Quiz, memory verses, bible story. I see the work with children as very important." (Free Presbyterian)

"To me religious and moral teaching go hand in hand. I don't think it should be given up. Children have to see that there is a purpose in life and Jesus is focal to that." (Presbyterian man)

"The Church has helped me to put a strong faith at the centre of my life. It helps me stay within limits. Without it I don't know where I'd be." (Methodist man)

The overriding impression in the Waterside was that for those in attendance at Church, their relationship to faith, Church and God was a central issue. Presbyterians tended to characterise themselves as 'evangelical' although usually with qualifications. Often there was a sense that the word itself was open to misinterpretation. There were also housing estates where attendance at Church was sporadic if ever. For many in Protestant areas the Church was peripheral to their conscious life. It is important to note however that hurts by Churches left deep scars in those who felt they had been wronged.

"My last and final criticism of the Presbyterian Church was a Wednesday night Prayer Group. Our Minister wanted a big gathering every Wednesday. Before this they had set up home cells. I had mine all set up and he wanted us all in the Church. He broke up my group. I had 2 who were coming to the Lord. They wouldn't go to the church because it's too hoytee-toytee. That Church is only bricks and mortar. The real Church is people. Breaking up that group was violence to me. I've not been back

to that Church since. I'm moving to another Presbyterian Church. When he took away my group from me I felt very threatened.." (Presbyterian woman)

"I have a mentally handicapped grandson. I took him up to the Hospital. I met a pillar of the Church up there and he said - 'May, I don' t see you at Church these days.' I says to him 'Do you want me to take him?', meaning my grandson. He says to me ' could you not get somebody to mind him? Do you not know how good fellowship is?' They talk about Prods and Taigs. If they talked about Christianity and faith it'd be a lot better." (Presbyterian woman)

"The thing that causes the most problems is the ministers. They say 'you have to go', 'you must go', 'you ought to be there'. To me its a voluntary thing. Church is about God, full stop. I believe in God very strongly, but the Church... no fun. My brother joined the cathedral choir. He took a lot of stick from the other boys in the choir. He was bullied and left. The minister came and asked him why he left. My brother was scared to tell him so he said 'I'd rather play football. The minister said straight out 'Well I know which is more important and it' is not football . ' Then my mummy said 'he's not telling the truth. He's being bullied.' The minister just said 'That doesn' t happen'. We said 'it does' but the minister didn't want to know. For me the biggest problem is the hypocrites because of all the backstabbing that goes on. It's not Christianity. There' is no charity in their behaviour. Another thing I don' t like is the accounts. They publish the names and addresses and how much you pay. I don't agree with it. The hypocrites look down the list. I've done it myself. I've looked down the list. Isn't that a terrible thing?" (Church of Ireland, woman)

"I had a daughter who had a miscarriage. She got pregnant out of marriage. Another member of the Church was lying in the hospital beside her. Our minister came in and passed my daughter because she was unmarried and went to the next bed. My daughter felt terrible about that. She said to me ' I felt like a leper.' It's like the Levi and the Samaritan." (Presbyterian, woman)

Of course, the demands on the clergy are enormous in this respect. Every flaw or mistake can have repercussions far wider than might be expected. Aside from the various sides to each case, perceived snubs or failings are considered important and remembered. In a sense it illustrates a desire to keep the Churches on a pedestal. The fact that the wound is so deep illustrates the degree to which people look to the Churches to act perfectly. This is certainly behind the overriding sense among Church-critics that the Churches are full of hypocrisy.

Nevertheless the Churches on all sides remain among the most important central points for their communities. The link between the two, the religious and political was alluded to by one person directly.

"The new chapel is called the St. Teresa's was opened in 1981 and is probably the most expensive building in the area. The chapel is served by two priests who reside in the adjoining parochial house. The chapel provides a meeting place for the residents and is well attended and supported (judging from the amount collected weekly in such a deprived area (approximately £2,000 per week) figure taken from parish bulletin) by the people area who clean the chapel on a voluntary basis. At times of elections, posters are displayed around and en-route to the chapel, so it is seen as a gathering point by the would-be politicians" (Craigneill resident)

The Church as gathering point for politics provides a clue about the nature of the link between the two. It suggests that at Church people do not only listen to the clergy but feel themselves to be together. The Churches are then important places for meeting, persuading and influencing others. This does not need to be a conscious manipulation. Indeed it probably works precisely because the political agenda operates below and within the religious purpose. The cultural and political importance of the Churches begins to be visible. Of course the influences will be different everywhere depending at least on the relationship of clergy to laity and the nature of events outside the Church.

On the Protestant side, the Churches are also present through clergy, ritual and regular services in 'Protestant Organisations' such as the Orange Order and the Apprentice Boys. In this case the inter-relationship of Church and politics is seen to be intricately interwoven into aspects of life beyond Church-buildings.

The Churches and social life

The Churches in Derry provide much of the structure of community life. As elsewhere this is based on the network of clubs, groups and organisations which are based in the Churches and which involve both active Church members and others who have association only through the organisations.

*"If you hadn't got a car you'd never go to Craigneill from Glendean. The predominant thing that would bind together are siblings and relations and the Church. There wouldn't be much social interchange apart from the Church. We also have Apostolic societies; we have St. Vincent de Paul. Those in it are from all over the place.. St. Vincent de Paul isn't officially under parish control but it works in the parish. Officially it's run from Dublin. The only time I saw Dublin involved was with the distribution of the EEC butter. They have a weekly meeting where they pray and then they have a meeting about who needs help and how to help. They often give things like a bag of coal rather than money... We also have the Legion of Mary. They're more spiritual but they do things like visit the old and the lonely. We have Youth clubs and things like that. We have a very reliable group of parish people. Basically what we're always trying to do is be aware of the needs of the poor. We're also doing work with the handicapped. It's the age of these groups. There's hardly a week goes by without a new group springing up." (*Catholic priest)

*"Most people would say that the Church has brought a heart to the Waterside. We've tons of organisations. We don't use them as a recruiting centre, but because our youth organisations have grown a lot of people have been affected. Their minister (me) was until illness an enthusiast." (*Presbyterian minister)

"We ran this course three or four years ago. It attracted mainly Grammar School pupils. They stayed for three or four years. They all did A-levels and faded out. I was anxious to start another but this time not for Grammar Schools only. We moved to Craigneill rather than Clonmore Avenue. We have attracted some of the Secondary ones. They get on very well. I'd also be involved in a woman's group on a Thursday morning. I hope it'll be a group to develop their own self-worth. I do family visitation. Only through meeting them in their own homes do you get to know them." (Catholic sister)

The Churches provide a wide variety of organisations in the Waterside. As elsewhere the organisations tend to be parallel especially between denominations but also between parishes and congregations of the same denominations. This is partly the result of tradition and also the result of fear. The Waterside Youth club is seen as Catholic territory. Because of fear of intimidation on the way to the club the young Catholics of Craigneill would be loath to go as well;

"We have a Youth Fellowship. Our folk wouldn't go to the youth club on the Glendean Road. There wouldn''t be much come and go. When I first came here there was a bit of rioting between Carnpatrick and Craigneill and I would go up and try and stop it. Because we'd had discos in the Church I knew them all." (Church of Ireland Rector)

"Waterside Youth Club is on Glendean Road. People from this area [Craigneill] wouldn't use it because mini-riots develop at flashpoints along the way. Waterside Youth Club is the parish club. There's also Kilfinn Youth Club. It's a controlled club, so it's Protestant so the kids certainly wouldn't go. Carnpatrick is tarred as Loyalist. There were nightly riots through the seventies, well stone-throwing. Everyone knew about the riots... Kilfinn Youth Club was wrong for the climate." (Youth Worker, Craigneill)

The Churches are part of integrated networks of clubs in their own communities. Yet even between Protestant Churches and between congregations mixing is normally confined to competitions or special events. This is 'normal', in the sense that clubs and societies in Churches belong to a parish or congregation everywhere, not just in Northern Ireland. The main difference seems to be that in the Waterside separation has serious undercurrents of fear not apparent elsewhere. Between Protestants there is some intermingling through Church events.

"We've two bowling tournaments every year and people come from all sides. That would be the extent of our cross-community relations.... Church attendance hasn't really dropped. We've built a new Church. The troubles hasn't affected attachment to Church. Nobody has ever used the Church politically. At this time of the year you have services for the Orange, Black and Apprentice Boys. Every Protestant Church takes part in the rota. Some of the Orangemen go to Church every week of course. The services would be on Sunday evenings because they wouldn' t all be one denomination. It's the done thing. We'd have more members not in the Orders than in them. The Orange people are very moderate. The Apprentice Boys are stronger. Ian Paisley has been strengthening his hand in them. The secretary of the Apprentice Boys is studying to be a Presbyterian minister. He had a brother-in-law shot. They emphasise that the scriptures containing all things necessary to salvation which I agree with." (Church of Ireland Rector)

The Apprentice Boys and the Orange Order are important parts of Protestant life on the Waterside. They act as umbrella organisations between Protestant denominations and between active and non-active Church goers. This integrating function remains important despite decline in membership.

The troubles have meant that the city centre remains underused, especially by Protestants who regard the City side as 'foreign territory'. The main competitors to Church organisations are therefore pubs and clubs. For young Protestants the flute and accordion marching bands also play an important part in cultural life. For young Catholics the rise of Derry City Football Club has been of major importance.

"There has been an unbelievable change. I've noticed that they're tidying up the estate. Vandalism has really dropped. There has been a big effect of Derry City Football Club. At breaktime people play football in the street not go around vandalising which is what they used to do. I don't think people give enough credit to the effect of sport." (Sec. School headmaster)

"Protestants don't involve themselves in the larger community. The activities on the City side, the Arts and Derry City are seen as irrelevant to them. They relate more to things in Coleraine, in Belfast and to Glasgow Rangers than to things here. People like myself are now saying 'lets get back into the city'. The Apprentice Boys have launched an exhibition on the siege and we're building a new historical and interpretive centre next to our premises in Society Street." (Protestant man)

"A disadvantage is that top-class athletics clubs are all nationalist. The best swimming club is nationalist. My son and his friend are the only Protestants in the Swimming club. The swimming club has a very high standard but there are location problems. A policemen couldn't pick up his children from the baths. My wife stupidly went over to collect them in her GB uniform. She was accosted by youths who accused her of being a policewoman. She was very shaken" (Presbyterian man)

The Churches are part of the backbone of social life in the community. Church attendance is not a prerequisite of association as we have seen with the Protestant organisations. The denominational divide is repeated between Catholics and Protestants with no large Intercommunity groups except in bowling leagues. The Parish in the Catholic community is the basic unit of local organisation. Unlike some areas of Belfast the gap between parish professionals and lay is not very apparent. On the Protestant side, Church attendance is less and membership of Church-based organisations is cemented by the Apprentice Boys, the Orange Order and the bands associated. While these are not 'Church organisations' their claims to the defence of scriptural truth and the support in religious circles means that the Church aspect is integral to their self-understanding. At the same time the Churches institutional influence over these organisations is not strong. Divisions between Protestants over support for the orders means that there is no 'Church position' on the orders.

The Churches and Public life

a. The Churches and community work, including unemployment and ACE.

The Waterside Churches have to minister in an area faced with an acute shortage of jobs, particularly in the late 1970s and early 1980s. In common with the rest of Northern Ireland the depression has hit hard. Traditionally Derry Protestants were employed. The latest recession has changed this picture with widespread unemployment hitting both communities. The Catholic community, victims of systematic discrimination in the city for some time, have long adapted to a life based on widespread unemployment. In many cases the women of the family have found work before the men, often in low paid factory work. The largest employers in the area are public sector, civil service, health service, DHSS and local government. The largest private employer is Dupont a major multi-national textiles manufacturer with a large plant on the Northeast edge of the city.

The result is a legendary reliance on government injections of funds and high levels of unemployment. The other semi-permanent feature of Derry life has been emigration and a serious drain of people away from the area to England, Scotland and America. Traditionally this has been associated with Catholic families. In recent times, the advent of a centralised university admissions administration for the United Kingdom (UCCA) and a general depression in the Protestant community has led to a serious exodus of Protestant young people, especially the highly motivated and educated.

Unemployment is regarded by many people as the real problem in the city, above any considerations of Intercommunity conflict;

"Craigneill/Brian's Hill has an overall unemployment rate of approximately 55% with the rate varying among different age groups. Unemployment increases to a staggering 68% for heads of household. Duration of unemployment is also high with 68% of those unemployed being long-term unemployed, i.e. out of work for 2 years or more. From these statistics it is self-evident the scale and seriousness of unemployment in the area." (Local report on the Craigneill area, March 1988)

"The biggest problem is no job in front of you. The choice open to them is not good. A lot of girls are into the factory or check-out Girls seem to do better than boys for jobs." (Female teacher, Craigneill)

"The tragedy is that the type of person, and I can think of 50, who've left Londonderry who've gone to Scotland and England, sadly won't come back and put input into Northern Ireland and Londonderry in particular. We can't afford it as a community. They don't come back. Those young people, 75% don't come back. Our leadership in the Church is middle-aged. The youngsters who do stay are not leadership material." (Presbyterian minister)

Unemployment and emigration automatically lead to a degree of poverty and demoralisation in the community. The advent of ACE has meant that funds have been provided from central government for Church-based projects. On the Waterside, the Protestant Churches entered into the question of coping with unemployment for the first time. The City side Catholic Church had long been involved in welfare advice centres and in coordinating social programmes. For the Protestant Churches this was a very new experience.

"A phonecall came to me from Bishop Mehaffy asking me to represent him at a meeting convened by Derry Presbytery. I met with the moderator of the Presbytery and the chairman of the Methodist circuit and two laymen from their Churches... Really the meeting was a talking shop. We had a lot of prayer. We realised that we couldn't move forward without the Roman Catholics. Bishop Daly obliged. We were lucky in the moderator of the Presbytery that year. We formed a standing committee. We saw that the economy was going so bad that we would hold a Day of Prayer in all Churches in the city on the economy. We decided to hold an ecumenical service and we invited David Bleakley down. It was very well attended...

We decided to lobby the DED. We discovered that the Jobmarket for Derry was on the West Bank beside the barracks behind three barricades. At that time there was no other Job Information Centre. People with security forces connections wouldn' t go. We told the DED .that we wanted a High Street Job Market. They couldn't provide that but they agreed to post all the details of jobs in all libraries and resource centres.

Clergy, we found, were very bad. They' re out of Grammar School, into College and then they're into looking after the unemployed. We organised group visits of clergy to job markets and to DSSOs. We took them in groups. We also ran courses with the Churches Central Committee on Community Work on counselling the unemployed as people. We did a survey of all the Churches asking us to tell us how many of their congregations were unemployed. On the Protestant side the figures didn' t tally. People weren't telling their clergy. They weren' t admitting to it. One person I met in the Crown Buildings didn' t want people to know. Another man I knew withered away and died. I made myself available and the clergy sent people to me. I put it down to the Protestant work ethic...

By 1982-3 the ACE scheme was becoming big... We discovered then that we had a blank area in the city the Waterside. The Shantallows, Creggans, Craigneills were very well equipped with Welfare Rights and street knowledge about dealing with unemployment. So we set up the Waterside Churches in Action..." (Male, ACE manager)

The Waterside Churches in Action (WCA) is the formal structure for Church ACE work, voluntary work and other schemes for the whole area. The committee now has a considerable budget and also maintains numerous attachments outside the Waterside. Unusually, the committee has the full participation of Catholic, Presbyterian, Church of Ireland and Methodist Churches in the area. This fact is, not surprisingly, always mentioned by everyone involved. The committee does not extend to the Cityside Churches although several groups on the west bank are linked to the WCA. The committee is composed of representatives of these four denominations. The group meets monthly and consists of four clergy and four lay representatives from each of the Churches and one co-opted member. The chairmanship is always clerical and rotates annually. Staff are also represented.

"We are unique in Northern Ireland in that there is active involvement of

*all. Each Church is represented at every meeting. The chairmanship is always in the hands of the clergy but it rotates every year. I find it very interesting that as each one comes and goes they have their own way of 'going mad' as ! say. Every year I say 'what is your pet theme?' ... This year its 'Care for the carers', or looking after our workers." (*ACE co-ordinator)

*"People prefer clerical chairs in relations with agencies. We've a rotating chair. It's very important that there's a RC priest as chairman. The year you' re chairman you're talking 10 hours work a week. It works." (*Presbyterian Minister, committee member)

The Committee moved quickly into the setting up of premises and a rapid expansion of the amount of work channelled through their hands;

"In February 1983 the committee came together to see about relevant action. They decided to give it one more go and open a voluntary advice centre in a flat above a pub. This horrified the Methodists and Presbyterians. They asked two of us to man it on a voluntary basis. It became clear that we would have to get into Welfare Rights..

We opened our doors from April 1983. From May it became clear that the need was there. It was suggested that it be opened permanently and that we use ACE. I was employed as an ACE worker. I was then long-term unemployed. We now generate £700.000 through wages, overheads and the European Social Fund. We have 130 workers. We also have the Voluntary Work Bureau in the City Centre and he has 185 Volunteers. We employ 121 ACE Workers, 5 Core workers and 6 permanent staff.

*We dealt with 745 people in 1983. Last year we dealt with 22,480. This is not only Welfare Rights. We cover Welfare Rights, a Job Information Service which is provided by the Job Market. People can make phonecalls here for free. At night our jobs board is placed in the window so we have a 24 hour service. Then we do home visiting, which I see as an extension to the weak in society bringing a Christian thrust to the work. As well there is a home decorating service, a gardening service, a small repairs service, a community garden and we have a training service for ACE workers. We try to work to improve their marketability. We want to care for the carers too. We could do more than that for them. We have an escort service for the elderly as well." (*ACE Coordinator)

"Early in 1983 I was invited to a meeting in the Methodist Hall. At this meeting, attended by representatives of the clergy and laity of the four main Churches in Waterside, the general discussion centred on the twin issues of unemployment in the area and the need for a local Job Centre. There was also reference made to the possibility of some kind of joint action by the local Churches to establish a centre where people of every denomination in any kind of social need could receive Christian help and practical advice... Little did the original committee members imagine that in five years there would be two offices in the city employing well over a hundred people and generating almost three quarters of a million pounds into the local economy." (Catholic priest, past chairman of WCA)

The Committee also took over volunteering for the whole city, Waterside and City side with an office in the city centre.

"We set up the Advice Centre on the Waterside. We were asked by the DED if we would take over responsibility for the Community Volunteering Scheme for Counties Londonderry, Fermanagh and Tyrone. We decided to run the scheme in two ways. We have the Volunteering for the City through the bureau. Then we developed the concept of a Volunteer Managing Agency. These all use volunteers. Through the DED we fund groups. We've lost Fermanagh and we've gone into North Antrim. We have 50 agencies where we have volunteer input - from Age Concern to Mencap. We give them money to keep them going in difficult circumstances. For example in one council with DUP control, a Citizen's Advice Bureau was set up. Because there were a number of Sinn Fein Councillors on the Management Committee the Council wouldn't fund it. So we stepped in. Another example is one where the army had a surplus but which they couldn't give directly to the community, no way. So they gave it to me. I will give it to a playgroup in the fullness of time." (Volunteer scheme co-ordinator)

The WCA has a volunteering sub-committee. The work of the Volunteer Bureau extends to setting up employment schemes in Coleraine between the Churches (111 ACE Workers) and developing schemes from Ballymoney to Enniskillen. All this is officially under the auspices of the Waterside Churches. The result is a strain between the scope of the co-ordinating body, the Churches and the job being undertaken.

For many in the Churches the WCA is a shining example of cross-community co-operation in the city, unique in Northern Ireland. For others, it is a flag of convenience which channels DED money into projects which could be done by community groups.

"There isn't a very strong ecumenism... One thing we have that is significant is the WCA Centre. It has been a great success story. In Ecumenical terms they are first of all employing people, Protestant and Catholic. We feel very proud of it." (Catholic priest)

"I think our contact is good on community work, especially down at Thomas Street in the Churches Centre." (Methodist Minister)

"The Advice Centre works. It's not just for government benefits. It's not a government quango, it's to minister to the needs of the community." (Presbyterian Minister)

"The example of Christ was a social ministry. I think that we can become so heavenly minded that we' re no earthly use. I'd like to think that my congregation knows this. I think that the WCA Centre is a tremendous example of co-operation." (Presbyterian Minister)

"I read about somebody who visited Thomas Street and was delighted at the 'cross-community work'. I'm a cynic. As far as I'm concerned I think the Churches have failed miserably." (ACE Worker)

"The 'Churches' label on this work makes no difference. It's an opportunity to work with the unemployed. The money is coming from the government and rightly so. Anybody else could have set up this office. It hasn't made any difference to the spirit or ethos of the work." (Volunteer co-ordinator)

"The Waterside Churches were approached by the DED to set up a volunteering agency. They didn't want to give the money to a community group." (ACE worker)

The difficulties in Derry as a whole, and the relationship of the Waterside to the rest of the city are highlighted by the problems faced by the Voluntary Bureau in the City Centre in recruiting Waterside Volunteers.

"The cross-community thing is wide open. Because of where we are in the city centre it's nearly 100% Catholic. At the beginning there were more

Protestants. I would have between 50 and 60 volunteers getting expenses each week. Only three come from the Waterside. So this is not really anything to do with anything cross-community. It's purely geographical and physical. Probably if the office was on the Waterside people wouldn't go across from here" (City Volunteering Co-ordinator)

The centre on the Waterside itself does appear to have people seeking advice and help as well as workers from both communities.

"Our workforce comes from the whole city. The friendships created in the 12 months last long past the twelve months. That too is a bonus. We're in this world such a short time and the hurt and hardship in the community breaks my heart... We get people in from the whole Waterside coming in here and everybody is equally welcome." (ACE Worker)

The political and spiritual impact of Churches are deeply entangled in this situation. Any gesture which includes Protestant and Catholic Church institutions in Northern Ireland is in itself cross-community. In this sense it has a symbolic political impact on the area. The employment policy of the Advice Centre is crosscommunity and the people using the services also come from both communities. This in itself is a matter for comment in Northern Ireland. The Volunteer Bureau on the City side has not been able to draw people from the Waterside largely as a result of political geography. Local people are clearly prepared to use the Churches facilities, mostly seeing it as a business transaction. Where this would involve a longer-term commitment to a city group, such as the Volunteer Bureau, Waterside Protestants have not availed themselves.

Church involvement in the ACE system amounts to the representatives on the committee (9) and the personal commitments of staff and workers, who may or not regard themselves as Churchgoers. Funding comes from the DED and a consultation at the centre covers areas covered by other non-Church centres. In this sense the WCA can be seen as a token gesture by the Churches in Waterside which diverts attention away from their real divisions and allows them to avoid real engagement with one another. Very few people in congregations and parishes regard the Advice Centre as a matter of personal commitment. The very fact of semiprofessional or at least paid care may lead to a disinterest in the rest of the community towards neighbourly care and may act to give an appearance of cross community care which belies a more prosaic reality: in a time of unemployment people will take ACE money from anybody. In addition the Churches may be acting to preserve their own sense of institutional importance by being the apparent benefactors of the community, in fact receiving money which would otherwise go to less hierarchical community groups with lay chairpeople.

At the same time it could be argued that without clerical leadership the firm cross-community stance of the WCA could never be repeated nor recognised. No other institutions have the same degree of support, the same symbolic cultural importance or the same general acceptability as the Churches. The very Church-based framework of the organisation may allow that meetings take place which might otherwise be impossible. The real meetings beyond the normal dividing lines may have more to do with the fact that Catholics and Protestants work together than in any Church input. Certainly changes have occurred;

*"People say that local peace groups and wee groups here and there are doing more than the official Church. I mean you can have all the bishops smiling and drinking champagne but it doesn't change a thing. It's not where the problem lies. It meant more to me when a lad from the Waterside came in here after two months working and said 'If I'd have known you were an f***ing nun I'd never have come in here"* (Volunteer co-ordinator)

"Yesterday a deaf girl who worked for us left. She was a brilliant girl. Very efficient, a secretary. So nice you could eat her. Her problem was that she couldn't answer the phone. But we are much better people because she was here. We all speak slower, we can use signs and she was always so happy. She made us happy." (ACE co-ordinator)

These small personal encounters with difference are certainly important. Nevertheless they appear to happen behind rather than because of the facade of organised ACE work, the result of personal relationship rather than government or Church-institutional programming. ACE for Churches also poses another problem; professionalism. The strength of Churches is traditionally the strong networks of community which they provide, and a sense of belonging. ACE seems to be an attempt to pay for actions which were once voluntary or the object of state funded jobs - visitation of old people, repairs, tidying up vandalism and so on. Badly handled, ACE may destroy the value of personal contact, making all the 'helped' the objects of impersonal attention only given because it is a job. At the same time it may act as a mechanism by which permanent jobs are replaced by temporary jobs at cheaper rates. They also stray into the domains of social and community work, both of which regard themselves as closed professions.

"We try to steer clear of professionalism because we don't want to be classed as part of the establishment. We are 'gifted amateurs'. I was also told by a Social Worker that 'you're not a caring service. You can't care, you're not professionals.' I said 'We're in 'he field of human concern". Mind you, the vast majority of professionals are very helpful. We refer to them and they to us. There's a mutual respect." (ACE co-ordinator)

Certainly there are fears that Church involvement means an extension of the economic clout of the institution against ordinary people. While such complaints are few and far between in Waterside though there are hints in local attitudes to the Craigneill Family Centre, the other major Church-based ACE-scheme on the Waterside.

The Family Centre in Craigneill grew out of the work of the parish sisters rather than that of the clergy.

"I was told that another sister wanted to set up a Family Centre up in Derry. I thought this was a great cause and I went up with a specific goal. She'd got a couple of residents together for a committee. We lobbied the Housing Executive for a house which we got and we lobbied for a seeding grant from the City Council which we got. This was in 1978. We started just the two of us and we got a 'Young Help'... Gradually we got furniture together. We appointed ourselves then. We got the local school principal interested and an accountant for a while. We got our chairs from a local activist in Brian's Hill. At that time the Community Centre was very powerful. We went to a to a particularly strong member of their committee and told him we wanted to set up and that we weren't in competition. From the outside it looked as though we were in competition. A lot of members of our committee would have nothing to do with the Community Centre. The City Council supported us, although every year they'd give out to us and tell us they were going to reduce our grant." (Parish sister)

The Family Centre is seen as part of local politics. The Community Centre was seen as having strong Sinn Fein links. The Family Centre was identified with the Church.

"When I first went to the Family Centre I would have been a bit

embarrassed because it would be seen as a bit Churchy, SDLPish. That has changed a bit since the sisters stopped being in charge. It's the only thing with ACE on the estate. The Community Centre was closed down. No funds. It would have been regarded locally as Sinn Fein. A lot of people wouldn't have let their children go to it. Derry City Council took it over and they open it up on certain days. The keys are kept in the Guildhall." (ACE Worker, Family Centre)

"The local Community Centre is presently closed down by the City Council. It was stigmatised as being run by Sinn Fein and as such never enjoyed the support of all the community. Some people would not attend the centre or allow their children to do so. The closing of the centre was the result of the committee falling away over a period of time and no new members wanted to become involved. Residents got together to protest against the closure but their action was not strong enough and was not supported by all residents. The community centre had been used for Irish Dancing, Bingo, Pre-school playgroup and Barnardo's had an after-schools project there." (Local resident, male)

"There's a Community Centre. The Craigneill Estate began in 1967. The Community Centre was thriving. The Community Association was running the Centre very well in the early 70s. In my opinion over a period of time the place was taken over by Sinn Fein. Between two and three years ago the City Council took over the Centre and closed it. Now the Council has re-opened it. Application to use it has to go to the Council. They hold the keys. But it's very limited use. A group of families and now a new Boxing Club use it. The Community Association fizzled out. It has not been in existence since the early 70s. The bulk of the population in the area don't want anything to do with Sinn Fein. The quiet majority want no part in that." (Local resident, teacher)

The Community Centre now stands as a mostly empty shell on the estate. The new Youth Club is in the Secondary School rather than the Centre. The Family Centre has become the centre for ACE work, Welfare Rights and other supportive facilities.

"If people want to contact an outside organisation like the Housing Executive they would normally use the Family Centre as they are seen to have more contact with outside organisations." (Local resident)

The split between the Church and Sinn Fein on Craigneill is much more heavily weighted in favour of the Church than in parts of West Belfast. The rivalry between the two groups is therefore less intense. The work of the Family Centre increased dramatically with the arrival of ACE.

"The ACE scheme took over in 1980. Our first ACE worker for Welfare Rights came in 1980. I got into Welfare Rights too and thoroughly enjoyed it and it was helpful too. We sisters did the course in Community Studies at the University. It was great cause we made good contacts." (Parish Sister)

"Initially this was started by two nuns as an Advice Centre. When the ACE scheme started we were able to build up to 21 ACE workers. I myself am funded by the Western Health and Social Services Board." (Family Centre Co-ordinator)

"We have various branches. We've Welfare Rights who deal with benefits. We're a referral agency. We're not professionals, we're a voluntary agency. We can refer them to people who do know something. We do some counselling. That was the initial reason why the Family Centre came into existence. There was nothing here. We have 2 visitors who go round Craigneill and Brian's Hill. It's a visitation service for the elderly and a drop in centre. We've just established a pensioners club. We're fund-raising for that and the WHSSB have shown a keen interest. We also have a children's Club for 6-11 year olds after school. It meets in the High school. The local Headmaster lets us use the school. He's great. The board and headmaster are very good. With just the two flats here we've no room. We have a summer scheme for 6-11 year olds. We also have a Drama group and a Discovery Group for 11-19 year olds linked in with the local Church. We also have a Community development worker. We run classes in the school with the Worker's Education Association and the Tech. We have crocheting, maths, keepfit and flower arranging. We've also set up a woman's studies group with the 'Tech. The core of it was the Mother and Toddler Group. It was a 10 week course originally. It was very popular. What happens now is up to them. The Community Development Officer is responsible for that. He puts out a newssheet. It's hand delivered to every house in this area, that's over 600... We also have an environmental team who decorate homes and tidy up the place for pensioners and the disabled. They also do gardens as well as internal decoration." (Family Centre Manager)

The Family Centre is the main employer on the estate. Apart from shops, school and the Church there is no employment directly on the estate. A Welfare Rights Service is well-used in such circumstances.

*"The aim of the Family Centre was to help people on the estate, to give people a place if they wanted help with welfare or a listening ear. It developed with ACE into a way of giving people employment." (*Parish Sister)

*"There isn't really anything for men. Maybe the football. As far as discussion is concerned they're immovable. Even the pensioners club would be mostly women. The young fellas are great - the environmental team is mostly young lads. The visitors are women. The Youth and Community and Community Development workers are men. The Youth and Community jobs aren't one or the other. The women are more full of chat for the visitors." (*Family Centre worker)

In 1986-7 the Family Centre initiated a survey of the area. The survey was a means of assessing local perceptions of priorities and of bringing together the various groups on the estate. The survey committee consisted of representatives of the Family Centre, Derry City Council, the local school, community centre, Waterside Youth Club, Parish officials, a local cooperative enterprise, the Forum for Community Work Education and a representative from the University.

*"The survey seemed to go on for so long... The ACE system didn't seem to work for the survey because people had to leave before it was done. The actual survey took a lot of time to do. Then we got the report published. The point was to find out the needs and to get the group together." (*Parish sister, Family Centre)

*"The survey was the ticket to get people to listen to us. Before people went to complain and nobody listened. Now they're going to call a public meeting and hope to restart the tenant's association. This is fraught with the danger that it might be taken over. We must get enough response in order to get the association to voice the opinion of the majority." (*Local resident)

"There is a lot of organisations doing their own little thing in their own

way but there was no collective action until the Top o' the Hill survey in 1986 and 1987. For the first time ever all the groups in the area met to discuss what should be done to improve living standards.. This excluded Sinn Fein who had members present belonging to other groups and were able to keep abreast of developments. We got together and managed to organise a very intensive survey which will be used to build a case for the area when looking for funding for employment projects from Government bodies." (Local resident)

The survey looked at many aspects of deprivation in the Craigneill / Brian's Hill area; housing, unemployment, social facilities, transport, shopping and amenities. Although, in a sense, the survey quantified what local people already knew, it had important results as a community venture. Through the survey, general complaints were expressed in formal language, suitable for dealings with public bodies. The Family Centre was shown to be the amenity used by the largest numbers of people in the area. Some 54% claimed to have some contact compared with 27% who had contact with the Community Centre before it was closed, 21% who used the school and 21% who attended parish hall social functions.

In 1988 the running of the Family Centre passed from the Sisters into lay hands. The Sisters remain represented on the Management Committee but the affairs of the Centre are co-ordinated by a lay person. The clergy role is also limited to membership of the management committee.

"We were set up by the sisters. The Parish priest was good to us, he nearly ignored us. We had a curate on the committee but he never tried to control the meeting. (Parish sister)

"We have membership which nominates the committee. People are members throughout the Waterside. In fact we only deal with Craigneill and Brian's Hill .. The membership would vote for the committee. We don't have that many members... Membership here is by invitation. It has kept out Sinn Fein. It's understandable. The fact that we've survived while the Community Centre closed is maybe because of this. The Committee does the asking. People can put themselves forward. I'm more pragmatic. I'm trying to keep the kids going and the pensioners going. We're just providing opportunities. We're not acting 'against' any big opposition. Some of them use the advice centre. I don't think there is any feeling of 'You don' t go near the Family Centre..' I don't ask the

workforce what their political affiliations are. That's not what we're about." (Family Centre Manager)

The Family Centre is in an interesting political position. Clearly identified with Church people, it is not regarded as being clerical except in a management capacity. This may in part be through the roots of the Centre in the work of nuns who have now withdrawn into a background role. The funding of the Family Centre has not come under any threat due to political pressure and the Family Centre, though Church, is not seen as an anti Sinn Fein statement.

Through the Family Centre, Craigneill has separate ACE work provision to the rest of the Waterside. Relations with the WCA Advice Centre are cordial;

"We've very good relations with the WCA Centre. There would maybe be an understanding that we work up here and they do down there." (Family Centre manager)

"We're good friends with the WCA Centre. I knew them all and I'd consult by phone. We'd a great relationship between all the centres. The WCA Centre did up our place for us. People in the Waterside Advice Centre might have been scared to come to Craigneill." (Sister)

The Family Centre in Craigneill predates the WCA Centre by several years. The Craigneill ACE programme was in operation before that of the WCA. The degree of social deprivation on Catholic estates has meant that the Catholic Church in Derry has a much longer tradition of social advocacy through Benefit Rights than the Protestant Churches. The by-product is that Craigneill-Brian's Hill remains a class and religious ghetto, into which outsiders, Catholic and Protestant have no desire or no reason to venture. Even in a cooperative project such as the WCA, Craigneill sits separately.

At the same time the Craigneill project, especially through the survey is much more integrally linked to the community in which it lives than the Advice Centre. This has to do with the size of the area served and of the relationship of the Centre to the community. The fact that the Waterside Churches project is a joint project of presbytery, circuit and diocese means that outside the officers and workers few people in the Churches feel directly attached to it. The Family Centre too is run by a management committee, by nuns and by ACE workers but it clearly belongs in the community of Craigneill/Brian's Hill. The Centre has clearer relationships with other local groups. Perhaps too the relationship of religious orders, in this case nuns, to a community is different to that of clergy and is not coloured by the same relationships of tradition or authority. A more visible clerical presence may add authority outside the area and at the same time it may unbalance local relationships. This does not appear to be so true for nuns.

b. The Churches and Schools

The Waterside area has numerous schools in both the controlled and maintained sectors. Under the Catholic parish come three primary schools and a secondary school while the State sector has two primary schools in and a secondary school. None of the schools are single-sex, but the divide between State and Maintained, Catholic and Protestant, remains intact.

The State schools in the area take different approaches to the involvement of clergy in their schools. Both have roots in Church schools which were transferred into the State sector at a late stage. Both primary schools have grown in numbers due to movements in population.

"I came here in 1972 when this school had under 300 children and now it's over 600. This is accounted for by population shift. That shift has stopped because the community is more polarised. More or less, there are very few Protestants on the City side." (Headmaster, Foyle Heights Primary School)

"About 40% of our children are from families who moved from the City side. There's a trickle still. There' is also a trickle of people moving to England, Canada and Australia. We've lost 4 families this week. It keeps my numbers nearly static. I would lose 25 children a year from the city and gain a similar number from the City side.. Numbers have risen steadily. We'll be 580 in September, our absolute maximum." (Headmaster, Cairnhanna P.S.)

The State schools are nearly entirely Protestant. Parents in both schools come from many denominations. The schools have taken different approaches to their relationship to the denominations;

"Input from the clergy of the Churches is that once a fortnight 6 clergy come in, 3 Presbyterian and 3 Church of Ireland. They take assembly. They take classes for half an hour. They represent the transferrers. The

Methodists are smaller. They've expressed no desire to come in. We've two clergy on our Board of Governors though they are not in the chair." (Headmaster, Cairnhanna P.S.)

"We have Nine Governors on the Board of Governors. We have 2 parents representatives one of whom is a DUP councillor but he's on as a parents representative. That was an organised strategy. Then we've 2 reps for the WELB a teachers rep and 4 transferrers from Second Presbyterian one of whom is the minister. Normally the ministers from the denominations would come in and take assembly. I never fully agreed with that. I did not like denominational segregation. I saw it as a way of checking up on Sunday School attendance... We have assemblies on a non-denominational basis. Every month we have a special service. We use two non-denominational hymn books, a bible reading and I give an address. I'm speaking out of a genuine desire to hold my school together. We also have a monthly class service where the children take their own service on their own theme, the theme being left up to the class teachers. The teacher doesn't do it, the children do. We have hymn practices. We also have ordinary assembly and we involve the children. We've tried to make it as meaningful as possible for the children... At one stage we invited the parents along but we found that it became competitive, a way of comparing class with class. We also have an end of term service. We invite parents along to our Christmas evening. We do not have any doctrinal instruction in the school. Any parent is secure in the fact that their children will not find their parents beliefs being challenged. The only people we can't wholly satisfy are the Exclusive Brethren and Jehovah's Witnesses. The transferrers had some concerns in the beginning but now they are happy. We do have Scripture Union, but parents choose. Mostly we do the Stranmillis course." (Headmaster, Foyle Heights P.S.)

The relationship of the parish to the school is much closer on the Catholic side. The school calendar is also designed to ensure a central place for the preparation for the sacraments and regular visits by the local clergy.

Two of the primary schools are immediate neighbours of Churches emphasising with geography the degree to which the two are culturally linked.

"We would have a close contact with the other parish schools. We did confirmation together. We took the lead this year. Every third year we would do the confirmation in our Church. There's a chaplain attached to

every school and he's in and out all the time. He's in, I'm sure, three or four times a week. he's very happy to come. The one before him was very good. I'd never have any gripe with the attention we get. I want the link with the school. We do a lot of religious things here, all over in the Church. We would assume that we' re part of the bigger community. Personally I think it's very important. I don't think you can divorce it if education is relevant to everyday life." (Teacher, Catholic P.S.)

The primary schools on the Waterside all appear to regard religion as an important part of childhood education. Nevertheless, the Catholic Schools accepted the Church's institutional importance in this task much more fully than did the Protestants. As we have seen the Scripture Union was important in the Protestant schools.

"I'm sure there are 50-70 Roman Catholic children here. The problem we do encounter is that the P3s need to make their first communion. Some take their children away. We have to proceed so that integration just happens. All the children will be treated exactly the same. That guarantee has never been broken. To me religious and moral education go hand in hand. I don't think it should be given up. I think children have to see that there is a purpose in life and that Jesus is focal to that.. The Churches must come together to show unity. The lead must come from them. You'd find elements on both sides who when they speak they just drive the wedge deeper and deeper." (Headmaster, Foyle Heights P.S.)

"I'm pleased that religion is going to be retained as a compulsory element. I'm pleased that parents have the right to opt out. In 'The Way Forward' they're hoping for a common programme but as the tenets are so different I can' t see much progress there, particularly as the view of the Catholic Church is 'What we have we hold'. I applaud the sentiment. I realise that its an important goal.. I feel it's a very important thing. We'd have, I hope, a fine balance between child-centred and bible-centred approach. We rely heavily on Stranmillis. Three of the teachers hold a Scripture Union group after school. It's very well attended. They have weekends away." (Headmaster, Cairnhanna P.S.)

The religious divide is reflected in the schools, the traditional pattern in Northern Ireland. The exception to the rule is the Model Primary School on the City side. This is a State school but due to an open policy and the increasing imbalance of population on the West Bank the school has a majority of Catholic pupils. The Waterside has no such experiments. *"This is a Protestant area. This would be seen as Protestant school. Integration isn't on geographically."* (Teacher, Cairnhanna Primary School)

The schools have taken different approaches to the initiatives under the umbrella of 'Education for Mutual Understanding' (EMU). Those who have engaged in the programmes have also sometimes faced opposition from some groups and parents.

"The Western Board has majored on EMU. Last year 30 children from here and another local Catholic school went to Buffalo, New York. The parents came over here and then we had a follow up. Last year we had a joint P6 project with Glendean Road based on the Folk Park [Omagh]. Now we're doing an IBM 'Ten Steps Award' with the new Strabane school in mixed teams. We've 180 pupils involved in that. Inter-schools activities are encouraged. Parents are given the option to withdraw. We would have a wee bit of tension with the Free Presbyterian Church. They have withdrawn their children." (Headmaster, Cairnhanna P.S.)

"There is the possibility of contact mainly on the sporting field; Netball tournaments, football tournaments. We also have 'Share days' in the school when children come from other schools. We also take kids to other schools. That again is a sensitive area because of the parents." (Headmaster, Foyle Heights P.S.)

"We've links through Football with Foyle Heights and Cairnhanna. We also had a great time with the Ulster Orchestra. This EMU is a load of bull. That has been going on for 25 years without the money. As somebody said it's enforced mutual understanding. I'd have as many links with Cairnhanna as with Holy Faith (RC). Any links I have aren't enforced. I know them personally. I haven't done anything with EMU. I don't see how we could take a sizeable number. I haven't got involved. I don't need to. I think it's a fashion. What gets me is that it's mainly about school trips." (Headmaster, St. Teresa's, R.C. P.S.)

The secondary schools in the area are geographical neighbours. The one can be clearly seen from the other. Kilfinn High School backs onto the Craigneill estate but is separated from it by fencing. St. Colm's is in Craigneill and serves a large catchment area. For the Catholic school the link to the parish is a matter of course. It simply 'is'. The prime importance of the secondary school to the community is through its organisations rather than as a meeting point. This is in contrast to the primary and nursery schools in the area where parents, particularly mothers meet daily while collecting children.

"One important thing about the primary school is that it provides a meeting place for parents of younger children who gather to take the children to school in the mornings. Also parents get involved in the School sports day and also are invited to school plays or performances. This does not happen at the secondary school. The only time parents come to it outside curricular activities is to complain or when they are sent for by the head teacher." (Local resident)

"We've a Board of Governors. It's made up of parish representatives, two clergy and two parents and reps from the Board. One of the curates is chaplain to the school. I encourage them to come in in the break time. There's very good support within the school. I think the parish/school link is very important. I'm not a great believer in segregated education. I do see the importance of having some separate education. I think it's important that people have freedom. I think it is a good thing that the Church has its say. In the end they leave it up to the teaching professionals. The freedom is there." (Principal, Catholic Sec. School)

The Protestant school also has clergy on the Board of Governors but the links and expectations are less than in a primary school. Religious Instruction is through Assemblies and through R. E. There was a strong sense that Religious Education was given a much lower priority in State schools though for some R.E. in school was very important:

"I was brought up in the Church of Ireland. I wouldn't see the Church as responsible for my developing interest in R.E. For me it was in school. When I was confirmed I was going through the motions. For me it was Scripture Union and teachers who influenced me. After doing 'O' levels I decided that I would like to teach R.E... When I look at Roman Catholic Schools in the City I get quite jealous of the importance the subject is given. Here there is always the feeling that it is an added extra." (Teacher, Kilfinn Sec. School)

School Buildings are also important resources in impoverished communities. The Secondary School in Craigneill is an important centre for the community on the estate, especially since the closing of the Community Centre. It is used for numerous after-school activities and by the full-time Youth Tutor.

"My main aim is to run a school-based Youth Club on three nights. That's the maximum time the WELB will allow for heating and lighting. Each night is two and a half hours. The age range is 11-18. I do some Maths teaching but that's limited to 6 or 7 hours a week. I also co-ordinate the use of the school by outside groups. Evening use by all groups has to be on three nights. We can use the place every day until 5.30. The Family Centre use the place for under 11s and other groups have used the place a few times. My priority is a good Youth Club. Success means bringing them through the door and offering them good social development. The image of this school is bad in Derry. The parents send their kids elsewhere. We're helping to try and raise the image of the school." (Youth Tutor, Craigneill)

Kilfinn has a controlled Youth Club in the school premises although the Youth Worker is not part of the teaching staff. This is virtually exclusively Protestant. Between the clubs there is not so much antagonism as a recognition of 'reality', that is of the fears which surround each.

"I think that the problem in Londonderry is that there are a lot of people who have been personally affected by the troubles. That effects the attitudes of course. You might have children of policemen sitting in front of you whose Dads have been shot. That' is where suspicion comes from. Among boys it wouldn't be manly to suggest that Roman Catholics were the same as them. These are people to be disliked, the enemy." (Teacher, Kilfinn Sec School)

"Kilfinn Secondary School is on the periphery of the Craigneill area. It is a controlled school which caters for the non-Catholic population. It also possesses a Youth wing which is supposed to service Craigneill but because of the religious divide the youth of Craigneill will not attend it." (Craigneill local resident)

The Youth Clubs have undertaken some cross-community work, but the image of the other local clubs as exclusive remains completely intact. Neither school works in EMU. They do co-operate in the Quaker Peace

Education Project which is based in the University, but these operate in the first instance through meetings of the pupils of each school on it's own. The climate is one of acceptance of the situation.

"We're not in EMU. We're doing a thing with the Quakers in the University, a separate scene. There's no trouble. The youngsters are aware of what it's for but they haven't come together with another school yet. The kids have grown up with it. They're just used to it. They accept it. They even accept the army walking through the school." (Principal, Catholic Sec. School)

"You need to keep every Protestant contact you've got. It's very difficult to get Protestant people to trust what lies behind any initiative." (Peace worker)

"When a Roman Catholic girl came from St. Mary's to talk to our classes there were 2 classes. One class is quieter and they were interested. Two of their parents wouldn't let them do the coursework though. In another class, two kids sat at the back with their arms folded. They were not objectionable but they decided that they were against it. It put me off a bit. I suppose I felt that if parents were against you what's the point? I suppose I don't like rocking the boat. The last headmaster when I told him I was bringing this teacher in said it was OK but warned me not to tell parents and just to let her appear. This Headmaster is an evangelical and doesn't seem to value cross-community work much. The main cross-community work goes on with St. Cecilia's through the History teacher." (R.E. teacher, Kilfinn Secondary School)

Cross-community education does exist, but tenuously. Nevertheless in Protestant circles it is often assumed that because the system is not explicitly 'Protestant' rather it is, officially, State that integration can take place within its structures. The fact that this State is viewed as a 'Protestant State for a Protestant people' is not recognised. The present trend among Protestants is a drift towards emigration from the area. Protestant pupils in the city have to cross the bridge to attend the only State Grammar School. There are numerous reports of people in their school uniforms being attacked.

"All my young leaders are secondary school educated. The Grammar

School people leave. My own children are examples. My son hates Londonderry, always has. He'll go as soon as he comes of age." (Presbyterian Minister)

"I'm on the Boards of three schools. I've learnt a lot about that system. At that level we have opportunities of uniting our communities through projects or holidays. We need to heal the wounds at that level. We won't do it with two systems. We already have the structures because you don't have Protestant schools. I'm convinced it has to be done at that level. At the third level of education it's too late. Our kids will go to Stranmillis or the University in Coleraine if they want to do teacher training but if they go for anything else they go to Scotland." (Presbyterian Minister)

The Catholic areas on the other hand seem to be experiencing an increase in confidence which is reflected to some degree in the schools.

"There's a surprising lack of vindictiveness given the social problems. I don't have any vindictiveness, no viciousness. You'll get a bit of graffiti in the toilets. I do admit to the influence and the good that the football thing has done. It's a very noticeable change. Even socially people will tell you that. It used to be that on a Saturday night if a police jeep passed there'd be stone throwing. Now you don't get that. The Security Forces would tell you that themselves. I've noticed it because it's given the kids something to lift them out of their depression." (Principal, Catholic S.S.)

"There's a lot of tick men going unpaid in the city when the team is playing away in the cup." (Local resident, Protestant)

This sense of progress in Catholic circles may reflect the increased confidence of the Catholic community in the city and the corresponding sense of defeat among Protestants. The Churches in the area seem to regard the schools 'settlement' as adequate in the sense that there is no great desire to change the structures. Perhaps this is because in the Derry situation, integrated schools would mean Catholic majorities even were integration to take place in the State structure. The Catholic Church in Derry has traditionally been outspoken in it's defence of Catholic Education. The apparent absence of interest in integration on the Protestant side may mean that it has disappeared as an issue for the time being.

c. The Churches, communities and violence

The Waterside has experienced considerable violence in the last twenty years. This takes many forms. The Church communities in the Waterside have all felt the effects of this violence and ministered to it. The number of incidents measured statistically has fallen considerably over the last 10 years. The depth of the scars, the memories of violence and the sense of fear and threat do not appear to be any the less because of that.

The Protestants appear to have dealt directly with violence in three main forms. The first is the violence which is integral to the present make-up of the Waterside - population movement which took place in an atmosphere of fear and has certainly left deep memories. The second is the violence which is directed against the security forces and their families and which continues to affect members of Protestant congregations and their attitudes. The third is the murder of relations of current members of the congregations. The depth of feeling about population movement is close to the surface.

"Less than 50% of my congregation are natives. Quite a lot have come from the City side. They maybe make up 40% of the people. They 'had to' move across. There just wasn't the quality of life for them as Protestants on the City side. Maybe 5-10% have come into the North from Donegal... The people who have come from the City side have been good Presbyterians. The City side Churches were the more established... Then there has been a movement of people out of the city." (Presbyterian Minister)

"There's hardly any of our people left on the City Side. I go to a Church on the West Bank but nearly all of us would live on the Waterside. I go because it was the Church I was baptised in, the Church my mother and father were married in and it's part of my history. I'm not really worried that we moved. There are certainly a lot who resent it." (local Methodist man)

"What I see is the insidious destruction of anything to do with the Union in this city and the nationalist attempt to visit the sins of our fathers on us, and I'm admitting there were sins... In the past, Protestants have tended to be intimidated into closing their doors because they were told they were bad people, perpetrators of heinous crimes. They try to scotch our tradition and we're very conscious that we have one. I believe that the Protestants themselves have allowed themselves to be driven into this

hole. Their leaders, Church leaders, have never concentrated on Protestant civic rights. They've done nothing to counter the movement of population or to counsel the people into changing or accepting the shift." (Local Protestant man, Church of Ireland (non-attender))

*"The Protestants have lost their confidence and it's going to get worse. They're withdrawing from everything. The City Council held a meeting on drinking and alcohol abuse and the Protestant Churches weren't even represented. I heard someone saying 'They're all Catholics.' This shows a very sad lack of confidence. Some won't even go across the bridge to shop. They've been through a very traumatic experience. They used to be the city now the boot is on the other foot. " (*Presbyterian minister)

"My Church is a congregation which moved from the West Bank... They moved in 1982 and I arrived only 5 months before. In the 1940s and 50s there were 500 families. !971 and 72 was a time of massive movement. Over 85 families moved in one week. Some didn't rejoin. We took 160 families in the transfer. We now have 400 families without any decline in other congregations. We're a mongrel Presbyterian Church.. Of our 160 families still in the congregation at the time of the move 110 already lived on the Waterside. All of the young families were over here... Last year a quarter of our congregation moved, fifteen families moved out of the city." (Presbyterian Minister)

*"I've very few families on the City side; about three or four. Over the last 20 years there's been a vast swing. People came across to escape the City side in quite large numbers." (*Church of Ireland Rector).

*"Over the trouble years we've seen a big movement of people out of the town and even bigger over the river. That was before my time. There's been no loss in recent years. Nearly all of the Carlisle Road Congregation lives in the Waterside but they go over on Sunday." (*Methodist Minister)

This experience of flight and perceived threat marks the Protestant psyche in Derry. The so-called 'siege mentality' was often referred to, although the nature of that siege must be said to have subtly changed. In a Protestants are having to come to terms with a sense that their longer besieged but overrun. In Derry, 'Not an Inch' has a hol a community who have given up their presence on the entir of the Foyle. There are now people who propose that the reconstituted a separate city. The result is pent up resentment in the community which is not always directed at external targets.

"I can look at the Roman Catholic Church with envy. They have organised, visited their prisoners, set up advice centres, dealt with unemployment. Our lot have a respectability thing. It's very important for the Protestant clergy and establishment. There's an attitude that they must distance themselves from anything that's illegal. While that's fair and right it's not our tradition in that we defied our king in 1689 and 1798. Their attitude leaves me in a quandary. They interpret respectability to mean that they do nothing. I think that every Churchman should have discourse. I am not theologically opposed to discussions with Roman Catholics. My anger is that the Protestant clergy and establishment do not wish to be involved with anything because they interpret the people as unsavoury and yet privately they support them. I've had experience of young Protestants being arrested, accused of membership of the UVF and the police say that the one thing 'we' haven't got is the Protestant clergy, and they do say 'we' and it makes me cringe. Bishop Daly does get involved - like in the Birmingham Six.. The Protestant middle class distance themselves from the working class because it's financially expedient. The lace curtain brigade will vote for Ian Paisley, they'll give voice in the Golf and Rugby Club but that's the limit. " (Local Protestant man)

"The Catholic middle class are much more open about their nationalism, whereas Protestants hide their light under a bushel." (Local Protestant woman)

The Protestants of Derry have withdrawn in large part from the life of the city. This was most acute at the time of the withdrawal by most Unionist Councillors, but it is also felt to be the result of serious intimidation.

"The siege mentality is an attitude of mind about the Protestants feeling that the community at large don't want them. Physically it's very real in the Fountain, it's there for a UDR man on patrol on the City side, for the farmer on the border who takes his gun with him on his tractor. The majority community of this city [Catholic] did very little to redress the problems for the people moving. They could have sympathised much more directly. An example of this would be where a young lad joins the army who lives in a mixed community on the West Bank. He cannot go home.

First Derry Presbyterian Church is bombed, all trappings of Britishness are denied, children going to and from schools on the West Bank are attacked. The City Council is obsessed with a Gaelic Culture which has very little to do with reality. It's more Irish-American than Irish. The SDLP could have given voice to this and could have tried to voice the fears of the Protestant community. John Hume is eulogised by people like Barry White but he could have done more. This total anti-Britishness which obsesses them is an anathema to the Protestants. In fairness they're under pressure from a fascist terrorist organisation... Pat Devine and Hume say that any overtures would have been rejected by Protestants. Of course the siege mentality would have meant some rejection but not only. There was great support here for one man, one vote. There was much less concern about Enniskillen, attacks on children going to or from school or deaths in the army. This has helped solidify the siege mentality. The column of the 'Derry Journal' consistently regurgitates the sins not only of the last 50 years but also 400 years. This does nothing to serve community relations." (Protestant, local school teacher)

"If what has happened to the Protestants of Derry is repeated in the rest of Ulster we will have genocide." (Local Protestant woman)

In the midst of this, the Churches live, their buildings on the City side often the last symbols of previous domination. In the Waterside the Churches therefore represent parts of the hard core of people all of whom know about the threat from the IRA and the reality of Protestant flight. In all the Churches the threat to the community is felt. It crystallises most sharply in experiences of the threat posed to families of members of the security forces.

"When I came here I had two dozen police families. Now I have two. Some of them are now in Eglinton and Limavady. I've had four police members killed. I had a UDR man, a very nice man, who worked in the Post Office, shot in the head. A Community Relations Police Officer was killed in Shantallow. We also have UDR funerals in the Church. We're lucky in the city that the UDA is not as active as elsewhere. These murders have an effect. Just because they're security forces..." (Church of Ireland

"There has been a movement of Protestants out of the city. W here there were 8 policemen. I now have 3. Those who have very particular reasons. It's a fact of life. Houses b

overnight. We're being policed by a police force from outside the city. There has been a fair movement of Roman Catholics from the City side. Behind me three houses have changed hands, Protestant to Roman Catholic. In one area a sympathiser of the IRA moved in when the police moved out." (Presbyterian Minister)

"Policemen move out. There are no police hardly left in Londonderry. There are no police on the City side. A lot live in Eglinton, Limavady and Coleraine. We would have had 35 police families. Now we have 15. We had a family the other day moved out. He has had so many threats he just can't stay. The IRA has just put such a threat on this life. He's a Derry man, she was a Derry woman. Those who have moved from the city have gone for good. Police can't sell their houses. The IRA maybe wouldn't know that they've moved. A policeman moving his house gets £1000 or £1500 less. In many cases people feel more vulnerable. For me I've a ministry to policemen who move through. I've a job to do. You either resent it or you get on with it. You' re ministering to people who move through." (Presbyterian Minister)

"Violence has driven people apart... Equally in the face of murder of security forces support for Sinn Fein has driven a wedge. People find it hard to understand why people vote for Sinn Fein even if they divide between violence and the rest of the policy. Support for Sinn Fein has become a wedge, people feel that it's a vote for violence. Of course on the other side the people feel that voting for the DUP's the same." (Methodist Minister)

The violence against the security forces is thus often violence to members of Derry congregations. The congregations under this threat draw closer together in the face of violence. The Presbyterian minister's choice of resentment or getting on with the job appears to be a false one. In fact many Protestants do both - resent and attempt to live on. What is, for a gunman, the murder of an impersonal representative of the British State has tragic consequences for relatives, friends and similarly threatened people on the other side. The murder of a policeman encapsulates the depth of the divide in perception in the violence in Northern Ireland. One person's British accomplice is another person's backbone of the congregation, doing his duty in the face of incredible danger.

"Perhaps the most shattering experience we had was when Corporal ***

was coming at 2 o'clock to collect the children in the minibus one day and he was shot dead one minute's walking distance from the school. Some children on their way home witnessed it. The other children in the school did not know that anything had taken place at all. Those who normally walked home were taken home area by area by a teacher. I issued a letter immediately after. The press were in here like a shot. I did not talk to them at all. I issued a letter to parents saying that I regarded my school as an island of normality in an uncertain society and that we resisted anything which might destroy that." (Principal, Primary School)

"The violence is real for some children in that two fathers have been killed, while others have been shot. Otherwise it's as normal as we can make it." (Principal, Primary School)

"The violence has had an effect. The congregation has known personal tragedy. Members of the congregation have been murdered. It has driven another section of the community into bitterness. I find the people who come on TV and say that they have no bitterness desperately false. I haven't met that sort of person. I had a personal friend who was murdered in 1971. I don't think I've ever forgiven them. It has brought this hardline paramilitary attitude. For me you can't have a Protestant paramilitary. you're a Protestant you can't be a paramilitary. Catholicism doesn't go with paramilitarism either. I can understand 'nationalist paramilitaries'. I can understand a man who joins the UDR or Police. I don't believe that the 'freedom fighters' have a cause." (Presbyterian minister)

This bitterness about a friend killed 18 years ago indicates the hostility which might exist in congregations who feel themselves to be permanently assailed. The continuing violence drives people into places of safety. The ghettos offer some security against personal attack and they reinforce community perceptions. Congregations can very easily turn into ghettos, places of safety where people try to make sense of their experiences. The universal experience of the police as victims in Protestant Churches makes it impossible to see IRA attacks on 'good Church members' as anything other than murder. It appears that Church gatherings in this climate reinforce rather than build down bitterness. Conspiracies which see the Roman Catholic Church as implicated in the predicament of Protestants have an authentic ring which is not contradicted by any experience when the only real contact with Catholic people is through the other end of a weapon.

In addition there is a clear distancing of the clergy, bastions of the Protestant establishment, from paramilitarism. Illegal actions are considered to emanate from sources outside the Churches. Such behaviour is considered reprehensible for practising Protestants. In contrast the Security Forces, particularly the RUC., are seen as the backbone of the community. Paramilitarism is 'bad', Security Forces are 'good'. The fact that this moral division is not mirrored in Catholic Clergy is a major problem. Middle class Protestants are extremely sensitive to criticism of the security forces and such criticism is read as at least ambivalence if not support for the IRA if it is expressed by Catholic clergy.

"Many of my people would see Roman Catholics as people who won't put their backs behind the Security Forces. They used to take as much benefit as they could get though. Now the Protestants are jumping on their bandwagon. The IRA would never have got as far if there had been more information to the Security Forces. We can't understand why the Roman Catholics don't back the authorities." (Church of Ireland Rector)

"I came into criticism when Dominic McGlinchey's wife was killed because I prayed for his children. I didn't pray for him. When I say that the UDA and the UVF will roast in the same hell they don't like it." (Presbyterian Minister).

"The Church of Ireland and Presbyterians would be mostly Official Unionists. We'd have some DUP members in the Church of Ireland but they don't come to Church. They claim they're loyal but they're not loyal to our scriptures. I don't know what they're loyal to. The good Church members are not fanatics." (Church of Ireland Rector)

"There are books by Avero Manhattan like "Catholic Terror today" or "Catholic Terror in Ireland". In the last of those you see what the Roman Catholic people did in 1641 and 1798 under the instigation of their priests. They'd see that it was instigated and blessed by priests. The IRA is the direct follower of this." (Free Presbyterian Minister)

"Our people are behind the Police again. After the Anglo-Irish Agreement they stoned them but now it's OK." (Local Protestant)

The Churches are in general the bastions of the 'legal only' approach. In this sense Churches probably act as restraining influences on some who might otherwise be tempted to take the law into their own hands. The Free Presbyterian Church and discussions within the Protestant organisations seem to be the borderline cases whose attitudes to the law verge on ambivalence.

"Protestants remember Bishop Daly with a white flag in the Bogside in 1969. We'd regard him as a political appointment. Maybe he's from an MA background in Belleek. Before the Roman Catholics didn't come out strongly enough against the IRA. If my boys were throwing stones I'd go out and sort them out. They [RCs] didn't come out strongly enough. They sat on the fence. Those funerals.. ., maybe excommunication is too strong but they could have prevented those military style demonstrations. The police seem to have to sit under their control." (Church of Ireland Rector)

On the Catholic side there are very different interpretations of and experiences of violence. The police and security forces are regarded as part of the problem by a large number of Catholics in the city. Certainly the security forces are an agent of violence rather than protection. Catholics on the Waterside also experienced political violence in other ways. Craigneill residents were intimidated by the presence of large loyalist housing estates next door. The estate had also experienced rioting on a regular basis in the early 1980s while there were a number of people from the area in prison for terrorist offences.

"The kids have grown up with it. They're just used to it. They accept the army walking through the school. I've seen a few instances of army harassment. Mostly they just do their job." (Headmaster)

"We used to be stopped all the time. We used to say to them 'Who's your wife in bed with at the moment?' That would drive them mad." (Local resident)

"News travels fast in the area. It has an inbuilt network where news reaches you very quickly. If the army or police were coming into the area or had a place blocked off people would establish very quickly what was happening. People would know who was lifted or whose house was raided shortly after or while the incident was happening such is the network. Crowds can gather at such incidents very quickly." (Local resident)

"This estate is very isolated... Carnpatrick is very Protestant. It puts a

barrier between here and the centre of the Waterside. The Youth Club is in the Waterside and our kids wouldn't go because they'd have to go through the Protestant estates. In the seventies it was a hotspot. Even now it's saturated by army and police. They blew up a house the other week.. It has a lot of army activity. There's always people being lifted. It causes a lot of resentment." (Local resident)

"One of the problems we have on this area is Sinn Fein. We're aware that they might try and use the Church as a crutch. The Community Centre was closed down because of Sinn Fein. It' s been re-opened strictly under the council. We've had no formal contact with them at all. Most of the active Sinn Feiners aren't practising. They don't look us in the eye. They walk past when they see me. We had a lad in yesterday who asked us to put an advert for the 'Colm Doherty Memorial Trophy' . Colm Doherty was an IRA man and they wanted to organise a football league. We said they couldn't advertise in the parish magazine.

Mind you, I'd feel that the people here are victimised. I came from the south. I was totally ignorant of Northern Ireland... When you see the police stopping the young fellows and making them take off their coats and it's freezing cold or it's raining. They do the recruitment for the IRA. I know that it's very hard though. When I go home to Donegal I sometimes zip up my anorak so that I just look like a young fellow. When they ask me where I come from I say Craigneill. Then they pull me aside. Then I unzip my coat and they stop searching because they see that I'm a priest. The other night I zipped up the coat and I was with an 18 year old. The police stopped us and asked us for identification. I said that I had none, the other lad had some. Then they saw that I was a priest and we were let off. The lad said to me 'Thank God you' re here. I'd have had terrible hassle.'

We meet the police with the Protestant ministers. Yet we feel that there's this antagonism towards us because we keep bringing up incidents. The Protestant ministers are very close to the police. There's this feeling in the meetings that we support the IRA. Yet I've never met an IRA man who told me. There's women on the estate get called 'whores' by patrol men in their jeeps. I understand why people hang on to Sinn Fein....

At the police meetings the Protestant clergy are very supportive of the police. We would be bringing cases to them. The problem is it's always the same. But the army doesn't patrol the Protestant estates in the same way. If there's a shooting the police come up here in droves. Sometimes you see the army outside the school while the kids are on there way in. It is getting a bit better. Sometimes the ministers wave but they are very stand-offish. I don't know what you do. But I suppose that's the point. You don't stop there, you keep going.

At heart I think things are moving. I met a soldier and he was a Christian. He said to me that there was a whole pile of religious people who went through his checkpoint and they never acknowledged him or never waved. He said that he didn't find it very Christian. I realised that I had only been seeing his uniform. I said that to him. I suppose it's hard not to be bitter when you see the way that they treat the lads around here. But what do you do? Why do the Security Forces ask the lads to take off their socks and shoes and stand in the street for hours? What is the purpose of it?" (Catholic Priest)

"The violence here reflects that in the rest of the city. There are no riots now. Army and Police raids are the only thing of significance. Unfortunately they're a fact of life. In a dictionary definition of violence the level has gone down. The paramilitaries have had a negative effect. There's so many normal, quiet people who're very afraid." (Local teacher)

"1981 was a dreadful year. Craigneill turned sour during the Hunger Strikes. There were riots every night. When Bobby Sands died it was terrible. We had to climb over the rubble to get into the Family Centre. It had an awful effect on Craigneill. There was one woman I heard telling her daughter 'Don't go out because there's all these masked men on the streets.' Her daughter just said to her 'Sure the masked men are all my friends!' " (Sister)

"The Hunger Strike was a very bad time around here. Rioting, stoning and so on. A lot of people moved out of Craigneill at that time, a lot of families with aspirations. A lot moved to Brian's Hill." (Local resident)

"If you live in Craigneill you can't help wondering if you live in a police state where the police have the power to do everything. The youth of the estate are very vulnerable to police harassment as they have nowhere to congregate other than the streets which makes them the targets of the ever present, ever vigilant RUC British Mobile and Foot Patrols. Harassment

is a daily occurrence in the area. If you ever go out of Craigneill, for any reason, you are subjected to surveillance and harassment on entering Thomas Street. I call the stop and search procedure harassment because my experience and the experience of others is that the police stop you (doing his duty) and already knows your name. They know who they are stopping and in my opinion they abuse their powers and see people from Craigneill as wearing horns on their heads. In my book they are enforcing the law fairly but harassing particular members of the community on a religious basis.

Daily harassment is one of the major talking points in the area, as is the 12th of August when the annual Apprentice Boys ceremony is held. On that particular day the boundaries of the Craigneill Estate are clearly evident to residents. They are enforced by the police. The Craigneill area is cut off for a full day in order to let the parade pass off peacefully and no movement is allowed in and out of the estate. The Quarry becomes the boundary. With the residents held in their own ghetto, the police and the Orangemen let the residents know who is the boss." (Local man)

Catholic people experience violence as part of everyday life peppered by incidents which bring back particular memories such as the Hunger strikes, police raids and also funerals. They certainly do not experience the security forces as their protectors rather as their intimidators and overlords. This different experience again encapsulates the different relationship of Catholics and Protestants to the State. The parish and congregational system means that the Churches, ministering and living within the bounds of only one side of that experience, come to reflect that experience in their outlooks. Funerals provide another example.

"Past differences are set aside when someone from the area dies. The wakes and funerals are attended by all with the bringing of mass cards to the wakes being the norm. Such funerals as those of IRA volunteers and that of Colm Doherty were significant to the area because of the circumstances in which they died and also the way their funerals were treated by the RUC. While residents may not have approved of their beliefs they resented the way in which remains were treated. All residents would have taken part or observed the funerals which were the focal point in the area. It is still alive in the minds of the residents today." (Local man)

In Protestant circles, funerals of IRA men are seen as repugnant because of the associated political display while the same funerals are seen by Catholics as 'sacred occasions' whose sanctity is destroyed by insensitive policing. In each case the question of who is committing the original or causal act of violence has a diametrically opposite answer according to where the commentator stands in relation to the violence.

The Catholic Church in the area regards itself as completely opposed to terrorism. In this regard they are parallel to the Protestant Churches. They would be criticised by militants in 'their own areas' because of a 'lack of understanding'. For Catholic priests the reality that their parishioners are harassed and besieged by various forces - economic or military - cannot be denied. For Protestant clergy the fact that their parishioners are also besieged by forces - terrorist, intimidation and emigration - is primary and they therefore support the police as instruments of stability. There is remarkably little appreciation of how this appears on the other side. We have already witnessed a degree of despair in the responses of Protestant clergy about Catholic support for the RUC. A similar despair is detectable in the views of Catholic clergy.

"I do any visits in the Protestant Carnpatrick area. It's very loyalist. I'd drive down no problem but I'd be scared to walk. You'd be worried you'd be putting a red rag to a bull... Catholics taking over their area and the like." (Catholic priest)

Many of the clergy, like many of the laity, do not know what it is to be a member 'of the other side'. The perception of Protestant ministers as to Catholic grievances breaks down over the security forces if not before. The perception of Catholics as to Protestant fears breaks down over the threat which the IRA poses to Protestants and the extent of the genocidal fear and hatred that it breeds.

Experiences of violence whether structural (discrimination, unemployment) or physical (Shooting, bombing, rioting, harassment) leave deep memories. What is done in revenge for the memory is never considered quite 'as bad' as the event which is remembered. A fundamental difference in the communities is the events which are remembered as assaults, clear instances of atrocity and which are justified or qualified or 'understood'. Thus Protestants understand why the IRA must be destroyed before there can be peace while Catholics understand that security force activities often push people into the IRA. Protestants understand why Catholics cannot be fully trusted while Catholics understand why state forces cannot be trusted. In this the Church professionals, clergy, appear to be as human as their congregations. When the Churches are asked to act against violence and the appeal is directed at the clergy or professional staff who are held to be the Churches by other institutions everybody might be in favour. What is understood as violence by the responding clergy may be entirely different. A Protestant acting against violence may wish to support a security clampdown, a Catholic may wish to raise the issue of police harassment. In this 'the clergy' or 'the Churches' are a true reflection of Northern Irish society and act no differently than other institutions.

d. The Churches and Inter-community relationships

The Churches have no 'policy' on inter-community relationships. The variety of attitudes within the institutions is as wide as the variety in secular life. There is no unity within denominations, let alone between denominations, in attitudes to inter-Church contact or to inter-community relationships. There is no such thing as 'the Churches' which have a uniform institutional policy or which could react uniformly to changes in government policy. The Waterside Churches contain representatives of many approaches to this issue.

"We've two bowling tournaments every year and people from all sides come. That would be the extent of our cross-community relations. We wouldn't go to the chapel because we've been brought up on our prayer book and we'd feel traitors to our reformation. We have a fear of swamping. We have no difficulties on a social level." (Church of Ireland Rector)

"I haven't found the siege mentality as regards my own people. I find them outgoing and community-minded. I haven't found any bitterness. When you haven't lived in Derry and you hear the name mentioned you'd think it'd be closed and people stick to their own. But I haven't found that. There's a great deal of co-operation between all the Churches." (Church of Ireland Rector)

"The security problem has driven people apart. People are embittered. Protestants equate the provisional IRA with Catholicism. I think this is wrong. I think Irish Catholicism is different from any other in the world. It's too politicised. For some reason the two religions have not been able to live together here where they've lived together everywhere else. It's not religious it's political" (Presbyterian Minister)

"I am an ecumenical. I believe in biblical ecumenism. In my day I've had all sorts of people in my pulpit including Free Presbyterians. I draw the line of course with Roman Catholicism. Some of the ecumenicals would not have Baptists or Free Presbyterians in their pulpits but they would have Roman Catholics. I am much more ecumenical than they are. That is the historical tradition. The Presbyterian people have been very friendly to Roman Catholic people. The Catholics talk about 'Catholics, Protestants and Presbyterians.' While they were very friendly they drew a line at worshipping together. You can be friendly with your neighbour but you don't have to go to bed with his wife. I am involved with Roman Catholics in social issues, in alcohol and drug education, in life, whatever. On social issues I've no differences. But I don't want them to sacrifice their principles for me or for me to sacrifice mine. I don't want to throw bricks. I'll meet with Roman Catholic people every day but I'll not be involved in joint worship." (Presbyterian Minister)

"I get on very well. I don't ask 'who owns this shop'. If it's good value then.. My next door neighbour is Roman Catholic. We get on very well. If you live in this city you have to get on with Roman Catholics. I get on fairly well on a Church basis. I think the bishop is very powerful. When I've been close to a priest he's been shifted. I'm not into joint services with anyone.. I've never found that my lack of joint worship has affected my relationships. I'm probably more bigoted than I allow. Inter-Protestant relations are 'all right'. We're brothers in theory but I'm not convinced. It's a bit of a sham. People baptise each other's babies. In public it's all good. In private it's not. The WCA Centre is very good. There is a genuine harmony. I dropped out of a trip to England recently to allow a Roman Catholic to go." (Presbyterian Minister)

"The other important thing is ecumenism. We're in a very mixed parish. We haven't a very strong ecumenism. This is a parish where there are strong political feelings. I'm going tonight to the opening of the Methodist Conference. I try to be meticulous about these things. Most of it's at that level. You haven't a lot of anything else. I suppose it's the political situation... I don't want to say too much about ecumenism. You get English people over saying 'why aren't you building bridges?' But we have to live here. My ecumenism is based on talking to everybody. I've never met any hostility. But there again I might not go out and talk to a group on the twelfth of July. Sometimes people say 'I didn't expect a priest to be like

that.' Apart from that we draw on all sections of the community for any skills or services like plumbers.
There's a lot of indifference in the parish. People are not all that worried whether you go to things or not. People from Dublin always think that it's important! Our people would be inclined to go to other people's things more than the other way around.. Personally I would go if I was invited. Sometimes it's not as easy for the other ministers." (Catholic priest)

"I find the Protestant ministers very stand-offish. They're polite, very nice but underneath they harbour a lot of anti-Catholic feeling." (Catholic priest)

"In the Churches, even among the Protestants, there isn't much official contact. We have a Protestant clergy council which meets twice a year. We have a joint Church of Ireland/Methodist Church outside the city. Apart from that people do their own thing. At the moment the Protestant Churches are working together aimed at a Billy Graham Crusade. The Roman Catholic Church was invited but wasn't interested.. I think the contact is good on community work down at the Advice Centre. We also have a an ecumenical convention for young people, Protestant. Apart from that there's a joint service in Galliagh [City side] once a year. Apart from that.. If the Churches are prepared to work together on the community work level then other opportunities would be given. To a certain extent the Roman Catholic Church is so big that they can do their own thing. We also have a clergy meeting, absolutely no friction." (Methodist minister)

"We are very opposed to Brian Mawhinney's proposals, as we put it de-Protestantising the Protestants. We see it as very important, standing up for biblical principles and values. More and more we see the intrusion of ecumenism through cross-community trips where children are taken to such shrines as Knock. What we see as the underlying principle of cross-community work is a total betrayal of what Ulster Protestantism is. The Catholic Church takes part on an equal basis without changing her motto 'semper idem', always the same. There is a distinct bias to Catholic history. Children are denouncing their Protestant heritage. Roman Catholicism is promoted as of equal standing to Protestantism." (Free Presbyterian Minister)

Among Church professionals then there is no common understanding of what the Churches should do to further or retard inter-community contact.

The WCA Centre is the largest joint venture but even here there can be problems. The centre actually involves very little Church input except through the clergy and Church funds. Yet Northern Ireland's cultural friction extends to petty-sectarianism. Even between the participants in agreed joint projects such as the Advice Centre there can be difficulties arising out of cultural principles.

"These [WCA] committees never get involved with any theological debate. We got some money from a brewery. The cheques was sent back because of Methodist and Presbyterian objections. Over £2,000 was sent back last year. The European Social Fund are notorious in how they pay out. Consequently one has to have an overdraft to cover the delay in payment. You get cast-iron guarantees from the EEC, the bank managers are OK and he says you need a mandate from your committee. But the Presbyterian Church cannot enter into a loan agreement or debt. Therefore they cannot sign for the loan. The Methodist Church feels that debt is nearly a mortal sin. The Church of Ireland would probably pawn the communion silver! The Catholics would probably run a bingo session. But we can't get a loan in theory. Church Unity is very difficult.

"In the Methodist minister's year as chairman he wanted to clear the debt of the Advice Centre. The Bank Manager was very annoyed! Then there was the Marriage Guidance Council and the Catholics. If the Ford Motor Company gave us a car we couldn't raffle it - the Methodists would withdraw." (WCA Worker)

The comic dimensions of these difficulties should not hide the serious consequences. One misplaced raffle could cause the collapse of the committee. The degree to which apparent detail becomes central illustrates the difficulties of cross community contact at any level.

In the Waterside the Derry/Londonderry debate has already proved how names become symbolic of the whole community's identity. The result is that cross-community work between existing institutions can only take place on the basis of 'lowest common denominator'. It goes as far as the point where the first and smallest principal of any participant is broken. The clergy, protectors of their institutions represent their institutions on such committees. Unless they defend the principles of their institutions or at least of their congregations they may come under attack from their parishioners. Therefore few Presbyterian or Methodist Ministers could allow a car to be raffled no matter what their personal view. The cross-community programme of the Churches comes to depend on ballot-tickets! Given the range of what is considered 'principle' the grounds on which cross-community work can take place is likely to be correspondingly narrow. For as long as Churches accept each other as of equal validity (e.g. in the social field) even if different, then cross-community work may not be even necessary. All may continue in parallel tracks with mutual respect and acknowledgement that differences 'are' but do not 'matter' in the sense that they are not better or worse or a reason to fight. Once fighting begins, and it is a question not only of difference but of 'better' and 'worse' then difference becomes 'sides'.

This is the dilemma of the Churches in cross-community work in a landscape of violent conflict. Their principles are regarded as 'correct' and those who do not hold them are regarded as implicitly or explicitly 'wrong' or 'less right'. This element of competitive 'betterness' begins in the sphere of raffles and in order to protect the principle the offended group withdraws. In inter-Church relations these issues arise time and time again. If violence did not exist in Northern Ireland Church bickering could be dismissed as an internal matter.

Criticisms of 'The Churches' attitudes as institutions come from all sorts of angles, from those who characterise their contribution to cross-community relations as extremely limited and those who regard it as tantamount to betrayal. Clearly each speaker has assumptions of what 'the Churches' are and should be.

"The Churches don't really support the work of our peace group. Our chairperson tried to get a service for all the dead going. Neither ministers nor priests nor bishops got together. They wouldn't do it. We started out in the mid 70s and we laid wreaths for all the dead in Northern Ireland. It was all we could do. The Churches wouldn't help us further." (Peacegroup member, Catholic)

"The Churches don't organise social meetings with each other at all. We wanted the clergy to meet the young constables and we got one priest who agreed to come. We spent two days phoning them up and they didn't want to know. The Church will send people to us but they don't want to dirty their hands. The Churches don't organise for their own Churches socially, let alone between them. Except for the Sunday School excursion. They don't organise anything between each other." (Teenage girl, Church of Ireland)

"The bishop [C of I] is a bit out of touch. Maybe he thinks that meeting Bishop Daly is leadership and the people will run and catch up.. I don't know. There are certain people wouldn't go to confirmation because he's there. They say he's more concerned about the others than his own flock." (Church of Ireland man)

"I do find a deep suspicion of Roman Catholics. Having said that, among the children there is a great interest to find out what Roman Catholics believe. One of the big hurdles is a fear about what other people on the estate think.. Last year for GCSE I brought in a Roman Catholic teacher to talk about Roman Catholic sacraments. But then I had about two parents who objected and I had to abandon that. I'd see the main thing that separates people is this fear of what people would say in their own communities." (Sec. School teacher, Church of Ireland)

"We are against romanism, ecumenism, liberalism and modernism." (Free Presbyterian man)

"I'm not happy with any efforts the Churches make. I see them as more of a stumbling block in this area. That at times is very difficult as I'm a member of the institutional Church as a member of a religious order. Most of us have moved out of our main house. The Bishop has got some nominal control at times but not too much. Sometimes I feel I'm a wee bit cynical." (Sister)

The Churches in the Waterside seem to move in many directions in relation to inter-community relationships. Because they are not government institutions but also communities in which each person relates to every other as an equal member, especially in Protestant Churches, there is no mechanism by which all Church members could be forced to adopt a certain posture towards community relationships. Any attempt by central government to overtly fund one Church-party against another could have an even worse effect. The Churches do not act uniformly. They are not simple bodies whose attitudes can be assumed to be held by every member. Their collective identity is in a common membership but not in common views. This means that any uniform government policy from outside, for example to provide money for cross-community initiatives, will have very different results in different places. At the same time it means that the Churches cannot claim to be having a uniform moral or political effect on their members even in the case of decisions reached by the hierarchy or General Assembly. A sermon by a bishop will not be heard by all members in the same way and the sermon can no longer be held to represent the views of the Church. The same is true of decisions by the General Assembly or General Synod. A resolution to improve community relations will be acted on by some and acted against by others. The idea that 'the Churches' are a monolithic institution which can deliver uniform political attitudes is to misunderstand them and their place completely. This is not to say that there are not general trends nor that Church community is unimportant. What the Church is varies from congregation to congregation and even person to person. The days of doctrinal unanimity, of automatic deferral to a recognised superior, if they ever existed, have surely passed.

4. Theological reflections in the Waterside Churches

In the Waterside diversity rests on a diversity of outlook, differences which make generalities about 'The Churches' impossible to make without serious qualifications. In this section we will be primarily concerned with matters of doctrine and the relationship of each speaker's Church to other denominations. The second major theme will be the clergy and on the nature of the clerical task as understood by the various clergy. Among the Churches there were different expressions of the Churches task in the Waterside.

"I would like to think that Presbyterians have a mission to this city. The Presbyterian Church as a whole is moving in a direction I don't like. The majority of ministers in this town would be in favour of friendly relations. I don't believe in cosmetic worship together. I believe in meaningful worship for example in the hospitals. The people who go to big public displays of togetherness have no problem about getting on with their neighbours. We don't impress people. We have very real difficulties between our Churches. But we do have more for us than against us. I don't want one big Church. I think we've something to learn from each other. I think we Presbyterians have a freedom to express ourselves because we're not bound by episcopacy. Maybe some of our younger men would benefit from a guiding hand!

Presbyterianism brings a strong vibrant evangelicalism.. I think the Church must be evangelical. We all start from the premise of John, 3:16 'whosoever believeth in him'. I think as Presbyterians we ask for a personal commitment to that. The Catholics say that you do it because the Church tells you. We ask people to examine scripture for themselves. It's very interesting that there are a number of people on the City side who have left the Roman Catholic Church and meet in 'Christian Fellowship'. They have discovered the personal relation to God through Christ. It also gives a certain democracy to Church Government, something that we offer." (Presbyterian Minister)

"I'm not convinced that Presbyterians have the ultimate and total Church. I do think it's got the closest to a biblical Church. I'm a convinced evangelical. I do think people need Jesus as saviour and Lord. I'm not interested in robotic Christians. I suppose it's a reaction to the Free Presbyterians. I'm sure the Lord allows us to develop our own personality - transformed not conformed. I have women elders although I'm a convinced evangelical. There is terrible peer-group pressure between ministers, a pressure to conform...

...I'm not into joint services with anyone. I'm convinced that ecumenism is more needed than ever. But I think it's a bit dishonest. I think there is a theological dimension but my final view has not been arrived at. I live with a lack of certainty. If my friends push me I'll end up with a harder view than I want to have. I've never found that lack of joint worship has affected my relationships." (Presbyterian Minister)

"That's the Church's primary task - the word of God to the world. The preaching of John Wesley and George Whitfield was responsible for tremendous social change. It also delivered Britain from the influence of the French Revolution. The social standards in Britain were different through the influence of the Wesleys. John Wesley used to preach to 20,000 people. The British Labour Party grew out of the evangelical revival. I think the work ethic, so strong in Scotland and Northern Ireland comes out of the same thing.

Yet preaching is the very thing that is caricatured. 'Don't preach at me'. Preaching is the very thing that is parodied. Take the Sunday issue. Somebody said to me that the way to destroy Christianity is to destroy Sunday because you lose the teachers and the chance of teaching.

The Church hasn't emphasised this enough. There are people who come to the Presbyterian Church and know precious little about the Gospel. If they go to evangelical Churches they know about being saved and precious little else. If they go to Liberal Churches they preach about being good or politics. I'm protected because I preach through all the books of the bible. Salvation is very important. It has to be life-related though...

..Here, Presbyterianism is very formal, very conservative with a small c. The Reformed Church should be reformed and reforming. Presbyterian life up here is lacking any kind of evangelistic outreach towards Roman Catholicism and towards their own people. Presbyterians in Ulster were always very radical. They've been influenced by the siege mentality. I have the sense that the people look over their shoulders at what the Free Presbyterians think..

..Evangelism is best done on a one to one basis with the people with whom you work. When you come to Church you should be taught the necessary tools. It doesn't matter whether you're a Roman Catholic or Protestant if you're a sinner. In a city like Londonderry which is terribly divided I don't know how you'd do this one to one thing.. I feel burdened by the fact that there are people in Londonderry who've never heard the Good News about Jesus. I don't believe that the Roman Catholic Church teaches it."
(Presbyterian Minister)

"All those people in the Church think they know it all. All my kids went to the GB and BB. All my grandchildren go too. It's meant to be their heart. After that it orientates them for later life. I think it's important that they're taken to Church not sent to Church. They need to be taken to Church by their mum or dad. When they get to 17 or 18 they come into the world with a Christian attitude. And then the Church slaps you in the face. But in the end the commitment is to God.. I've completely pulled out of Church because people look down their nose. Then they try to force me to Church. I'm still a practising Christian. I always say 'We'll have to pray about this'. Without prayer it's nothing, but the Church.."
(Presbyterian woman)

"If I did go to a mass there would be questions. I wouldn't be going to mass. Reconciliation is 'in' but we can't just throw away our doctrines. All our views are based on the bible. They believe in the story in the tradition of the Church. I wouldn't go as far as the Archbishop of Canterbury in recognising the Pope as head of a new Church. Some Church of Ireland would waver a bit more. I don't see mine wavering. I

remember a lady in Donegal saying to me that the Roman Catholics have no religion they've so many practices." (Church of Ireland Rector)

"I would think that one of the most important aspects is a ministry of reconciliation - to God and to each other. This has to be one of the most important. You don't go about it in a big dramatic way. I'm not really keen on vast marches. I tend to work more quietly. I think it's only when you know people individually that you can build up trust. It's a slow thing... I think people still look to the Church. They look for a lead in community matters. I don't think the Church is as authoritarian as it was fifty years ago. If the clergy speak the people don't necessarily jump. The relationship between clergy and people now is probably closer..

..There would be a fair number would have little attachment, just baptisms and ceremonies and so on. I don't just ignore it. I would always invite people to Church. I don't go down and read the riot act. I don't stand up in the pulpit and read the riot act because you're talking to the converted. They're not against the Church. I think that Church attendance is important. It's important that people feel that they belong somewhere. The whole business of building up a community of people who believe in God.. I do think that Churches should be places where people are wanted and needed. I think fellowship is important. Those who go to our parish have a fairly strong sense of fellowship. Sometimes it doesn't run through everybody." (Church of Ireland Rector)

"I do find Christian communities. Maybe not in the Church so much but in other activities. I would attend a bible study group of people from different Protestant denominations. I attend a Presbyterian 18-30 Fellowship, Those communities fulfil that side of things. I would be sympathetic to the idea that Churches are communities. But I think that the Churches fail, maybe because of a lack of commitment, an evangelical core. Unless people are encouraged to be committed..." (Church of Ireland woman)

"We would see the New Testament as a balance between offering the Gospel to save the souls of people and also ministering to the whole person. John Wesley opened up hostels and so on. Wherever there was social need we've done things..

..Historically the Methodist Church is non-aligned. The Church is not so aligned with Unionism. We've been able to be a bridge Church. We're

seen to house Roman Catholics in our hostels. They see that we go for need not religion." (Methodist Minister)

"The Church has been very important for me. But there's not many Methodists around here. I do find a community around here, but where I live on the Housing Estate it would be laughed at. We're very involved in social projects and in ecumenical work. The Bishop [R.C.] opened our conference this year, welcoming all the delegates to the city. I have been involved in a number of cross-community things which I can talk about in the Church but I can't talk about on the estate." (Methodist man)

"I don't think Free Presbyterians like to be dictated to. In our Church anyone who holds an office has to be a saved person. They have to have a born-again experience. This is a biblical experience. John, 3:3 'except a man be born again he shall not see the Kingdom of God.' So everyone from our Church Officers and our communicants on.

I personally received at 3 years of age which was very young but my mother was a saved person. In Second Timothy, 3:13 Paul wrote 'that from a child you knew the holy scriptures.' From an early age I knew what it was to sin. Just coming on three I had personal faith in the Lord Jesus. Of course at that particular time I hadn't a comprehensive knowledge of the Word of God. But that's true of most people who are saved. It's only after study of the Word..

...On a Tuesday morning we meet for prayer, praying for a revival such as there was under Whitfield and Wesley. The Free Presbyterian Church doesn't exist just to break things apart and pull things down. We have a biblical mandate to challenge error but we do build up an alternative. That is seen on Tuesday when we have an outreach. We are the only one's going around doors in this city except the Jehovah's Witnesses and Mormons. We have a prayer meeting and Bible study on Wednesday. On Fridays we've a children's meeting, young people's meeting and revival meeting. We do some open air work..

....We want to remain in the bible. The reformation, when Calvin and Luther and Knox attacked Rome was marked by reform in the spiritual and the physical realm. The bible in Jude 3 exhorts us earnestly to contend for the faith which was once delivered unto the saints. It speaks of the role of the watchmen in Ezekiel 33, 4 - 6 when danger is looming we have to sound the trumpet. We have a God-given responsibility. We are ambassadors

for Christ. That is why we take such a strong stand against modernism, liberalism, ecumenism and romanism....

Our objective would be to see evangelical Christianity reinstated, to see the mainline Churches abandon their march towards Rome. Our preaching is full of the Word of God, our sole rule of faith and practice. It means we reject man's opinion and the impact of tradition and the apocrypha. Our message is not confined to the mere Love-texts of the Word of God or the Unity texts of the Word of God which ecumenicals pluck out of context. We believe implicitly in the Word of God but at the same time we recognise that there is also a balance to Love in that God is also Light. God's attributes of Power, Might, Wisdom, Love, Justice and Truth are all on an equal footing. There is none of his attributes pre-eminent. He demands punishment for Sin. The bible says 'The wages of sin is death'. God does not tolerate sin. His truth militates against sin yet he exercises love, mercy and grace. In the cross of Calvary we see all these things. Christ bears our sins. God could not dismiss the penalty. But we were not required to pay it, Christ took it for me. He received the punishment. God's truth was upheld. The ecumenical movement have a lop-sided approach to the attributes of God. They explode his love to such a degree that they destroy justice. They make him love sin. They even destroy hell." (Free Presbyterian Minister)

"The way to talk to people is anything but moralising, my natural way I must say, coming out of my training. 'You must not, you should not do that. You don't go up and say 'Were you at mass?' They just seize up. It has no point. I discovered this in a dramatic way. I met this young guy and just started talking to him. Two years later he came back to me and he said 'sure, you know me'. Young people behave differently. I thought that it was a great thing that he came back. You establish a trust, a contact. Young people come to me, often because I've done a wee thing for them.

The way forward is difficult. We are lucky that the great majority of our young people go to Church. We have to be careful that we don't drive the young people out of the Church. I don't want to dilute the thing but you don't ram the thing down their throats by making a big 'YOU MUST'. The onus is back on the clergy and the support groups. We have a lot of that back-up such as marriage groups who give people marriage guidance. We try to meet people at all the important times of their lives: birth, baptism, marriage, first communion, marriage, bereavement, death and so on." (Catholic Priest)

"I would have had a vision of what it means to be part of a team, a collaborative ministry. I would have had that vision. Clergy, laity and religious. But we're not on the same wavelength. I'd have found this diocese very traditional. The 'practice of the faith', attendance at Church is very high. I think the clergy live out of a different model of the Church than I would envisage. I'd see my role as orientated towards the marginalised, those outside the official Church. That's my particular orientation. Through group work, one to one, through overall care, concern, compassion. I'd also see my work in evangelisation, through pre-sacramental preparation of parents and so on. I'd see these as very vital moments in the life of parents to look at their life and faith. A lot of parents left school at 14 or 15 and their education literally stopped and certainly their faith development stopped. They may be mature adults but their faith is not mature..

...We get on with the clergy OK but there is no formal structure of a team. I meet them regularly on a one to one basis but not in any pattern. My dream would be that you'd have some form of pastoral council, a co-ordinated effort. We interact with agencies, St. Vincent de Paul, Playgroup, school and so on but we don't have co-ordination. We have huge gifts in Waterside. The extent of the parish has advantages and disadvantages. You do have the educated group within the parish. Certainly they run the St. Vincent de Paul and they're dedicated and excellent people. You lose the bond too though..

..Our task as religious is different from the clergy. The priests in their education would be much more focused on the formal, hierarchical Church. The sister is much more on ground-level. This is where I'd love to see the priest depending on the individual not just concentrate on liturgical celebrations and ask people why they don't come. We say that someone has 'marriage difficulties' but I think we have to enter into that. I think that there's another way of finding God. If the liturgical celebration is not a part of daily living it's not mature, it's a habit." (Sister)

"We had an instance of this power struggle recently. Our superior thought she'd set up a chat group with religious and clergy in the diocese. She thought out of courtesy she'd mention it to Bishop Daly. A few weeks later all the clergy got a letter from the Bishop telling them to invite all the

religious to a meeting in their parish. " (Sister)

Each of the Churches has clearly got very different ideas of priorities for ministry. Preaching, community, social outreach and saving souls, pastoral care, regular attendance, sacramental preparation are given different priorities by different people. Within denominations there is no coherence either.

Within the Catholic Waterside very little was known about the content of Protestant religious sensibilities beyond an acknowledgement that they existed. 'The Church' is a vast organisation large enough to be concerned with internal matters rather than external relations with other Churches. This creates it's own difficulties in terms of power struggles between different levels of authority. Nevertheless the fights about theological and religious priorities are internal to the Church. Protestant critiques of the Church seldom featured in Catholic considerations. To a large extent the Catholic Church is dominant enough to suggest to its members that it is the people. This is not the same as saying that Protestants pass unnoticed but rather to see 'Protestantism' as somehow peripheral to the Church. Politically, Catholic clergy act to voice their 'pastoral concerns' for their flocks. For Protestants this reinforces the sense of Church domination of Irish society and reinforces the belief that an Irish Republic has no place for them. In Derry this is underlined by the sense, often repeated, that Bishop Daly is the most powerful person in the City. Protestants, on the other hand, are very aware of the Catholic Church and of the influence of the hierarchy in the lives of Catholic people. They adopt differing degrees of distance to the Catholic Church in their outlook.

"Our views of the Catholic Church are well known. We don't see it as a religious body. We see it as a subversive organisation and we think that this is proved by history." (Free Presbyterian Minister)

"In ecumenism, Roman Catholics wouldn't have to drop so much as me because they agree with me. It's what they add on that worries me. Everybody is interested in the Catholic/Protestant divide. I can't see why there can't be mutual acceptance of both and that they're different. I've neighbours living beside me, Roman Catholics. We're great friends.. I regard the Roman Catholic Church as a Church in error. I think that they're so much in error that they unChurch themselves. It's an awful tragedy. If you add on to something that is perfect you destroy the perfection. There are 3 marks of a Church: first that the Word of God is

faithfully proclaimed. Second that the sacraments are administered as Christ proclaimed and third that they administer discipline. The Roman Catholics don't preach the Word of God and they've seven sacraments and not two." (Presbyterian Minister)

"I'd have friends I wouldn't bring together. There's this suspicion that you can't be a Roman Catholic and be saved. You can't be a Roman Catholic and have a personal relationship with Christ. This is not true. I've met many Roman Catholic people whose Christianity is very important to their lives, more important and more serious than it is to most Protestants. Where evangelicals are positive is that they encourage people to take Jesus seriously and to question their commitment to God." (Church of Ireland Woman)

"I'm a firm believer in Church unity. For an outsider to look at the Church divided into denominations and in our country you get the impression that they're at each other's throats, it doesn't do the Church any good. Unity is a long way away. I don't believe that we can just jettison what we believe in and bind ourselves together in an orgy of sentimentality. We have to accept that there are differences. In the meantime we accept what we have in common. True unity will not be man-made but God-given." (Church of Ireland Minister)

"When I was in a job before, not in Northern Ireland, I did a lot of work together with a Roman Catholic priest. We used to be a kind of double act and we shared the same building. We were great friends and we used to do chaplaincy work together. That's not to say there weren't differences but we had a strong personal bond." (Presbyterian Minister)

"I wasn't brought up to hate Roman Catholics just to know that they were different. We're more sacramental than the rest of the Protestants. Our folk would be closely linked to the Presbyterians. The majority wouldn't normally go into a Free Presbyterian Church. They'd go into a Free Presbyterian Church before they'd go into a Chapel!" (Church of Ireland Rector)

"I don't have any problem with inter-denominational things. This is only my view. I don't agree with all that I see but it doesn't mean I can't be there. I've preached in St. Eugene's Cathedral and I go to the service in Galliagh. I don't feel compromised. Some of us would be criticised for

being seen with Roman Catholic Clergy. I've been at so many funerals. In five years I've been to many things and I've never had anybody in my congregation come to me and say I shouldn't be doing it. In fact I've had the opposite. People come and say 'I saw you'." (Methodist Minister)

Often both Catholic and Protestant make allowances for religious differences by claiming that this does not affect them in the social sphere. The Catholic Church's claim to universal authority as a Church is mirrored by Protestant attempts to save the souls of 'lost' Roman Catholics. Often, both proclaim that these religious claims can be set aside and areas of co-operation found which do not challenge these central assumptions. The truth is that both cannot be permanently true. There is an inherent disequilibrium between groups who seek to 'win' over one another. Either the fight will re-emerge on the social level or the claims of mutual exclusiveness will be dropped.

One of the problems for Churches in Northern Ireland is that the option of separateness, 'simply' living as neighbours minding our own business is constantly overstepped. The implicit or explicit wish of all the Churches seems to be to convert the members of other Churches or to claim a superior vision. At the same time, the geographical separation is not absolute and so issues from mixed marriage to general access to power whether local or national constantly challenge simplistic notions that we can live apart on a daily basis. The Northern Irish Churches act as if the other Churches in the same place were somehow 'peripheral'. This creates the illusion of universality and yet every day the reality re-emerges that Northern Ireland is a mixed society. Even today, the Churches have been unable to live with pluralism within Christianity, let alone inter-faith pluralism. Perhaps this dimension of Christian division, present if submerged elsewhere, only becomes important in the violent circumstances of Northern Ireland where theological division is seen to compound social division..

The theological difficulties bind the social difficulties together and help to create a sense of belonging and identity within each community and a sense of difference between the two communities. These differences are differences between better and worse. My group is not 'just different' but somehow 'better than' the others. Every time my group is then attacked without justification as I see it, I am reinforced in my view that 'they' are the problem. Relations which are entered from positions of superiority and inferiority are bound to be competitive. Thus Church competition merges with community separation based on 'betterness' and inter-community relationships are to be built on this basis.

Theological differences in Northern Ireland are important even for people who have nothing to do with Churches because they inform how we identify each other. Fears of the other group arising out of violent contact are given theological justification and explanation. Thus secular fears of the Catholic Church merge wit h Protestant theological opposition to Catholicism. Churches seem to compound and rationalise fear. It is this suspicion and fear which people take into cross-community relations and which may limit the relations from the start. In this context, Churches which attempt purely social cross-community work and who have no intention of wrestling with their theological certainty that they are right must inevitably give a double message on one level or another. This has bedevilled the Churches from the start and perhaps explains the inability of the Churches to separate themselves from the divisions in the community. Indeed, they share them, even if they are differently articulated.

We can now examine some of the attitudes of clergy about their social task and their place in society. This may help to shed light on the thinking behind clergy attitudes in community life. Again, it must be said, that here there are distinct differences between and within denominations. This too confirms the curious paralysis of the Churches as social institutions in Northern Ireland.

"The ideals of priesthood I had in seminary are very different from the reality. You become a public image. You're not your own. People call. There's so many duties. Subconsciously I'm carrying a lot of comments about priests that I heard in the past that I am trying not to be. Then when you're trying to relax and the phone or the bleep goes. Others meet you as 'the priest' or 'the person of God' coming to meet you. The priest is a representative of God with the people. We say the prayers when the people are so weak. The priest is at the wake, he leads the coffin, he takes the mass, he leads the house and says the farewell prayer.. People are so weak in death. When I see the people's belief it's very beautiful.

When you're in civvies you're just somebody. When you're a priest people look. If people saw me coming out carrying booze out of an off-licence that's when I feel the pressure.

I wear the collar. It allows me to dress simply. But it means you have to live up to a certain thing. You've got to be kind. You've got to be gentle.

The struggle is to put on the mind of Christ. By my own preaching and living, I have to do it myself. That would be the hardest. I'm just trying to 'be in God'. When I'm not living in prayer it doesn't mean anything. Every Sunday seems to come so quick and you have to take on this public image. If I'm not praying then I'm becoming God not God is God. The cross is there but the chains do set you free.

How to be myself? Not to feel guilty when I put the feet up? People don't understand the priesthood. They see the big car and they think you're loaded.

I've no real 'mates'. They've all come and gone. Family becomes very important. You can go there to relax. It's hard to mix in the parish. I have to be free for everybody. I have to be isolated to be free for everybody. There's a contradiction there. I can't be too palsy walsy with people or others won't be free to come. The parish does become your home." (Catholic priest)

"The primary task of the minister is to bring the people at the coal face into contact with Christ in the bible. I can't be in Maydown or Coolkeragh but there are people in my congregation who are. I have to give them something to bring into their work, the information. Then you help people in their crises. We don't have bishops. With elders he's primus inter pares: a pastor, a preacher, a leader. Under God he keep the people fed with information. I believe the Church today should have 'body-life'. In the Church people should use their gifts. I wouldn't do certain things, not because I'm above them but because I'm doing other things. What normally happens is that ministers get involved in many things which take them away from their primary responsibility - preaching. Hence the decline in preaching. Billy Graham was asked what he would do if he started again. He said that he'd preach less and study more. The trouble is that people don't get around to doing what they're meant to do. My primary task is preaching. That's the Churches' primary task : the Word of God to the world." (Presbyterian Minister)

"My job is to shepherd my own flock and to make them more Christ-like." (Church of Ireland Rector)

"I don't visit in black suits. This is me as I am. They [the Congregation] will put you [the minister] on a pedestal if you let them. I go for a team

ministry. We try and let people speak. In my services we try to have some relationships between all the people there. Most people want to be on a pedestal. I'm sure of that. You watch some of them go into a pulpit and they change - voice, attitude. I think people find it hard to get to know two people in one body. Most ministers don't let the congregation see their other self.

The job of a minister is to build up the Church. Not the bricks and mortar. The minister should be delighted if people come to full Christian maturity even if that's more mature than the minister himself. I sometimes wonder if ministers worry that some of their members might not do their job better than them. I enjoy pastoral work. I'm better with people in their homes than in Church. In ministry at the moment we're looking at how to get people to move from membership to leadership. My Church has done very well in my absence due to illness. They took their own midweeks and attendance improved! I felt wick about it and thanked the lord about it. I'm very interested in the renewal of the Holy Spirit. It's not always easy for people in Londonderry. I've learnt from illness that I'm dispensable. I've learnt about my own limitations. I've learnt that my strengths don't lie where I thought they did. I've learnt to relax. It's been a very humbling experience. It's remarkable. I've been a better Daddy. I'm not quite sure I'm the same person I was seven years ago." (Presbyterian Minister)

"As far as I am concerned my principle task is to care for the people in my charge. I do so spiritually as well as other areas. People are a unity and to break this up into sections is hard. We care for the whole person. Obviously to conduct the worship in the Church is part of it. I've also to let people know that the Church is always available to all and sundry." (Church of Ireland Rector)

"The Minister should be a director, directing people, encouraging. All too often we develop a one-man ministry. We run around like blue-assed flies. When we get into a pulpit we're there giving a Word of God. I remember a professor of mine always said 'If a man hasn't been alone with his God and his bible then he has nothing to say in the pulpit.' Past generations had a greater knowledge of their dependence on God. Somewhere we've lost our dependency on God. We've replaced it with a dependency on the Government. We have to believe in the sovereignty of God but we also have to believe in the depravity of Man." (Presbyterian Minister)

"I see my job as a shepherd. I hope I measure up to it. I think that people are very proud of their Churches. They don't want shabby Churches. The people are very proud of them." (Catholic priest)

"Those attached to the Church look to the clergy to give a lead. I'm not so sure about those outside the Church. They expect us to speak on all moral issues, though not in a party-political manner. Church people look to us still. It's very much an ecclesiastical city in the sense that the Church is called upon to be involved at every level. The Church is given very high profile." (Methodist minister)

When 'the Churches' are asked to adopt a public profile inevitably The Church' is clerical. In this sense it is essential that those clergy are seen to be representatives of their people. In as far as traditional authority structures still exist, the appearance of clergy at events may result in the acceptance by Church members that this is a correct posture, 'simply because' a leader does it. Where these traditional structures do not exist the result may be a distancing of clergy from people meaning that the representative value of the clergy is reduced or rebellion in the Churches, as has happened in nearby Limavady Presbyterian Church.

Conclusions

We have already identified differences between denominations and within denominations. To this we can add different understanding of clergy and different relationships in each case between clergy and laity. All of these differences mean that Churches cannot function as 'interest groups' or 'trade unions' or 'lobbies'. Nor can they be assumed to hold similar 'policy views'. The Churches claim an allegiance which goes beyond these concepts, in the same manner as the democratic system or the state claims an allegiance beyond party interest. They cannot then be used as such by parties or groups within government. Parties or groups within government will almost certainly find willing friends and allies in the Churches and they will also find sworn enemies.

An outside body will not be able to persuade people inside Churches to act differently if they claim a higher authority to interpret doctrine than the Church authorities themselves. Thus they cannot 'force' Churches to adopt particular policies towards community relationships. Government can offer assistance to particular initiatives they choose to support or can choose to work outside the Churches altogether, offering an alternative. In Northern Ireland this is a difficult course to effect given the entanglements of history, culture, politics and religion.

The Waterside Churches live as part of the people of Derry. They can no longer be said to 'be the people' nor can the Waterside be understood without an understanding of the roots of these relationships both Catholic and Protestant. Whether the allegiance to Churches is active or nominal, a question of political identity or personal belief it nevertheless exists. An attack on the Catholic Church, for example, can easily be interpreted as an attack on the Catholic people. Protestant Church behaviour is seen as a matter of the utmost importance by Protestants, even those whose attachment is nominal. The Churches were part of the siege of Derry also.

The four largest Churches on the Waterside have a community work programme together which is impressive by its scale. It is fraught with many possible pitfalls. Its existence is a matter of some comment, especially the degree of commitment to it by the Waterside Church authorities. Nevertheless, it does not, nor can it, build community between the Churches except between the workers. Church institutions are involved, a number of people are deeply committed and the mass of the Church goes on in blissful separation, perhaps now with a better conscience.

This is not to deny the symbolic relevance of the initiative but to make a sober assessment of its possibilities. It is important that statistics on numbers inquiring do not blind us to limitations in the field of cross-community work. It is possible that the Churches committee is the tip of a larger iceberg a small outworking of deeply rooted community relationships. It was not my impression that this was the case. It is important to be clear about this if the WCA Centre is not to be seen as a sham.

The Protestants of the Waterside have lived through a whirlwind over the last twenty years. The community has the feel of a group who are not yet sure whether the wind has abated and have decided to keep their heads down and their mouths shut. There is a 'provisional' aspect to the present composition of the city. Within the Apprentice Boys there are moves to re-establish a presence in the city with a refurbishment of their headquarters. The incident of the changing of the city name opened up deep divisions within the Protestant community which have not been healed. The Churches themselves reflect these divisions. The Free Presbyterian Church is a small group. Their intense Protestantism and determination to defend Protestantism appeals to a community under siege. Their insistence that the larger Churches may be about to sell out to 'Romanism' has the effect that other Churches begin to 'justify' themselves in the face of this charge. Their impact is thus much greater than their size. In a city haunted by images of 'Lundy' these charges are very poignant.

There deepest effect seems to be on elements of Presbyterianism. Such charges stir up unease. The Presbyterian Churches in Derry have serious divisions between them in attitudes to cross-community relations and to the Roman Catholic Church. The Church of Ireland reflects serious divisions. The Methodists are a smaller, more intimate congregation whose very 'irrelevance' may make their position vis a vis Roman Catholics easier.

The Catholic Church has risen in stature with the political rise of Nationalist Derry. Long the most powerful protector and shelter of the community in the days of Unionist domination, the now permanent control of the council by Nationalists has allowed the Catholic Church to appear the most powerful body in the community. Given that the alternative leadership might be Sinn Fein this is often seen as a contribution to peace. At the same time it reinforces Protestant views that Nationalism is Catholicism and reinforces Free Presbyterian attitudes that behind Nationalism and IRA Republicanism lies the Catholic Church. Long years of clerical leadership have had an important impact on the relationship of clergy to people. One is reminded of the relationship between the Polish Catholic Church with the Solidarity Trade Union where the Church provided continuity and shelter through changing political circumstances. The result is a sense that the Catholic Bishop is the city's most powerful figure.

This appears to be true across all class divisions in Derry. While it is true that Church attendance in Protestant working-class areas is much lower than before, the Protestant organisations, the Orange Order and the Apprentice Boys, seem to extend the reach of the Churches into these areas too. Among Catholics, there is only circumstantial evidence of a serious erosion in the loyalty accorded to the Church. Even the clergy appear to be secure in their belief that young people will continue to go to Church. As such, the Church remains crucial vehicle for so-called 'vertical integration' that is the integration of all classes into one identity. Certainly there is absolutely no evidence of any cross-community class party emerging in Derry. Indeed the Protestant Churches tend to be less opposed to integration than many working-class non-Church Protestants. The monolithic quality of Derry Catholicism as seen from the outside may itself be the main reason for the continuation of Church influence among Protestants. However, the failure of Unionist politics in the city, coupled by the growing sense of 'creeping Irishness' in the city, leave the Churches as the most coherent Protestant institutions in the city.

The political importance of the Church makes ecclesiastical relations politically important. Both traditions minister to people under threat: the Protestants to the siege, to a sense of impending genocide the Catholics to a history of systematic discrimination and humiliation. All of these memories have been revived to make sense of the violent experiences of people over the last twenty years. The Churches memories do not appear to be any different to the memories of people in secular life. Indeed if anything the opposite is true. The Churches are the vehicles through which memories are given continuity, where solace is sought and where deliverance is prayed for. In such circumstances the Churches are not places to look for people to challenge old patterns of relating. Theologies are sought which make sense of experience and which place the blame firmly where it belongs - in the actions of 'the others'.

The question of who is primarily at fault and who has to change first is never forgotten. Joint services and actions which never wrestle with this underlying problem can always be accused of fence-sitting or irrelevance. The Churches then co-operate in the space left between them - community work. Of course, this too may lead to change in other spheres and it may not. We must be careful not to mistake a surface appearance of willingness to co-operate for a willingness to extend co-operation beyond certain well-understood limits.

SECTION SIX: REFLECTIONS, THE CHURCHES AND INTER-COMMUNITY RELATIONSHIPS

'The Churches' are central to Northern Irish life, both historically and in the present. Attempts to ignore or bypass them will always founder on the reality of stubborn belonging which has characterised Protestants and Catholics. But this is not to say that the Northern Irish conflict is 'religious' in a simplistic sense. In the sense of doctrinal holy war it is not. In another more profound sense, the churches are integral to the experiences and understanding of people in Northern Ireland. They are places and groups which channel, shape and direct the experiences of life in Northern Ireland. Of course this reality cannot be separated from experiences outside the churches in economic, social and political life and in family and community structures. Nevertheless the relationship of church and religious experience to these other aspects is an organic one in which one relates to the other in a web which cannot be reduced to one of its parts. Analyses which ignore this web of human experience by insisting on the centrality or primacy of one part over another part will always end up driving out the aspects of life which cannot be fitted into the ideology or theory. Religion, demoted to superstition in the vocabulary of the 'enlightened' elite, is an early casualty.

Ultimately the churches are integral to the identities of who belongs to 'us' and who belongs to 'them', the division which continues to dominate much of public life in Northern Ireland. In that sense too the institutional churches are part of the power conflicts which dominate and divide Northern Ireland past and present.

'Socialisation' is not sufficient as a description of this experience. The person 'becomes' in the course of these experiences, changing and being shaped by life. The reality of evangelical changes in people's lives cannot be 'denied'. The explanations which are provided can be challenged but the experience cannot be dismissed if we are seeking to be scientific. One person's religious experience does not simply or only mirror society but contributes to it. Churches are part of the shaping of person and society in Northern Ireland. In other words not only people are 'socialised' but society too is made what it becomes. The term 'culture', favoured by anthropology, has both personal and societal dimensions and intimates the dialectical relationship between the two.

For this reason 'The Church', let alone 'The Churches', is always elusive if we try to confine it to 'Institutions' or if we imply that their sole importance is 'personal'. Both interpretations fail to grasp the essential 'Both ... and' quality inherent in the churches claim as social organisers and guardians of a reality which transcends all social institutions and penetrates into every institution and person.

The churches in Northern Ireland are the oldest indigenous social institutions in the land and they are communities of people where values are passed on, friends are made, community is experienced and times of supreme personal and societal importance - baptism, first communion, marriage and burials - are shared. Even for those, mainly Protestant, who no longer maintain any active link to a church or to belief, the churches are pervasively present and important. Identity remains most accurately gauged by denomination. Friendship, marriage, residence and school remain stubbornly loyal to religious barriers. Whether religious or non-religious, Protestants share the same fears. 'The enemy' is common and in the ghettos which ensue the presence or absence of certain churches is the most tangible symbol of difference apart from the colours of kerb-stones and slogans.

Of course the Northern Irish conflict cannot be reduced to an inter-church war any more than Irish culture can be reduced to folk music or Protestant culture reduced to flute bands. In this view, the concept of 'Culture' must be more universal. The Churches are central to culture in Northern Ireland, to the shape and forms our lives take whether we are or are not believers. Like music and the presence or (official) absence of contraception they are clear markers of difference, a difference in whose wake everybody lives.

Violence which drives the groups apart unites those being attacked in a defensive alliance. Differences within groups are denied or repressed when attack is most acute. Thus religiosity or lack of it is a subordinate issue where the matter of common survival is at stake. Of course, paradoxically, the appearance of difference is complemented by the growing reality that everybody's lives are more and more the same - lived in the shadow of fear and murder to a greater or lesser extent. Fear and violence seem to make everybody the same.

In this context, the Churches in Ireland cannot be overlooked. Historically, colonial domination in Ireland was most acutely applied in the sphere of religion. The Penal Laws discriminated in public life on grounds of religion. Elsewhere in Europe, colonising powers discriminated against particular groups on the basis of language. In Ireland, anti-Catholicism became synonymous with anti-Irishness. Thus political and social economic difference was expressed in denominations and cultural and personal experience was shaped in this light. The eruption of violence between these groups, understandably understood by the rebels as a socioeconomic and political struggle, was and is experienced by Protestants as murder and rebellion which requires a defensive response, or more security. This in turn sets up further alienation in the Catholic community creating more violence and more response. Even more, fear and violence ensure that people in both groups try to ensure that every possible risk is avoided. Who constitutes a 'risk' is defined by their community of origin. The cleavage of religious origin marks the best indicator.

This cleavage over religious roots sets up two semi-autonomous worlds, symbolically attached to each other. The presence or absence of threat and/or violence in relationships now structures the experience of each community in two exclusive forms. For Catholics, violence exists in relation to the British State, to Unionist power and to Protestant paramilitaries. For Protestants violence exists in the IRA., Catholic theology, the threat of the Irish Republic and international misunderstanding. Each person may concentrate on particular aspects of the threat, and what is common is that there is this threat. Secure relations are now much easier to build within rather than between the experiences. Of course this means that each community becomes structurally similar but this similarity is never experienced. What is experienced is absolute opposition.

In this context the most important badge of difference is religion. The nature of church contacts at institutional level is determined by relations within each church. The 'Both social and personal' nature of churches means that while the churches are institutions they are also the people and the relations between them. Where people are under threat so the churches reflect that threat. In churches where the congregations choose the minister (e.g. Presbyterian) this may be particularly acute. Eventually those who come forward for professional jobs in the institutional churches (e.g. clergy) come out of these experiences also and the union is complete. Theology and politics come to be one. For Catholics this may be a theology of popular justice, for example liberation theology, which seeks to justify Catholic outrage as that of the people of God (the Poor?). For Protestants this may be a theology of siege which seeks to justify Protestant experience as that of the people of God (the Israelites?). Both give support, intellectual backing and faith to others whose theology may be weak but whose knowledge of violence and fear is strong. In general, however the church institutions have also sought to uphold the remains of social order in a period of social disintegration. This difficult task of seeking change and maintaining order has often led to them appearing to speak schizophrenically. The serious problem is that their is no agreement on who should change and how.

Churches are perfect refuges from siege. In the calmness of weekly service, in the wholeness of community life there is a respite from the siege and embattlement outside. Also in church membership is a guarantee that nobody belongs to 'the enemy'. The group is united in their opposition to the enemy. More importantly, violence to a member or to a member's family is here experienced as an attack on the group. Similarity within the group (i.e. the threat to all of us is confirmed) is matched by a magnified difference between the groups, a difference which is paradoxically similarity. In such an atmosphere those who equivocate are isolated and can be regarded as 'weird' or more sinisterly as 'quislings'.

Churches are also perfect bases for claiming the moral high ground, for rallying the fainter-hearted to the flag. The Penal Laws experience is a classic example. Theologies which emphasise not only difference but superiority have fertile ground. A political centrality for the churches also beckons, not simply in the nature of politics but in the content. On the one hand, by becoming involved in the content of politics, theological fears of 'priest-domination' become factual. On the other, in the face of raw 'fear and threat' which are not articulated but nevertheless present, explanations which lead to a stiffening of resolve, a will to resist and defend have a ready audience.

a. The Protestant Churches and inter-community relationships

The role of Protestantism in the ideology of Northern Unionists has long been a matter for academic discussion. The rise of Ian Paisley as the most visible, and most popular, leader of Unionism and political protestantism has meant that a simple dismissal of the link is always likely to prove untenable. Recently, Steve Bruce tried to show a coherent link between Free Presbyterian Calvinist ideology and the politics of Ulster Protestants. In so doing he does not adequately explain how it comes that a small extreme group can come to articulate most appropriately the fears of a broad section of society such that even Unionists who are opposed to Paisley and Free Presbyterianism are forced to acknowledge his primacy. The presence of Paisley certainly ensures that the 'Protestant' part, the religious tinge, does not disappear on the Unionist agenda.

The Free Presbyterian Church remains and has remained a tiny minority among Protestants. Despite the proliferation of a number of large buildings throughout Northern Ireland the membership of the church is less than a tenth that of the Presbyterian Church and less than a quarter that of the Methodist Church. At the same time the Free Presbyterians personify the political face of Ulster protestantism. How does this come to be?

In our investigations we found that 'protestantism' is more easily defined in political terms than in theological terms. The unity on the evil of IRA violence lives side by side with great variation in theological outlooks. What violence has done is to turn those religious Protestants, who from religious reasons seek to secure protestantism by any means, into prophets and defenders rather than lunatics and extremists. For people outside Northern Ireland the appeal of Ian Paisley is difficult to understand. He is portrayed variously as a fanatic, a fascist, an ayatollah and a lunatic. For Protestants inside Northern Ireland he clearly has a different image unless we are to conclude that they all share these characteristics.

We also found that Church people react out of their situations much as non-church people. Where this leads people to seek religious reasons for their fate the dangerous combination of certainty and rightness raises its head and some at least view a response as holy war. The history of Ireland and Britain makes this combination relatively easy in Northern Ireland.

The churches in Ireland have a tradition of being part of the people. Unlike elsewhere the churches have retained an important social position. We have seen how this means that the churches have found it difficult to respond in a manner which marks the churches out as different to any other social institution. Indeed they are so close to the events that they are blamed for them in many quarters. This explains the persistent use of the word 'Protestant' and 'Catholic' as shorthand to describe the 'sides' in the political arena. The churches have certainly not been able to break this association.

In our survey we found that anti-Catholicism in theological terms was fairly widespread among Protestant clergy, especially Presbyterians. Many of the same people declared a willingness to work with Roman Catholics in 'non-controversial' spheres. Such a viewpoint poses problems in that it implies that protestantism is closer to God, to Truth than Catholicism in an absolute sense. This already makes relationships between people difficult. In the context of violence where people divide on religious lines in their attitudes to, for example, the security forces the religious superiority very quickly becomes social and personal mistrust leading to all of the symptoms we have observed.

Many Protestants have experienced at first hand the murder of their friends, relatives and colleagues. The besiegement of Ulster Protestants is a fact for many of the congregations and parishes of Ulster. As we have repeatedly shown, churches provide safe havens, anchors of security, identity and belonging from which the 'enemy' is excluded. Only 'Us' are in the church. In this context an attack on one by someone outside is experienced as an attack on our church membership. Churches are expected to provide comfort and sustenance in times of trial. This they do. Clergy and people experience the same part of reality. Most importantly, the collective bond is closer between church members than it is between 'British People' in Kent and in Dungannon. People in Kent and Dungannon simply do not have the same enemy, except perhaps after the successful IRA attack on soldiers in Deal. Mostly many Ulster Protestants experience violence against them but the same is not true of all British people. Ulster Protestants are therefore more reliable allies in the will to resist the onslaught than the British as a whole. Indeed as the British seem to distance themselves evermore from the experience of Ulster Protestants, so Ulster Protestants must rely ever more firmly on their own resources. Thus Protestantism becomes firmly mixed up with identity because it is the most coherent identity in the face of violence.

Of course this begs the question as to how avowedly non-religious people fit into such a scheme? What they share in common with the church goers is the sense of besiegement and violence. They too have been abandoned by Britain or at least recognise the increasing distance. The Protestant perspective, while never wholly believed, provides a coherent political body willing to fight to defend Ulster. This aspect of protestantism appeals to a beleaguered and angry people. Loyalism is thus careful to maintain its links with protestantism. It ensures a broad front of people opposed to the violence of the IRA and provides a coherent and determined intellectual basis for opposition.

Politically the 'Protestant' label is a flexible tool. It is supportive of the Union but allows for a 'back-up clause'. If Britain fails then protestantism will continue to fight for Ulster against the IRA. Campaigns for an independent Ulster never gather sufficient support in themselves and yet integration into the United Kingdom as integral to England has never appeared likely or plausible. Protestantism has the advantage that it combines opposition to the IRA with a number of political alternatives. Hence it is grounded in self-confidence not dependent on British help. This means that Protestant opposition to Catholic power is a rock on which opposition to the IRA can be firmly based. Its political appeal in an uncertain context is obvious.

The most obvious gap is that protestantism is defined in terms of domestic politics rather than in terms of the churches. The churches as institutions have somewhere disappeared into oblivion. Protestantism becomes the experience of violence by Catholics and republicans as much as a faith and manner of living in all contexts. In order to understand this it is necessary to employ our distinction between the churches as institutions and the churches as people. The churches seem unable to extricate the faith of the church from the desire to defeat the IRA. A 'United Ireland' can be feared in political and religious form and the churches appear largely to allow this confusion to stand. In the context of regular murders the anger of congregations is also likely to mix up political and faith positions if the 'IRA' are seen as Catholic and evil.

The Presbyterian Church is the largest Protestant denomination. Like the Free Presbyterians, and before them, the Church claims to originate in the teachings of Calvin. Similarly both call upon the Westminster Confession of Faith as a central tenet, albeit with significant concessions for interpretation within the Presbyterian Church. Presbyterianism has a democratic structure with considerable autonomy for each congregation. The Church has a governing body, the General Assembly, which meets annually. Within the instructions of the General Assembly each congregation has considerable independence. We have seen that this means that congregations vary from place to place. From one congregation to the next the atmosphere, history and theology may vary considerably. This local freedom means that the church has an identity in its government but that many things may vary from place to place. Elsewhere in Europe, Calvinist and Reformed churches still oppose Rome but within a framework of recognising some common ground and areas of agreement. Nowhere has it meant the ending of the existence of reformed churches. Rather it means that religious denomination is no longer a reason for war.

The clear difference in Northern Ireland is the presence of considerable violence. In a context of increasing ghettoisation, continuing burials of colleagues and a clear sense of Protestant identity against catholicism violence the enemy comes to mean the IRA and the Catholic community. Increasing separation means that empathy breaks down between communities, bitterness grows and theologies which emphasise Protestant separateness have a willing audience. Indeed theologies which appear to suggest an openness, such as varieties of ecumenism, are identified with appeasement. The very decentralised nature of presbyterianism means that congregations call ministers after their own image. Beleaguered congregations may call ministers who will bolster their resolve. Theologies which identify the experience of Protestants with that of the children of Israel, God's chosen people, have a ready audience. Catholics who challenge security forces actions or bury members of the IRA are seen to be part of the attack on Protestants. Theological objections to Catholicism are reinforced in practice by the political actions of priests. The Catholic hierarchy becomes an insidious political force proved by its domination of the Irish Republic and their permanent presence in Catholic areas. Theological fears are backed up with empirical evidence. More and more young people from these real and theological experiences feel called to the ministry and the cycle continues. The result is a binding of minister, elders and congregation in a stand against 'evil'. Less and less people have any experience of a more complex reality.

Of course this only reflects part of the Presbyterian experience. The last twenty years have seen the opening up of massive divisions within the Presbyterian Church. Many of the ecumenical ventures in Northern Ireland, e.g. Corrymeela, grew out of Presbyterian roots. At the same time our survey showed that Presbyterian clergy were by far the most likely to refuse any theological contact with Catholics. The result is a church which is institutionally large in which the institutional apparatus has no final authority. Any church 'power' always depends on the acceptance of the churches' 'authority'. Presbyterianism, more perhaps than any other denomination, seems unable to speak with one voice.

There are several implications of this. First Unionism and Protestantism continue to be closely identified now reinforced by the reality of violence. Violence calls forth deaths and the dead are buried by clergy. The death is remembered by the congregation as one of 'their' dead, always unjustified to some degree. In Presbyterianism this is particularly true for the security forces. The Minister is expected to proclaim the death unjustified. A series of attacks from the same source is liable to bring forth calls for the murderers to be stopped. In Northern Ireland these calls are directed at political sources. In Presbyterianism the calls are directed against the I.R.A., couched in terms of 'more security'. This besiegement, so clear to minister and congregation has its political expression in Unionism. The interplay of history, violence, experience and justification all serve to defend the besieged.

Any resolution by the General Assembly in just about any sphere will always be hedged around with large levels of dissent. A 'policy' on inter-community relations which the General Assembly adopts is likely to have very differential effects. The Church continues to exist as an institution but the reality of this church is likely to be different in different places. Attempts by the General Assembly to comment on the political situation expose division. The church institution is powerless to stop itself being taken over by congregational experience. The 'Presbyterian Church' as institution becomes identified by default with the response to violence. This happens most acutely at funerals not in the General Assembly. The political place of the church as defender and comforter is magnified with every death. Other strands of theological thinking are more submerged and the fear and anger expressed at funerals comes to dominate. The political hatred of the IRA seems to have a church counterpart. Any contact with contaminated bodies (e.g. the World Council of Churches, the Council of Churches for Britain and Ireland) becomes suspicious.

The size of the gap between the Church as an institution and its ability to influence its members contrasts sharply with the Free Presbyterian Church. Unlike the mainline churches the Free Presbyterians are able to produce a uniform 'party line' on anti-Catholicism and the implications in political terms. This in turn threatens to be an attractive alternative to Presbyterianism in the event of the Presbyterian Church failing to back up the Protestant experience. For Presbyterians this is a particular risk because of the claims on the roots of Calvin and the Westminster Confession as well as similarities in church government and cultural style. Thus Free Presbyterianism comes to exert a considerable influence on some Presbyterians despite attempts to draw distinctions. A Free Presbyterian jibe that the Presbyterians are no longer loyal to their Calvinistic roots seems to set up uncertainties in many minds especially given Paisley's apparent ability as a prophet of the Protestant predicament.

Theology which sees in Roman Catholics only a mission field and in Roman Catholicism apostasy, never deeply buried in Ulster, is now widespread, respectable and influential. This means that future contact between Presbyterians and Catholics is also pre-empted except where conversion is central. In this view, Presbyterians who continue to seek relationships with Catholics are people who would appease the devil. Between the devil and Christ there can be no compromise. Translated into politics this has no end except the eternal fight of good and evil where even victory will be won only at the price of eternal vigilance. While this is the view only of a minority of Presbyterians, in the context of violence any refusal to meet the other on an equal basis is read or can be read as part of the conflict. Thus the refusal of Ministers to meet priests or of Presbyterians to meet Catholics has political ramifications which are hard to separate from theological considerations. Effectively Roman Catholics are 'unclean'. The experience of violence confirms this and allows those who wish to avoid theological contamination social licence to do so. The social status of the clergy in rural towns means that this has massive social and political implications. Political and theological protestantism are now very often the same.

The result is that the Presbyterian Church cannot separate itself from the Protestant experience of violence. It constantly speaks to and from this experience. Once it does this it is no longer any different from the Free Presbyterian Church unless a clear distinction can be drawn between Free Presbyterian and Presbyterian political attitudes or interpretations of the gospels. This not being the case, the Free Presbyterians often appear to be more coherent Presbyterians. The institutional weakness of the Presbyterian Church means that its statements are likely to be weakly oppositional to the Free Presbyterians (so as not to offend sympathisers) or weakly supportive (so that Free Presbyterian statements are clearer and more politically coherent.) The result is the worst of all possible worlds for the Presbyterian Church. The church is now enmeshed in the political conflict and the largest Protestant church is powerless to act as an institution in the situation. Conversely, religion can now be blamed for the conflict and the Presbyterian Church cannot act to stop this.

The other Protestant denominations do not exhibit quite the same level of crisis. Various interpretations can be advanced for this. In the case of the Church of Ireland, the Church has never been identified with 'Ulster' to the same degree as the Presbyterians. The 'Irish' and 'British' dimensions to the church past and present means that the Ulster experience is qualified. Secondly the hierarchical nature of the Church of Ireland means that local experience is always supplemented with the experience of the hierarchy who are close enough to have some authority and far enough to allow experiences to impinge on their reactions. The hierarchy are linked with the Anglican Communion. The Presbyterian Church has progressively cut its links with other bodies outside Northern Ireland. The essence of Presbyterianism lies in its congregational structure. The essence of Anglicanism is a broad church held together by an undogmatic hierarchy. In the context of radicalised congregations the Presbyterian General Assembly must bow. In the same circumstances, the hierarchy can act as a restraining influence. This may also mean however that the Church of Ireland leadership is no longer closely bound with its grassroots membership. We have seen evidence that public gestures by Bishops may not meet with universal approval from those further down the hierarchy. The Church of Ireland as an institution is also unable to 'deliver' a political unanimity on inter-community relationships. What is possible is an appearance of greater cohesion. Thirdly, the Free Presbyterian threat is much more distant. Theologically, historically and conceptually there is very little overlap between the Church of Ireland and the Free Presbyterians. The Free Presbyterian claim to represent a 'pure' form of Christianity cuts little ice in Anglican circles. For them Paisley remains a political figure of limited theological importance. Indeed although the so called Anglo-Catholics are a small minority in Northern Ireland an awareness of this dimension of theological thinking within the Anglican communion may ensure a degree of separation in the political field.

The Church of Ireland has, like other Protestant denominations, also failed to draw any clear distinction between protestantism and unionism. It too is characterised by weak institutions and dominated by funeral orations. Violence has clearly emphasised the church as refuge and sanctuary. The church clearly plays a part in the community under siege. However, the doors are never as tightly shut for the Church of Ireland as for Presbyterians. The historically broad base of theology, the Irish dimension and the existence of hierarchy have kept the Church of Ireland active on the international stage at a time when most Presbyterians have withdrawn

Methodism too has retained an Irish dimension to a greater degree than Presbyterianism. The Methodist Church is everywhere too small to be the numerical or political heart of Protestantism. Historically Methodism spread in a totally different manner to Presbyterianism or Anglicanism. Irish Methodism does not seem to be officially identified with political protestantism. In common with the Church of Ireland, there is theological difference between Methodists and Free Presbyterians. This is not to say that Methodism in Ulster has no connection to political protestantism but the structure and nature of that relationship is different to the Presbyterians or Church of Ireland. Traditional Methodist roots in the working classes mean that the Methodist church has maintained an active 'social' ministry. This has often been non-sectarian in character. We saw that social concern has remained an important strand of Methodism. The relatively small size of Methodist congregations may prevent the sense of 'besiegement' that seems to develop in Presbyterian and Church of Ireland circles. The policy of constant change of Ministers may also ensure that Methodist congregations remain open to outside influences from time to time. Of course the Methodist church is weak as a political institution. It is not a part of Methodism to be a political party. Methodists have not attempted to use 'Methodism' as a political philosophy and so the public profile of the Methodist Church is lower than the smaller Free Presbyterian Church. This does not mean that Methodism is irrelevant but that its importance is pervasive rather than apparent.

The most important external changes in Protestantism have been secularisation and the growth of smaller, mostly evangelical, churches and house groups. This disintegration of Church structures does not mean that 'religion' or even 'the churches' are irrelevant. It does seriously change the nature of the nature of what 'Church' is. The churches may become more disparate, more chaotic organisations paralysed from 'doing' anything except in small groups. Thus we can explain the paradox of huge social presence and paralysed central church institutions. Violence has everywhere had a differential effect. It has united some together in opposition to the enemy, it has sent others looking for an emotional experience of religion, it has alienated many from Christianity and it has led others to seek ways to work across denominational divides.

The denominations which all arose and developed in historical contexts shaped the structure of Northern Ireland society. The impact of violence has seemed to splinter the denominations. At the same time the churches have in places become places of close political and personal identity at local level. The Churches are called to interpret and minister to their congregations in this context. What precisely the ministry will be will depend less on denomination and more on the particular outlook, experience and history of each congregation or parish.

'Denomination' has become a poor guide to political or social position. One Presbyterian Church may be totally different to another. The Church of Ireland exhibits the same tendency. The Free Presbyterians are unique among the small churches in their claims to fulfil or interpret a political role in Ulster. Unlike the larger churches they are also effectively unanimous in their antipathy to Catholicism. This gives them a political weight which is far greater than their denominational strength and effectively cripples the Presbyterian Church as an institution.

The larger Protestant church institutions cannot guarantee that the response will be uniform among their congregations and parishes. A government looking for partners in inter-community relations policy will have to take this into account in the formulation of policy. Repeated calls for 'The Churches' to do something are probably too late and possibly concentrate time and effort in inappropriate areas. They may rest on an inadequate media-led image of the churches which wishes to turn them into identifiable political parties which can be understood as pawns or kings in a game of chess which is controlled by political factors. This is not to say that the churches should not act together. Rather it is to recognise that they cannot at present and that changes may happen at many levels. By concentrating on large institutions alone opportunities may be lost and an unwanted publicity given to the most politically coherent institution, the Free Presbyterian Church.

b. The Roman Catholic Church and Inter-community relationships

The Roman Catholic Church has experienced the violence of Northern Ireland mostly from a different perspective to that of the Protestant Churches. 'Catholics' make up the other party to the debate. In addition Catholicism is fundamentally different from Protestantism in structure in that 'Protestantism' is a generic name for numerous churches each separate while 'Catholicism' is a unitary structure which is organised internationally, nationally and locally both in parishes and in religious orders. For these reasons it is easier to deal with Roman Catholic experiences of violence and intercommunity relationships in a separate section.

As we outlined, the Penal Laws and the colonial experience shaped much of the Catholic Irish identity. Unified by O'Connell in a national campaign for Catholic Emancipation, Pan-Catholicism has become synonymous for many Protestants with Irish Nationalism. The depth of Irish attachment to Catholicism is famous throughout Europe and Irish religious are scattered throughout the world. Furthermore, the Irish emigrants to the United States established their communal lives and identity around the construction of churches. This testifies to the cultural centrality of the church and has led to a high political and social profile for the hierarchy in Irish life.

As we have time and again confirmed, the Catholic Church in Northern Ireland is central to community identity and community life. The church is very well attended and virtually the entire community is baptised and has regular links to the church. There is as we saw considerable evidence that this may be changing among young people in Belfast though there is very little evidence of serious change outside the city. Experience of the Church is universal at some level in the 'Catholic' community. More, perhaps, than protestantism it is the universal glue of the community, an identifiable part of private and public life at many levels. Politically, the Catholic community looks in different directions republicans who justify political violence, nationalists who detest it and Catholic unionists. Two issues unite the bulk of the community - Catholicism and violence.

The experience of violence in Catholic areas is fundamentally different to that of Protestants. Unlike Protestants, Catholics do not focus on the IRA in the same manner. The IRA, as we saw, are far from universally admired or respected. Indeed they are more often despised. Nevertheless IRA violence is seen in another context, particularly focused on the security forces; RUC, UDR and British Army. All three are widely regarded as 'external' to the community and as contributing to the growth of the IRA. Particularly in the city ghettos the security forces are seen as forces to harass and intimidate the local population.

The church in this context acts as the institution which continues to represent the population to the authorities. As we saw in Derry, this means that they act as advocates in cases of harassment, a task which does not occur in anything like the same proportions in Protestant areas. Thus at one and the same time the church can be portrayed as the State in nationalist communities and as refusing to put its back behind the forces of law in the battle against terrorism. This same double-bind re-occurs in various forms over schools, ACE schemes and issues such as the hunger strike. Furthermore, in the Protestant community the State relates directly to its citizens without institutional intermediaries. In the Catholic community the intermediary place of the church increases the institutional power and profile of the church. This gives the hierarchy a public profile as political actors which confirms to republicans that the church is a conservative agent which, as was claimed in one of our studies, works to secure the British Empire and at the same time confirms to Protestants that the Catholic Church is a huge political power, the real enemy behind the IRA. If you are looking for such evidence in a siege or in the context of a struggle for justice of which you are certain there is ample evidence for both. Ironically the Catholic Church is regarded then as the representative of both States in Northern Ireland. By Protestants it is regarded as the precursor of the Irish State. It is also seen as the real power. In places such as Derry where the local Catholic majority can exercise some limited political influence, the high profile of the Catholic Bishop is seen as evidence of this. Where nationalists gain power so the church takes over. At the same time local critics of the church in West Belfast regard the church as the agents of the British State in Northern Ireland for their refusal to back ACE schemes whose funding was curtailed under suspicion that they had paramilitary links. Both and neither would appear to be true, but the field for conspiracy is immense.

The violence has put serious strains on the institutional authority of the church. The spread of English-based metropolitan culture through television and radio has added to the strains on catholic perspectives. The result is an increasingly difficult situation, particularly in inner-city areas of Belfast and the peripheral housing estates. The church is also engaged in propaganda to stop the spread of modern ideas regarding divorce, birth control and abortion.

We found that the church is now part of serious local struggles in Belfast. The violence has had a very disruptive effect in the Catholic community. Policing is now effectively in the hands of local paramilitaries. Daily violence is common through car-theft, punishment shootings, intimidation and security force patrols. Public life in these areas is held together by common norms of behaviour between neighbours and a moral code which is most firmly stated by the church. The church is the centre of local opposition to Sinn Fein.

Government policy on the funding of community groups and the attitude of the Greater Belfast local councils has meant that many community groups are starved for statutory funds. This is based on suspicion that public money was buying weapons for the IRA or at least allowing paramilitaries to develop deep community roots and a higher local profile. Much of the alternative funding for these areas, among the poorest in statistical terms in the United Kingdom, has been channelled through the church. This is particularly true of the ACE schemes. The churches' presence ensures that the money does not fall into paramilitary hands. At the same time it gives the church authorities considerable economic control in their areas, it concentrates high-ranking positions into clerical hands and it has polarised local attitudes to the church particularly among young people. The result is that the church authorities are seen to be ever more powerful and resentment of this control seems to be growing. Sinn Fein have managed to raise their profile locally as champions of the people's groups and have won votes locally on such issues.

We also found disintegration on a number of other levels. First family break-up is now increasingly common in Catholic areas. Divorce has begun to be registered in schools. Secondly, church teaching on contraception and family planning is widely ignored in many urban areas. Thirdly the political and economic power of the church have led to well-publicised attacks from local people such as Father Des Wilson who have accused the church of kow-towing to the British State. He has also sought to import some of the ideas of liberation theology and apply them to Catholic West Belfast. The result is an ambiguity on the violence of the IRA.

The implications of all this are difficult to assess. It is important to note that as the Protestant churches vary from place to place, so too the Catholic parishes are different. Outside Belfast we found much less evidence of any serious power struggle between the church and other groups. The ACE problem did not appear to be as acute. This was mostly because the church was widely accepted in a cultural sense as the moral authority in a manner which no longer applies in Belfast.

The Catholic Church is thus much more visible as an institution than the Protestant churches. The hierarchical structure of the church enables a more definite media image in the persons of Bishops and Cardinals than the Presbyterian or Methodist structures. This reinforces any Protestant fears that the church as an institution is to be feared. Control of schools, ACE schemes and many social services by the church may reinforce Protestant views. The modern media portrayal of 'The Churches' as the church leaders may also account for some of the misleading ideas of the actual nature of the church and the nature of church leadership. It also sharpens the view that a church is a political party. The situation becomes more complex again when the church authorities are actually granted temporal economic control, which allows the media image to exist against a background of some truth.

The Catholic Church has been most insistent that the Northern Irish conflict is not religious. This may be true on one level and yet, as we have seen, some important people, mostly extreme Protestants, dispute this. For most Catholics the problem is one of injustice, a permanent state of second-class treatment in all spheres. It is a political, social and economic matter. In this context inter-church relations are important to show Christian charity and to underline that the church opposes the use of violence but they are not the core of the matter. Nevertheless the theologies of Irish Catholicism continue to display a considerable amount of the 'superiority' we noted in protestantism above.

A continuing claim on the superiority of the Catholic Eucharist must imply that the Catholic version is closer to 'the Truth' than various Protestant interpretations. The continuing pressure that children of a mixed marriage be brought up as Catholics is a further signal to Protestants that the Catholic Church is imperialist and regards them as inferior. Schools policy is also controversial. The church claims that it is important to protect a different ethos, 'of love', but continues to be extremely hostile to integration with Protestants. Finally many Catholic clergy still refer to ecumenism as the 'return of the separated brethren' and regard their institution as the visible form of 'the one true church'. Together with the political, social and cultural authority now exercised by the priesthood, Protestant militants can easily construct a convincing case that 'Home Rule is Rome Rule'. All of this is certainly present in inter-community relationships in Northern Ireland.

Over the last twenty years, catholicism has also thrown up its own form of militancy in the form of types of liberation theology. Developed in the Latin American context as a theology for the poor, it has been translated into a theology which claims to fight for the poor in Northern Ireland. The poorest are identified with the Catholics of the ghettos and their struggle is said to be 'just'. In some forms this then becomes an apologia for IRA violence. The justice of the cause justifies everything. In a sense it is the mirror of Protestant siege theology. 'The poor', an identified group, are justified everything because their cause is righteous. They are the true 'children of God'. In siege theology as we saw, Protestants take the place of the poor. If siege theology provides a political justification for siege defence then this form of liberation theology provides a justification for besieging. Thus Protestant accusations that Catholicism is indifferent to the murder of Protestants are given renewed force. Any attempts to clamp down through security policy will reinforce the arguments for liberation theology. In fact they appear to be twins.

It must be stressed that liberation theology plays no part in official church statements. Indeed most of those who claim a link to liberation theology would be highly critical of the official church. Nevertheless its development is an important strand in the continuing interrelationship of religion and politics in Ireland. The church hierarchy have been more concerned to see the establishment of church approaches to family and personal life especially as the church authorities are seen to be ignored by large numbers of Catholics especially in the area of family planning.

Many Roman Catholic clergy, as we saw, are actively interested in extending the scope of their social activity. This reflects the poverty of many parishes in Northern Ireland and the high levels of unemployment. Once the ghettos have been established the issues of poverty and the related problems become the most urgent questions in daily life. As we saw in Belfast and Derry, Intercommunity relations are considered relatively unimportant by many in comparison to unemployment. The daily violence on the estates combined with 'ordinary' parish work means that anybody working here is likely to get caught up in questions and have little time for inter-community relations. Most people in ghettos have developed lives which take little account of the existence of another community. This is of course true everywhere but in Northern Ireland this means the parallel development of antagonistic communities who oppose each other politically along these lines.

Ghettoisation means that inter-community relations have to be fostered by deliberate means with all the problems this entails. In the context of poverty the enthusiasm for such efforts may not be widely spread. Catholic areas of West Belfast fall into this category in a classical manner. The church is the only local agency which can focus such activity and it too is mostly active to preserve the fabric of daily life internal to the ghetto. In this context church attitudes to protestantism expressed in terms of theology, schools, human rights, violence and the constitutional status of Northern Ireland are all 'political'. Of course churches in other places have attitudes to political matters but the different context of Northern Ireland gives such involvement a different dimension.

Final Remarks

The Northern Irish conflict is not about 'theology' for most of the people here. For nearly all nationalists it is expressed in political and socioeconomic terms. For most Protestants it is a battle to defeat the IRA murderers, to save Northern Ireland from the Catholic Church and the Irish Republic. And yet the nature of Northern Irish culture, the division of experience by religious tradition in relation to the British State and Irish Nationalism mean that the churches are integral to the division unless they can separate themselves and their faith from an identity with a political goal i.e. United Kingdom or United Ireland. In as far as they do not or cannot do this their actions are part of the political relationships between the groups and indeed they become the organising principle of that division even if people are virulently atheist. Theology then plays a role whether people know it or not.

Catholicism is clearly political in a different way to protestantism. There are no leading politicians who stake their position on a defence of Catholicism. Nevertheless the Catholic Church has a much higher profile as a social, political and economic actor than the Protestant institutions who are content to hand over most of this activity to 'their' state. In this sense it has a political reality to be attacked in a far more concrete sense than protestantism. Thus those Protestants who fear catholicism can credibly claim a Catholic political goal. The existence of the Irish Republic with its 97% Catholic population ensures that Catholicism is shown to have political aims by looking across the border. How a State made up of so many Catholics might avoid reflecting Catholic teaching has not yet been explained.

Religion and the Churches thus have a crucial part to play in inter-community relations but this cannot be forced. Policy and practice can only be successful if the change is desired.

Notes

1. For a development of this thesis see Frank Wright, 'Northern Ireland: a comparative analysis", Gill and Macmillan 1987.

CONCLUSIONS

1. The place of Churches in Northern Ireland Society

a. Churches remain the largest non-governmental institutions in Northern Ireland. They are present in every part of the country reflecting the historical importance of the Church as a social and cultural organiser. In Northern Ireland they remain central to society.

b. Churches are the largest organisations with voluntary membership in Northern Ireland. In comparison to England, Scotland and Wales attendance and the importance attached to it remain high.

c. Churches are important parts of the Northern Ireland economy. Much work in Churches by Church members is unpaid, clubs and societies generally have voluntary leaders and Churches employ many people. In addition Church collections raise considerable funds for a variety of other organisations particularly registered charities. (See below for ACE)

d. Churches are centres of important and lasting networks of relationships. In rural areas extended families, friendships, social activity and business contacts are all related to Church. In urban areas the first three continue to be true to some extent.

e. Churches are crucial markers of identity in Northern Ireland. They are one means by which the political complexion of an area can be gauged. They are central to the different experiences of children growing up through schools and youth activities and as refuges in times of trouble. Marriage, friendship, school and even career are often formed in the communities in which Church plays a part.

f. Churches carry many of the cultural memories of Northern Ireland through an institutional continuity which stretches back to the sixteenth century. They thus have an institutional authority which predates the people alive today. They are thus also entwined with the cultural and political history of the people.

g. In rural areas Churches remain important parts of the social order. They have an authority and respect based on a widespread acceptance of their moral leadership. In such settings the clergy are considered very important local figures. To some extent this has broken down in urban areas particularly among working class men. Nevertheless their authority is considerably greater than the institutional authority of Churches in Great Britain. No single Church can claim the attendance of the Roman Catholic Church in the Irish Republic and so ecclesiastical authority in the North is more fragmented though not necessarily less public.

h. Churches have suffered seriously under the impact of violence. In many ways the experience of violence has affected the Churches more profoundly than the Churches have affected the violence. The institutional coherence and popular authority of the central Church leaderships has declined and in a society which is marked out by the number of violent deaths the theological difficulties are serious. How does a religion based on 'Agape' account for the present spread of terror in a Church-dominated society? Violence naturally varies from place to place and the response to it is similarly variable. The result is that congregations and parishes are very different from one another even within denomination. Denomination cannot be taken as an absolute signifier for political or social position. Popular experience of 'the Churches' is therefore likely to be very different in different places.

i. Precisely because the Churches are spread so widely throughout Northern Ireland, when taken together, they reflect all of the strands of Ulster politics within their institutions. Churches as institutions have been unable to make any clear or consistent difference between a 'Christian' response to violence and politics and a 'non-Christian' one. As such politics appears to dominate the Churches more than vice versa.

j. There has been some disintegration of Church structures and authority in recent times. Protestant Churches continue to struggle with falling attendances in Belfast and the growth of small House Churches beyond any central institutional control while the Roman Catholic Church suffers from serious political trouble in West Belfast and a widespread flaunting of its authority particularly in areas such as birth control.

2. The Churches and inter-community relationships

a. The Churches are often blamed for a conflict in which the most consistently perceived dividing line is between Catholics and Protestants. Certainly they seem to be unable to convincingly rid themselves of this association. Funerals and orations at them seem to be the focus of the most public duties of the Church in this context. The Churches association with funerals and with responses which flow from violent deaths mean that they too are integrated into the whole 'system in turmoil'. At the same time, many clergy have tried to use funerals as places for appeals for an end to reciprocal violence. The importance of such occasions cannot be overlooked.

b. Protestantism is said to be more political than Catholicism. This arises from the fact that some, particularly around Ian Paisley, express their outlook in theological terms. The fear of 'Rome' is certainly not mirrored by a fear of institutional Protestantism on the Catholic side. Nevertheless, as an institution, the political profile of the Roman Catholic Church is much higher than that of any Protestant Church. In the absence of a State to which many Catholics owe their unconditional allegiance, the Church has become the main institutional organiser. The result is that any Protestant fears, whether expressed by Church-goers or atheists, appear to be confirmed from the perspective of someone looking for evidence of Church-domination in nationalist circles.

c. Churches have a vast network of associated clubs and activities. Many of these are confined to members of the parish or congregation and nearly always attendance is determined by the divide evident between Catholics and Protestants. Church activities are as divided as those of other organisations. In a context of violence and fear, the congregational and parish system seems to mirror and institutionalise the political and cultural divisions of Ulster. There appears to be only occasional congregational commitment to programmes of meeting and encounter across congregational boundaries, nor has there been any consistent encouragement for this from Church leaderships.

d. The Churches in Northern Ireland have not regarded Inter-community relationships as a matter for particular programmes of action. Churches have seldom produced proposals for new initiatives which involve congregations and parishes at a systematic level. Even ACE programmes undertaken on an inter-denominational basis tend to be limited to a small number of people. Serious discussion about the relationship of Christianity to the question of inter-community relationships have been limited to small groups and to particular congregations and parishes. Discussions on the task of the Churches in a divided society have seldom taken place except between clergy. There is very little evidence that parishes and congregations provide places for serious debate on the function of

Churches in inter-community relationships. In a society in which community divisions mirror denominational divisions this is a notable omission. It may be that the Churches fear serious institutional division in the event of discussions on this subject becoming widespread. It is clear that neither clergy nor laity have sought to open up such discussions.

e. Church leaders have been associated with calls for an end to 'violence'. Nevertheless, this has not been accompanied by major changes in the pattern of Church relationships. The Churches remain identified with particular sides and there are few consistent indications that this has radically changed in the last twenty years. The result is that a whole dimension of Northern Irish cultural life acts to reflect community fears and experiences but is seldom an active forum for reflection and discussion on alternatives, except through the conversion of others. This applies also to controversial questions of social, political and economic importance. The result is that Churches have tended to concentrate in one place, people of similar understanding or experience as it affects these areas, rather than be places of meeting with differences. In this context, Churches have a tendency to become protective fortresses for threatened people rather than places of open and profound discussion.

f. The question is often asked, 'What impact do the Churches have on violence?' Our research suggests that there is no single clear answer to this question. We can also ask 'What impact does the violence have on the Churches?' Over the past twenty years, divisions within the Churches have continued. At an ecclesiastical level, contact between Churches remains tentative, particularly between Catholics and Protestants. Within official Church circles, such contact has largely been limited to clergy and Church employees and has not extended to widespread interchange between the laity on a congregational basis. There appears to be little internal unity within the Churches, as to what Churches should do in regard to inter-community relationships. The result is a highly differentiated picture, with each congregation and parish adopting different approaches.

g. In ecclesiastical terms, there is some evidence that some in the Churches have moved further apart while others have engaged in common ventures. This confirms a general picture of fragmentation within the institutions with regard to ecumenism and inter-community relationships. Our evidence shows that large numbers of Presbyterians are unwilling to have any religious co-operation with Catholics. At the same time,

Catholics are regarded by many as more interested in preserving the denominational purity of schools than in seeking other ways. The dominant emphasis appears to be on institutional purity above inter-denominational engagement. In this context, inter-denominational contact between Churches is always limited in advance and is seldom entirely free of defensiveness.

h. From our research, it is clear that theological reflection by many clergy is focused on defence of clear doctrine rather than on repentance and change. In most theological thinking, there is a clear assumption that change, whether political or theological has to be undertaken by 'the others' first. 'The problem' is usually located in the doctrines, attitudes and actions of the others, whoever they may be. The corollary of this is that the speaker is always unable to act, because the other has to change first.

i. At the same time, it remains true that, in some areas, the Churches contain and support the only people seriously committed to inter-community relationships. In ghettos the opportunities for contact between people have to be organised. Churches are sometimes the only bodies undertaking this. At one and the same time, even in neighbouring parishes or congregations, the strongest opponents to any contact between Catholics and Protestants may be within Churches. Schools programmes for Mutual Understanding (E.M.U.) may be most strongly opposed and most strongly supported in Church groups.

j. Schools remain a major focus of division in Northern Ireland. Church involvement in schools means that this is a major focus of Church institutional power in Northern Ireland. Many Protestants do not recognise the fears of Catholics in regard to the State system and demand integration through the abolition of Catholic schools. Often they do not acknowledge even the Protestant-technocratic-British orientation of State schools. Most Catholics proclaim that their schools have a different ethos which must be protected. Nevertheless if the ethos is one of 'agape' it is difficult to see this in operation in the manner in which they are defended. There is no common agreement, even within denominations, as to what could or should be done about schools in Northern Ireland.

3. The Churches and "Action for Community Employment" (ACE)

a. The Churches have been given considerable influence through the expansion of the A.C.E. programme. This has had serious effects in some areas. For Churches in general the limited number of people involved means that the appearance of Church involvement in community work may be restricted to very few people. In other words, although the ACE project runs through the institutional 'Churches' it has very little real impact on the life of the congregation. This varies from place to place. Nevertheless, it is hard to see any distinctive 'Church' contribution to many projects except that Churches have widespread networks and are generally trusted by local people in areas associated with 'caring'. As a means for the Churches to be 'relevant' it can only ever be partial and temporary.

b. The Roman Catholic Church is now the largest provider of A.C.E. jobs in West Belfast. Government policy has been to restrict the funding of community groups because of fears that money was used to support paramilitary groups and their political wings, particularly Sinn Fein. One of the results is that many local people resent the Church monopoly, often represented in clerical chairmanship of every financially viable local institution. Given the difficulties of setting up projects without Church backing, many community activists find themselves in opposition to Church and State. One of the most obvious results has been that the Church has become involved in local political battles with Sinn Fein. The expansion of the Church into the economic sphere by association, is regarded by many community activists as anti-democratic given existing clerical influence over schools and youth facilities.

c. In some areas the Roman Catholic Church has been the refuge for all those opposed to the I.R.A. In many working-class areas it is the only local institutional opponent. Nevertheless, the politics of ACE resources has at times resulted in local community-activists resentment against the Church authorities which may be expressed as support for Sinn Fein.

d. The Protestant Churches are not popularly identified with ACE in the same manner. Where Protestant Churches do have ACE schemes, they often do so together or in areas where other groups (e.g. community groups, local council, Chamber of Commerce) also have active projects. The Protestant Churches are not regarded as the sole providers of community assets. Furthermore, there is usually more than one Church institution in

Protestant areas, which prevents the same sense of 'monopoly' emerging. The result is that local power battles are not focused on the institutional Churches in Protestant areas to the same extent as they are in Catholic areas. This difference may further compound Protestant views of Catholicism as political domination. Nevertheless, it remains true that the larger Protestant Churches are widely regarded as the Unionist establishment at prayer. Among clergy this would include outright opposition to loyalist paramilitarism. Withdrawal of ACE funds to groups suspected of paramilitary links has been less marked and where it has happened, the Churches have not been the focus of local anger.

4. Policy implications

a. A community relations policy towards 'the Churches' has to take account of the vast real differences which exist from congregation to congregation. A blanket approach can only result in unpredictable and possibly harmful results. The central institutions cannot control these results.

b. None of the Churches in Northern Ireland has developed a clear policy on inter-community relations. This may be because of the fear of institutional division. Nevertheless, the result is that the Churches are usually reactive rather than pro-active in the area of inter-community relationships. The Churches could be encouraged to present their own proposals for the involvement of Churches in policy changes. Unless there are widely-supported and well-known Church policies on inter-community relationships, institutional relations involving the Churches are likely to be unclear, unpredictable and unsatisfactory.

c. Inter-community relations cannot be improved by a policy which assumes that the Churches *in toto* will act in a manner significantly different from other secular institutions. Churches are organised on a parish and congregational basis and the experience of Northern Ireland is that most tend to reflect, more than they transcend community divisions. In the past some congregations and parishes have sought to reduce community boundaries while others seek some security behind reinforced separation. In secular society, reinforcement of boundaries might be called ghettoisation. Reinforcement of community boundaries is often an expression of deep fear and anger as a result of violent experiences shared by the congregation or parish at the hands of an identified enemy. This variation within institutional Churches must be recognised before any serious policy towards 'Churches' can be formulated.

d. The Churches can be encouraged to expand inter-community relationships in their areas. Conditions on inter-community dimensions to Church-based programmes attached to financial support seem an appropriate instrument. These can build on the large numbers involved in Churches and utilise the very well-developed structures and wide acceptability of the Churches. It is of major importance that 'encouragement' by financial or other means does not become force and that Churches are left to 'opt in' to possibilities on offer from the government. Northern Ireland Churches historically react in a defensive manner if change is seen to be imposed on them. It is imperative that the Churches be seen to take responsibility for their own commitments and choices in the area of inter-community relations.

e. ACE funding has led to very serious problems in West Belfast. The centralisation of control in the hands of the clergy, seen as agents of an institution, rather than local people has had many negative effects. ACE funding policy is a very blunt instrument, and the concentration of resources in clerical hands creates serious political imbalances within local communities. The government's policy aim, that money should not fall into paramilitary hands, is translated in many areas as the political vetting of the entire community. The result is a further alienation from Church and State in many places. Much thinking is needed to find ways of redefining Church involvement in order to avoid the sense of exclusion which now embitters many community groups, perhaps by encouraging more creative partnerships at local level. This is not to say that the Church should not be involved, but the nature of that involvement might be more flexible.

Glossary

We are grateful to Professor Ron McAllister, of Northeastern University, USA, who pointed out to us that there were a number of terms used in the text which are only comprehensible to a local audience. This Glossary is intended to provide some explanation for some of these terms.

P1,P2..P7: Northern Irish schools are divided into Primary (aged 4-11) and Secondary (aged 11-18). Primary school is divided into seven classes called Primary One, Two, Three and so on. In common speech, these are reduced to P1, P2 and P3. P1 is for four year olds, P7 for 11 year olds.

Grammar Schools:
Secondary Education in Northern Ireland is selective. At the age of eleven, pupils may take a qualifying examination, known as the 'eleven plus'. Those who pass the eleven plus, qualify for State-funded places at the provinces Grammar Schools. Those who fail the exam go to Secondary Schools.

Education and Library Boards (ELBs):
Educational Administration in Northern Ireland is organised on a regional basis. There are five Education and Library Boards who control large budgets for schools, youth work, student grants and so on.

Tech: Local short form for 'Technical College', which provide continuing education for adults, school leavers and work training. Usually located in major centres of population.

EMU: Education for Mutual Understanding. Government-backed programme to encourage a cross-community dimension to formal education. Operates at the level of curriculum and in joint projects between schools, including contact schemes.

District Council: Northern Ireland is now divided up into 26 District Councils which have authority in a limited sphere of local services. They replaced the old County Councils, which formed the basis of Northern Ireland's alternative name, the Six Counties.

Health Board: The provision of public health facilities is administered at local level by four regional Health Boards who allocate resources within their areas as part of the National Health Service.

DSSO: District Social Security Office. Local Office for the provision of social services and the processing of claims for social security benefits. Also known as 'the dole' or the 'broo'.

Job Market: Local centre for the Government Department of Employment. Advertises vacancies and monitors unemployment locally.

ACE: Action for Community Employment. Government Scheme for the long-term unemployed. Partially funded by the European Social Fund. It has become a semi-permanent feature of the Northern Irish economy. Each scheme is locally managed, often with Church involvement.

NIVT: Northern Ireland Voluntary Trust. Independent Funding Body for Voluntary Groups engaged in the field of Social Services in Northern Ireland.

VSB: Voluntary Services Belfast. Co-ordinates volunteers in a variety of projects throughout Belfast.

Corrymeela: Christian Community based throughout Northern Ireland with a residential centre near Ballycastle. Often used by community groups as a residential resource.

BB,GB: Boys Brigade, Girls Brigade. Uniformed youth organisations based in Churches. Virtually entirely Protestant. Also exist outside Northern Ireland.

Orange Order: Protestant Organisation originating in Armagh in the late eighteenth century. Historically regarded as the most visible integrating institution for all Protestants and Unionists particularly in Northern Ireland. Regarded by many as the real power under the Unionist government. Of late it has appeared to be in decline, although membership of Flute Bands, linked to the lodges remains strong.

Gaelic Athletic Association:

Also known as the GAA. Established in 1887 to promote Irish Games, especially Gaelic Football, Hurling, Gaelic Handball and Camogie. Controversial in Northern Ireland because of the stipulation that no member of British Crown Forces (i.e. RUC, UDR or Army) can play the games.